New Challenges of North Korean
Foreign Policy

New Challenges of North Korean Foreign Policy

Edited by
Kyung-Ae Park

First published in 2010 by
PALGRAVE MACMILLAN®
in the United States—a division of St. Martin's Press LLC,
175 Fifth Avenue, New York, NY 10010.

Where this book is distributed in the UK, Europe and the rest of the world,
this is by Palgrave Macmillan, a division of Macmillan Publishers Limited,
registered in England, company number 785998, of Houndmills,
Basingstoke, Hampshire RG21 6XS.

Palgrave Macmillan is the global academic imprint of the above companies
and has companies and representatives throughout the world.

Palgrave® and Macmillan® are registered trademarks in the United States,
the United Kingdom, Europe and other countries.

ISBN: 978–0–230–10363–4

Library of Congress Cataloging-in-Publication Data

New challenges of North Korean foreign policy / edited by Kyung-Ae
Park.
    p. cm.
    ISBN 978–0–230–10363–4 (alk. paper)
    1. Political culture—Korea (North) 2. Korea (North)—Foreign relations.
3. Korea (North)—Politics and government. 4. Ideology—Korea
(North) I. Park, Kyung-Ae, 1955–

JQ1729.5.A91N48 2010
327.5193—dc22   2010008381

A catalogue record of the book is available from the British Library.

Design by Newgen Imaging Systems (P) Ltd., Chennai, India.

First edition: October 2010

10 9 8 7 6 5 4 3 2 1

Printed in the United States of America.

CONTENTS

ILLUSTRATIONS

Graphs

Tables

Figures

PREFACE

North Korea's foreign policy behavior has long intrigued scholars, puzzled laymen, frustrated negotiators, and aggravated policy-makers. The world has regarded North Korea as an unpredictable rogue state and a source of conflict and alarm to the international community. Controversies surrounding North Korea's nuclear facilities and missile technology have persisted for the past twenty years, and Pyongyang again sent shock waves through the international community in 2009 when it tested a second nuclear device and a barrage of missiles. Subsequently, the Six-party Talks became deadlocked and the international community began to implement unprecedented tough sanctions on Pyongyang after the UN Security Council adopted Resolution 1874.

In addition, Kim Jong Il's illness triggered fears of instability in the North Korean system and even a sudden collapse of the regime. With the United States and South Korea producing contingency plans for a possibly chaotic post-Kim Jong Il era, concerns over Kim's health reignited a debate over the succession issue and rekindled interest in the impact of the succession on Pyongyang's future foreign policy directions.

In the midst of the escalating tensions, however, North Korea initiated a peace offensive toward the United States and South Korea in the latter part of 2009, following former president Clinton's visit to Pyongyang in August. His visit aimed at securing the release of two American journalists who were collecting information on the plight of North Korean refugees along North Korea's border with China. In the middle of unprecedented confrontational bilateral relations, the journalists had been convicted of illegal entry and "grave crimes against the Korean nation." The release of the journalists set the stage for a renewed bilateral contact and subsequently led to the visit of President

Obama's envoy, Stephen Bosworth, to North Korea in December, which marked the first direct high-level contact of the Obama administration. Bosworth's visit was intended to convince North Korea to return to the Six-party Talks, and was followed by Washington's announcement that it had reached a "common understanding" with Pyongyang on the need to resume the Six-party process.

Pyongyang's overtures continued into the beginning of 2010. In a New Year's message, it called for "an end to the hostile relationship" with the United States and for reconciliation with Seoul, skipping its usual invective in the message against both countries. It expressed its strong desire to improve bilateral ties with Washington and Seoul to ensure peace and stability on the Korean Peninsula. Whether North Korea's latest conciliatory gestures will gain momentum for a new breakthrough in Pyongyang's relations with the outside world remains to be seen. North Korea now stands at a crossroads, and many internal and external challenges facing Pyongyang will reorient its foreign policy in the coming months and years.

This book brings together the work of ten of the world's foremost scholars and leading experts on North Korea. The contributors of the chapters are longtime analysts of North Korea and most of them utilize firsthand knowledge obtained from their visits to Pyongyang, from which this book particularly benefits. The book provides an assessment of the domestic and international challenges to North Korea, which will inevitably affect the way North Korea relates to the outside world. Witnessing the rapid changes in North Korea's foreign policy environment, the contributors of this book critically analyze the key factors and issues that are shaping North Korea's foreign policy behavior and its future direction. The authors examine the implications of the domestic challenges posed by the changing national identity and ideology, people's exiting the country, economic stagnation, and the military-first politics, for Pyongyang's foreign policy. They also offer insight into the impact of various external challenges on Pyongyang's foreign policy, such as China "rising," multilateralism, and leadership changes in the United States and South Korea, and assess Pyongyang's strategies for coping with these challenges. As such, the book exposes North Korea's major foreign policy challenges, which Pyongyang is currently facing in dealing with its changing domestic environment, the new world power structure, and the new administrations in both the United States and South Korea.

Earlier versions of the chapters in this book were presented at a conference held at the University of British Columbia. Thanks are due not only to the contributors whose chapters appear in this book, but also to all the other participants of the conference, including Dae Seok Choi, Gon Namkung, and Dongho Jo. I would also like to acknowledge Insub Mah who supported the project with invaluable intellectual conceptualization during the various stages of this project. For the financial support that enabled us to proceed with this project, I express my deep appreciation to the following organizations: The Academy of Korean Studies, Ewha Institute of Unification Studies of Ewha Woman's University, Institute of National Strategy of Sungkyunkwan University, Hwajeong Peace Foundation, and the Ministry of Unification of the Republic of Korea.

KYUNG-AE PARK

PART 1

Challenges From Within

CHAPTER ONE

Socialist Neoconservatism and North Korean Foreign Policy

RÜDIGER FRANK

Introduction

The North Korean intercontinental ballistic missile (ICBM) test of April 2009 and the nuclear test of May 2009 have rekindled interest in North Korea's foreign policy and its domestic origins. As usual, there are more questions than answers, but we can now even less afford not having the best possible understanding of current developments and future actions. This chapter therefore aims to contribute to the debate on the following questions: What has prompted North Korea to intensify its nuclear program? What are the domestic drivers of such a policy? How does this fit into the overall picture of North Korea's foreign policy? We will do so by having a closer look at the domestic developments of the past years, which have shown tremendous dynamics, from initiation of reforms to their subsequent reversal. A quantitative analysis of North Korean propaganda supports our qualitative assessment.

No matter which of the major theories of international relations is applied, domestic developments usually play a major role. This is particularly true for a short-term and midterm time horizon. While liberal thinking from the outset assigns a pivotal role to individuals, even (neo-)realist models, which tend to focus predominantly on interstate relations, need information about national interest and the various perceptions related to this. A constructivist perspective helps to appreciate the emergence and formation of values and interests beyond the mere question of power maximization and regime survival. While we will mostly focus on very specific questions in this paper, it is nevertheless helpful to understand that these issues can be applied in a larger theoretically informed context.

In principle, we argue that, after a brief reform period, North Korea is now returning to the specific, orthodox form of socialism that has been created under Kim Il Sung since the late 1950s and was applied until about the mid-1990s. In fact, North Korean propaganda repeatedly referred to the 1950s and 1960s as their new point of reference (discussed below). The ideological doctrine of what we call "socialist neoconservatism" in the sense of a return to conservative, non-reformist socialist values is closely connected to all the issues that are currently of interest to analysts of North Korea and strongly affects economic policy including inter-Korean cooperation at Kaesŏng and the resuscitation of the Ch'ŏllima movement. This new old trend in ideology also informs our interpretation of the nuclear and missile tests of 2009, as well as the overall analysis of North Korea's foreign policy and its behavior in the Six-party Talks.

Ideology Is the Key

It is often not appropriately appreciated that socialist ideology is far more than a bizarre feature of political and economic systems that are alien to most individuals in the West. Ideology is or has been the central issue for all socialist societies, since it represents the core around which everything else is grouped, including the all-important legitimacy of the leadership, economic policies, or foreign affairs.[1] If we want to understand how individual policies should be interpreted, their placement within the realm of the ideological substructure of the affected society is crucial. It is no coincidence that one of the standard works on socialism identifies a dominant ideology as one key characteristic of all such systems.[2] Kornai argues that, eventually, socialism develops into a good of intrinsic value. North Korea (or the Democratic People's Republic, DPRK) is no exception, although we would suggest that due to the semireligious nature of the *chuch'e* ideology and the cult around Kim Il Sung, this statement applies at an even higher degree than in most other socialist systems that we have known.

For many decades there has been only one monolithic ideology in North Korea that was supposed to be shared by everybody regardless of age, profession, or social rank. Individualism was and still is

regarded as negative behavior and is displayed as inferior to collectivism (*chiptanjuǔi*). The DPRK constitution of 1998 reflects this in
article 63: "In the DPRK the rights and duties of citizens are based on
the collectivist principle, 'One for all and all for one.' "
From a systemic point of view, this monolithic ideology is North
Korea's biggest strength and, at the same time, its greatest weakness.
It has managed to keep the country together despite severe shocks and
hardships such as the collapse of the socialist system in Europe around
1990, the death of Kim Il Sung in 1994, or the famine of 1995–1997. On
the other hand, while the foundation on which the North Korean system is standing ideologically is very strong, it consists only of one "leg"
or pillar. In pluralist societies, even though single ideological approaches
and political ideas might fail or get out of favor, this will not shake
the stability of the whole society since there are so many other ideas
and ideologies that still remain intact. This is why developed democracies are enormously robust and crisis prone despite the relative weakness of the single elements of their ideological foundation. If something
goes wrong, the leadership is replaced, not the political system as such.
Citizens as a group are usually very little preoccupied with ideology,
although they might have strong ideological positions as individuals.

The situation is much different in socialist countries. As long as their
core ideology is not threatened, they can ensure stability of political
power for a considerable time even if the government fails to deliver
on economic promises, since leadership, political system, and ideology
are seen as forming one entity. But as soon as ideology gets shaken, the
whole system is in danger of collapsing. In fact, this is how we can interpret the sudden implosion of the socialist systems in Eastern Europe.
Along the same logic, Kim Jong Il urged to preserve a conservative attitude and not begin to follow the deadly trend of reforming socialism:

> The most serious lesson of the collapse of socialism in several coun-
> tries is that the corruption of socialism begins with ideological
> corruption, and that a breakdown on the ideological front results
> in the crumbling of all socialism's fronts and ends in the total ruin
> of socialism…If it secures ideology, socialism will triumph; if it
> loses ideology, socialism will go to ruin…If the ideological bul-
> wark falls down, socialism will be unable to defend itself no mat-
> ter how great its economic and military power may be.[3]

However, a few years later, he violated this principle by introducing the
North Korean version of the 1979 Chinese reforms. It is still relatively

unclear whether he initiated or just tolerated the changes, whether he had this in mind since his visits to China in 1983 but had to wait until he came to power, or whether the 2000 summit with Kim Dae Jung influenced his decision. It is relatively safe to assume that the famine in the late 1990s played a major role, at least as a catalyst. In hindsight, we now know that the economic adjustment measures were indeed (just) another perfection drive, that is, an attempt to make the system work and not to replace it.[4] Reforms not having gone far enough, the return to orthodox positions was inevitable, including a sharply reduced propensity to risk-taking, innovation, and dynamism. We therefore call this new old policy line "socialist neoconservatism."

Conservative, Orthodox Socialism

What exactly is North Korea returning to? What is "conservative socialism" in a North Korean context? Without a doubt, North Korean socialism is closely connected with the person of Kim Il Sung. We know that during his guerilla days, and as a member of the Chinese Communist Party, he has been heavily influenced by his senior Chinese comrades and their views.[5] We also know that he later spent considerable time in Russia, where he was trained according to the prevailing Soviet doctrine of that time—something that can roughly be described as Stalinism, although the term carries meanings that make its application to other cases at least questionable.[6]

But we should not forget that Kim was born in 1912. By 1945, he was just thirty-three years old, and he could have by no means expected that he would indeed be able to triumph over all his formidable political competitors and become the de facto leader of North Korea a few years later. It was the combination of the feeling of betrayal, as the Soviet Union did not participate in the Korean War, Stalin's death in 1953, the Twentieth Party Congress in Moscow of 1956, the fierce fight with the pro-Chinese and the pro-Soviet factions of the Korean Communist movement, the chaos emerging in China during the Great Leap, the disappointment with the Soviet complacency in the Cuban missile crisis, the fear of the new military government in South Korea since 1961, and the general unease regarding Moscow's new line of collective leadership and peaceful coexistence that prompted Kim Il Sung to develop and emphasize his own Korean version of socialism that later became known as *chuch'e*.

As his life experience under Japanese colonialism and his frustration with Korea's division after liberation explains, Kim was driven by nationalism and the fear of a loss of independence. The role played by the Great Powers in Korea since the late nineteenth century made him xenophobic. But this does not mean that he had developed his blueprint of a Korean version of socialism right after he left his home village of Man'gyŏngdae for the Manchurian exile in 1925, although official North Korean propaganda would like to make us believe so. Rather, he was very happy with adapting the Soviet model in the early years of North Korean nation building, not only because this would grant him Moscow's generous economic support and military protection, but also because this was the one model that he knew and that obviously had worked. North Korean official historiography produces a very different picture today, but this should not obscure our view of the fact that, until the mid-1950s, Kim Il Sung saw no reason not to follow the Soviet example.[7]

We would therefore suggest the emergence of the "*chuch'e* system" as the time when socialist orthodoxy was created in North Korea, that is, roughly from the mid- and late 1950s until the early and mid-1960s. This orthodoxy had its roots in Stalin's system that was quickly getting out of favor after 1956, but it was not a copy of it. We have discussed the crucial function of a stable ideology in a socialist system. Kim Il Sung could not be as risk-taking as the Russians or the Chinese were, since his legitimacy was shaky after a factional fight and the lost Korean War (although he had quickly declared it a victory). Mao could afford to destroy public order in China, since he knew he could restore it. Kim Il Sung would not dare to gamble in a similar way. Among the other restrictions he had to consider was the problem of a divided country that required very specific measures, such as a heavy nationalist component. The fresh and painful experience of Japanese colonization, coupled with the absence of Soviet support during the Korean War and the feeling of being stuck between two major adversaries, made national independence another key element of his blueprint for the perfect system. Thus, North Korean socialism developed and was taking shape by the late 1950s and early 1960s.

Despite their uniform description as being "socialist," which we regard as correct, no socialist country was similar to the other. This became particularly obvious in the post-socialist transformation period.[8] Within the socialist camp, North Korea had always stood out as being particularly unique. The DPRK neither joined the Warsaw Treaty nor was it a full-fledged member of the Council for Mutual Economic Assistance (Comecon). Kim Il Sung refused to follow the Soviet process of de-Stalinization. Around the time when the Chinese started their Hundred Flowers Campaign, North Korea experienced a coup against Kim Il Sung. The coup failed but created a sense of insecurity and prevented North Korea from joining the Chinese experiments too enthusiastically. Hence the Ch'ŏllima-Movement of 1958 was reminiscent of the work-harder-campaigns in the Soviet Union and Europe[9] and not of the much more extreme Great Leap Forward, despite similar terminology. The Chinese Cultural Revolution of 1966 was not accompanied by any comparable event in North Korea.[10] However, around that time, the *chuch'e* was developed into the indigenous form of North Korean socialist ideology, declaring North Korea's ideological independence from both Beijing and Moscow.[11]

Marxist or Leninist ideas about socialism shaped the image of a socialist society in East Asia since the successful October Revolution in Russia. But, very similar to Neoconfucianism centuries before, only few intellectuals fully understood these relatively complex thoughts. The vast majority of uneducated, underprivileged farmers, workers, and guerilla fighters conceived the concepts in a very rough and simplified form. The ambitious and self-confident leaders, such as Mao Zedong and later Kim Il Sung, deliberately altered these foreign thoughts to make them fit the realities of their own societies. This included, but was not limited to, the substitution of "working class" (a key concept for Marx)[12] with "masses," a much more flexible term that would be applied to the farmers in these underdeveloped countries.

This "creative" application of Marx's theory has not been confined to China and North Korea; in fact, Lenin was the first leader who made theory fit the reality of his country. But the old terms were kept for a long time, leading to considerable confusion about what "socialism" actually is. Again, Kornai provides a very useful reference point.[13] Combining the logic of economics with the reality of socialism, he has identified a few key characteristics that despite all diversity are necessary and sufficient to describe a socialist society. They include the undivided power monopoly of the Communist Party, a dominant ideology, state ownership in the economy, and central bureaucratic coordination. The details, such as names of the parties or of the ideologies, differ, but the essence remains the same, and so do the consequences.

Not everybody agrees with such a position. The modifications to socialism in individual countries are seen as so profound that they prompted an academic discussion about socialism as such, asking whether we shouldn't rather speak about various kinds of socialisms.[14] We will not indulge in such a debate here, but it is helpful to be aware that the question of what socialism means has not finally been answered. We avoid the related controversy by using North Korea itself as a reference point. When we argue that North Korea is returning to orthodox socialist positions, we refer primarily to North Korean socialist conservatism as it emerged since the late 1950s until the early 1960s in response to the events as mentioned above, in particular the Korean War experience, the 1956 Party Congress, and the emerging Sino-Soviet split that posed a serious challenge to North Korea. Orthodox socialism in North Korea combines elements of Stalinism, strong defensive nationalism, xenophobia, and Neo-Confucian traditions. This type of socialism could be observed until the death of Kim Il Sung and the beginning of the famine in the mid-1990s.

In the *economic sphere*, this includes central planning and central coordination, state ownership of means of production, a focus on heavy and chemical industry at the cost of light industry, the logic of "big is beautiful," and a preference for investing into production versus consumption. In such an environment, money usually plays a secondary role, and individuals adjust their behavior in a way that makes them much less sensitive to price changes than their peers in market economies. All economic activities are controlled and coordinated by the state; private trading and production that could serve as an alternative source of power or ways of upward social mobility do not exist or are severely limited.

In the *political sphere*, there is the undisputed power monopoly of the Communist Party, in the case of North Korea, the Korean Worker's Party (KWP). An important feature is that the political system of North Korea is (still) leader-based. The Party as such plays the role of supporter of the supreme leader. Unlike most other socialist countries, in North Korea the Party apparatus itself has little real power over top-level decisions. In the Soviet Union, in its satellite countries, and even in China, the Politburo (or its Standing Committee) yielded real power. Party Congresses were convened regularly to disseminate new strategies and to consolidate internal organs of power, such as the Central Committee. Power struggles took place within the elite over control of the Party. In North Korea, socialism could be maintained despite the absence of a Party Congress since 1980 (!) because the KWP plays a much less decisive role as a subject; it is reduced to the status of an object and an instrument, although it is as such still a very powerful one.

In the *ideological sphere*, socialist countries usually present a monolithic model as discussed above. In North Korea, socialist ideology is particularly closely interwoven with nationalism. In fact, nationalism is the dominant element, which is why the North Koreans have shown a

remarkable lack of sensitivity when meddling with the core principles
of socialism in a Marxist-Leninist sense (discussed below). Jorganson
therefore appropriately described *chuch'e* as "country-specific ethnic
nationalism" (not socialism).[15] Again, North Korea is not alone in this
respect; however, here we find a major difference to the satellite states
in Eastern Europe, which had to be careful not to offend the Soviet
Union by overly nationalist tendencies. It is also helpful to remember that, in orthodox socialist theory, socialism and nationalism are
mutually exclusive concepts. Class by definition reaches across state and
national boundaries; common interests are based on common class, not
on common ancestry, culture, or tradition. Few socialist systems could
hence afford to publish statements such as "our party puts forth the
army, not the working class, as the leading force of our revolution," or
"the nation is over class and stratum, and the fatherland is more important than idea and ideology," and walk away with it.[16]

Socialist Neoconservatism in Ideology

Reform according to Kornai means that one or more of the basic characteristics of a socialist system are changed deeply and lastingly.[17] China
has shown that it is possible to eliminate state ownership and bureaucratic coordination and to replace the dominant ideology with patriotism, while still maintaining the power monopoly of the Party. For a few
years, it seemed that North Korea would try to follow a similar path.[18]

However, since around 2005 and increasingly since 2008 the North
Korean leadership has been trying to turn back the wheel of time.
Today we see a complete reversal of the policies of 2000–2004. In
January 2001, Kim Jong Il wrote in the *Rodong Sinmun* that "Things
are not what they used to be in the 60s. So no one should follow the
way people used to do things in the past."[19] However, in March 2009,
during a field guidance, he declared that officials should "energetically
lead the masses by displaying the same work style as the officials did in
the 50s and 60s."[20] Within a few years, he had come full circle.

A single quote is, of course, not enough to prove such a major ideological reversal. A more precise way to quantify ideological developments is an analysis of official North Korean media, such as the
publications by Korea Central News Agency.[21] The Internet presence
of this source is based in Japan and used as a tool of propaganda specifically for Koreans in Japan and South Koreans, but it reproduces articles
by North Korean media such as *Rodong Sinmun* and *Minju Chosŏn*. As

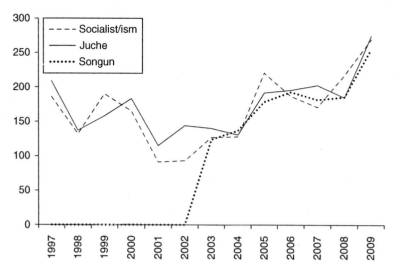

Graph 1.1 Analysis of official North Korean media (KCNA).

such, it is genuine and provides a glance at the development of official ideology in the DPRK. One example is the utilization of the terms "socialism," "*chuch'e*," and "*sŏn'gun*" by North Korean state media. As Graph 1.1 below shows, their appearance has doubled (!) between 2004 and 2009 (n = about 1,200 in each period). This graph is based on the English-language edition of the Korean Central News Agency (KCNA) Web site. It is interesting to see that the term *sŏn'gun* (or "military first") has only been used since 2003, while in the Korean version it first appeared in 1999. This suggests a certain connection to the reforms, although the menacing term suggests otherwise.[22] But myth-building has already started. Current propaganda claims that its roots can be found during Kim Il Sung's anti-Japanese campaign, that is, in the 1930s. In March 2009, KCNA reported about a newly published book that divides Kim Jong Il's *sŏn'gun* leadership into five stages: (1) When Kim Jong Il grew up between 1942 and August of 1960; (2) when Kim Jong Il actively promoted the *sŏn'gun* revolutionary cause of Kim Il Sung from August 1960 to June 1982; (3) when Kim Jong Il further developed the *sŏn'gun* politics in depth, defended Korean-style socialism, and gave full play to its advantages and vitality from June 1982 to December 1994; (4) when Kim Jong Il enforced the *sŏn'gun* politics in all fields, thus overcoming grave difficulties from January 1995 to December 1998; and (5) when he pushed

forward the cause of building a great prosperous and powerful socialist nation through the general advance of the *sŏn'gun* revolution from
January 1999 until the present time.
As mentioned above, socialism in North Korea is connected to
nationalism. This is reflected in the term "our [Korea-] style socialism" (*urisik sahoejuuʹi*). It has been used in only less than five KCNA
articles in the last quarters of 2001 and 2002, but the number rose
to over twenty-five in 2006 and jumped to more than thirty in the
first quarter of 2009. The development goal, dubbed *kangsŏng taeguk*,
has been supplemented by the term "socialist" and is now again called
sahoejuŭi kangsŏng taeguk (socialist prosperous and strong great country). This term has witnessed an even more obvious intensification, not
being mentioned even in a single KCNA article in the last quarter of
2002 but jumping to over one hundred in the same period of 2008 and
two hundred in the first quarter of 2009.

In late 2007, a decades-old slogan reemerged that had already been
criticized back in the late 1950 by East German diplomats: "Let us
produce, study and live like the anti-Japanese guerrillas!" (*saengsando
haksŭpdo saenghwaldo hang'ilyugyŏkdaesigŭro*).[23] Among the newly emerging old buzzwords are "single-minded unity" (*ilsimtan'gyŏl*), "collectivism" (*chiptanjuŭi*), "self-reliance" (*charyŏkkaengsaeng*), and "mental
power" (*chŏngsinryŏk*). The North Korean media increasingly quote
older, more conservative articles of Kim Jong Il, most of which deal
with *chuch'e* and the leading role of the Party. Also notable is the connection between *sŏn'gun* and *chuch'e*. We witness a reinterpretation of
sŏn'gun, possibly in preparation for the post-Kim Jong Il period. Rather
than an ad hoc measure to cope with the difficult situation of the late
1990s, it is increasingly transformed into a timeless ideology along with
chuch'e.

Conservatism in North Korea, too, goes hand in hand with tradi-
tionalism. On October 29, 2007, *Rodong Sinmun* emphasized that the
chuch'e idea means "believing in people as in heaven." This is not a
new expression, nevertheless it provides another interesting parallel
to Korea's past.[24] Supporting the notion of a partial return to even
pre-socialist traditions is the reintroduction of a Confucian holiday
on April 4, 2008, when for the first time in North Korean history
Chŏngmyŏng (tomb sweeping day) was officially celebrated. This is
remarkable because it reflects the readiness of the leadership to openly
embrace traditional concepts to support both the nationalist agenda
and ideas of filial piety. The latter is directly related to the two leaders
Kim Il Sung and Kim Jong Il. In April 2007, *Rodong Sinmun* carried a

short article reminding its readers of *Chŏngmyŏng* and its old meaning, especially tending to the graves of ancestors.[25] *Chusŏk*, the Korean equivalent to thanksgiving and the most important holiday in South Korea, was covered by *Rodong Sinmun* on September 14, 2008 as a "folk holiday," continuing the reintegration of traditional customs into ideologically and politically correct life in North Korea. *Chusŏk* had been reintroduced as a public holiday only in 2003, fourteen years after the rehabilitation of the Lunar New Year in 1989. In this respect, North Korea clearly deviates from what we would typically expect to be orthodox socialist positions, that is, the condemnation of religion as "superstition" and "opium for the people." In North Korea, folk traditions are used to reinforce nationalism and hence are acceptable.[26]

An excellent example to quantify the changed paradigms in North Korea is a look at the titles used for Kim Jong Il. As Graph 1.2 shows, in the period of roughly 2000–2005, he was mainly addressed by the "worldly" title "Great Leader" (*widaehan ryŏngdoja*). Since 2006, there has been a sudden drop in the frequency of "leader," and instead we note a sharp increase in the use of the "religious" title "General Secretary" (*ch'ongpisŏ*).

This is a clear sign that the period of pragmatic reform is over and marks the return to a renewed focus on ideological rigidity and purity.

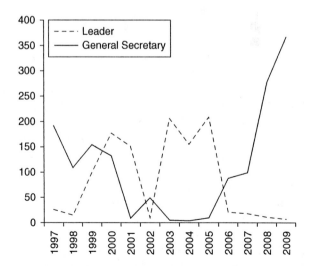

Graph 1.2   Titles used for Kim Jong Il (Leader and General Secretary).

Socialist Neoconservatism in the Economy:
Ch'öllima-2

The economy of North Korea is not doing well. This is hardly new; however, there are various degrees of "not doing well." After having survived what seems to have been a major food crisis, or even famine, around 1995 and 1997, the North Korean leadership is rightfully worried about a repetition of such a situation.[27]

A glance at the North Korean assessment of their economy's performance is provided annually by the reports held at the parliamentary session around April. The budgets reflect what we could call macroeconomic data for the DPRK.[28] Since there is almost no private economic production, there are only the state sector and the military sector. The latter is usually perceived as being relatively large and includes all kinds of enterprises. For obvious reasons, data on this part of the economy are unavailable. But with the rest of the economy, including trade under state ownership and control, the state's budget is comparable to the Gross National Product (GNP) minus the military sector. The rate of increase of budget revenue would hence be a rough equivalent of the GNP growth rate. From this perspective, based on official North Korean statistics extracted from the Korea Central News Agency (KCNA) Web site and the annual budget reports, we see that the economy has been growing (and was expected to grow) at an extraordinary pace in the double-digit range since the beginning of the reforms in 2002, but declined sharply in 2006 to a modest 5 to 6 percentage points.

In the economy, too, we note the reemergence of orthodox socialist positions at the expense of reform-oriented appeasement and flexibility. Kim Jong Il had stressed in 1995 that "Private ownership inevitably gives birth to individualism and bourgeois ideas...Socialism is incompatible with private ownership and the capitalist market economy."[29] It was therefore exciting to read that in January 2002 *People's Korea* quoted Kim Jong Il as pointing "to the fact that foreign trade should be conducted in accordance with the mechanism and principles of capitalism." However, this is being retracted again. The most significant development in North Korea's economic policy in 2008 was the return to a paradigm that was at least half a century old. In line with the neoconservative trend in ideology, in December 2008, Kim Jong Il resuscitated the North Korean version of the Chinese Great Leap Forward, this time called "great revolutionary upsurge" (*hyŏngmyŏngjŏk taegojo*).

The key event to launch what we call "Ch'ŏllima-2" was Kim Jong Il's visit to Kangsŏn, the home of the original Ch'ŏllima movement, on December 24, 2008. The workers there allegedly adopted a letter that was later used as an example and source of inspiration all over the country. They wrote: "There is no fortress unconquerable for the DPRK as long as the seasoned and tested leadership is provided by the Party and all the servicepersons and people are single-mindedly united and the DPRK has matchless armed forces and the tremendous potential of the independent national economy."[30]

This movement is clearly and openly reminiscent of the North Korean version of the Chinese Great Leap Forward. The original Ch'ŏllima movement was started by Kim Il Sung during a guidance at the same Kangsŏn Steel Complex in 1958. It was less extreme than the Chinese example but exhibited the typical economic rationale of classical socialism: in the absence of capital and other resources, labor was to be utilized extensively, bringing into play the socialist ideology and, less openly stated, the repressive system of the socialist state. Kim Jong Il chose the same place for his campaign and explicitly referred to the example fifty years ago. Ch'ŏllima-2 is replacing the creative application of market principles. North Koreans have meanwhile even been asked to join typical mass campaigns like a 150-day-battle in agriculture, which was followed by another 100-day-battle. We will not have to wait very long for signs of exhaustion and typical counterstrategies, such as faking production results and withholding performance.

The preparations for such a movement were already visible earlier in the year 2008. On March 9, *Rodong Sinmun* marked the tenth anniversary of a "work harder campaign" called the "Torch of Sŏnggang" initiated by Kim Jong Il during an on-the-spot guidance at the steel mill at Sŏnggang in North Hamgyŏng province. A few days later, on March 24, *Rodong Sinmun* urged that all people should make a leaping advance in building a socialist economic power with the same vigor with which they brought about the "Great Ch'ŏllima Upswing" in the latter half of the 1950s. The readers were informed that, through the spirit of Ch'ŏllima, North Korea was able to complete its industrialization in only fourteen years. On May 15, *Rodong Sinmun* stressed that more propaganda and agitation work would help to achieve economic success and to leap forward as in the 1950s and 1970s. On October 20, a KCNA article quoted Premier Kim Yong Il as stressing the importance of applying socialist principles in operating the economy, and referring to a thesis by Kim Jong Il on this issue. According to KCNA, "The participants discussed how to strengthen the state's central-oriented control and supervision of economic projects, while emphasizing ways of agitating the people's collective spirit along with (economic) collectivism."

On November 22, 2008, KCNA published an editorial, reminding readers of the "Kanggye spirit" shown by Kim Jong Il ten years ago during the famine, the period known as the "Arduous March" in North Korea. It praised the people in Chagang province, who "are not interested in increasing individual wealth," so nobody should "think of whining, dependency on others, fantasies of money and trends pursuing capitalism." In early December, calls to adhere to a socialist economy were renewed. *Rodong Sinmun* wrote that the current situation makes it imperative to stick even harder to the socialist economic principles.

The reports about the activities of "youth shock brigades" (*ch'ŏngnyŏn tolgyŏkdae*) as reported in a KCNA article of December 14, 2008 are reminiscent of the logic of the Chinese "Great Leap Forward": "There are neither difficulties insurmountable nor fortress unconquerable for them as long as they remain united as firm as a rock around the great Party." The same is true for "reliance on the masses" as well as "single-minded unity" between the KWP and the Korean people. References to Ch'ŏllima, the symbol of labor-centered mass campaigns created in 1958, were found in less than ten articles in the last quarters of the years 2000 through 2007. Since the end of 2008, their number exploded to reach over forty in the first quarter of 2009.

Economic nationalism is the policy of the day. It seems that, by the end of 2008, economic policy in North Korea has come full circle since the 1980s. Economic difficulties were met with the half-hearted establishment of Joint Ventures (law of 1984) and economic zones like the one in Rajin-Sŏnbong in the early 1990s, the so far failed zone in Sinŭiju, or the industrial complex in Kaesŏng since 2004. The famine of 1995 was countered by increased reliance on international economic aid, market-oriented reforms since 2002, and close inter-Korean cooperation since 1999–2000. As the negative effects of these measures became obvious, and especially since the U.S. attack on Iraq in 2003, the North Korean leadership has decided that this path was too dangerous to follow, and resorted to a combination of nuclear blackmail, the policy of exclusion of South Korea, socialist neoconservatism, and a return to mass-driven attempts at improving economic efficiency with a focus on human resources.

Why Socialist Neoconservatism?

As we have seen, North Korea has been returning, since about 2005, to conservative, orthodox positions after a brief era of reform and new thinking that became visible around the time of the first inter-Korean summit of 2000. This is not to say that the summit led to the reforms, although it might have been a catalyst; rather, we would argue that the summit is one of the first signs that such a new thinking was gaining influence in Pyongyang.

The detailed reasons the reform path has not been continued are subject to ongoing research. We assume that, as it is often the case, the background is multicausal. As Chun argues, the very existence of South Korea creates an environment that leaves little room for a strategic reorientation after an unsuccessful transitional phase.[31] In other words, unlike China, North Korea does not have the option of a trial and error policy. Furthermore, it is unlikely that the U.S. attack on Iraq in 2003 has left no impression on policy-makers in Pyongyang, who have shifted their priorities from preventing another "Arduous March" to preserving the independence of their country, which was designated as part of the "Axis of Evil" and as a rogue state. The frequency of use of militant language in KCNA articles illustrates this: from 2001 to 2009, the combined use of the terms "front" and "struggle" has almost tripled, and its use is still twice as high as during the famine year of 1997.

Last but not least, it seems that despite all studies of the Eastern European, the Chinese and the Vietnamese experiences, North Korean policy-makers were surprised by the devastating effect the new economic policy had on the ideological coherence of their country. In combination with the unexpected serious health condition of the top leader and the unresolved succession issue, this has led to a destabilization of the domestic situation that not only prompted a return to "safe" old policies but also to an increase of tension in foreign relations.

As was to be expected, the reforms after the 2000 inter-Korean summit and the measures of July 2002 have created a domestic situation that became increasingly risky and burdensome for the leaders in Pyongyang. Despite the failures and shortcomings of the reforms, in a relatively short time North Koreans discovered, many for the first time, that there is a life outside the grace of the state. They suddenly and quickly realized the power of money. Their value system changed accordingly and moved closer to what most of us consider as a given. The socialist system of economic management and political guidance started looking outdated. The formerly largely egalitarian society experienced a swift diversification, with winners and losers, many unanswered questions, and growing individual ambitions.

To make matters worse, tens of thousands of young North Korean women had a chance to experience, on a daily basis, the benefits of a hypermodern South Korean working environment at Kaesŏng. We can only imagine how profoundly that changed their minds, and what kind of stories they told at home, acting as multipliers. Mt. Kŭmgang was a famous recreation area for North Koreans—until it was turned into a money-making business catering to the class enemy. Later, tour buses from the South entered not only the scenic yet isolated mountain but also the densely populated city of Kaesŏng. North Koreans on their way to work were stared at like animals in a zoo. This strongly reminds the author of his own experience of life in East Germany, when a cash-hungry government opened its highways for transfer visitors from West Germany. Hearing about the affluence on the other side of the Iron Curtain was one thing, seeing the advanced design and technology of Mercedes, BMW, Audi, or Volkswagen cars broke the heart of millions of family men who were crammed behind the steering wheel of their outdated Trabant. Their reaction was not to turn around instantly, drive to Berlin, and oust the Politburo. But they accumulated this frustration until there was a chance to let it out in the autumn of 1989.

North Koreans so far had little opportunity for similar experiences, so we should not underestimate the effects of marketization, the Kaesŏng zone, and the tourism projects. As stated above, it was not to be expected that this would lead to an immediate reaction. But, as in other formerly socialist countries, it is unlikely that all citizens have remained completely silent. We should not forget that the true believers in socialist societies, especially, used to write angry petitions to the higher levels when they discovered grave deviations between theory and reality. We have no reason to expect that this would have been any different in North Korea. Reports from the provinces must have been flooding Pyongyang, telling about new kinds of crimes, growing dissatisfaction of losers, and reckless behavior by winners. Local functionaries were frustrated by all the anger directed at them, and some will have passed it on to the higher levels, alerting the leaders in Pyongyang to the damage they had inflicted upon their legitimacy.

With its distinct institutional heritage, specific geopolitical situation, and, not least, aiming to gain ideological independence from the Soviet Union relatively early, North Korea is a case of socialism that exhibits a particularly large number of peculiarities, the nationalist *chuch'e* ideology and the hereditary leadership model being just two of them. However, this should not obscure our view of the fact that it still does match the criteria of a socialist system as outlined by Kornai.[32] Moreover, the monetization and partial marketization that the country has undergone in the past years have led to a significant societal transformation that we should not ignore. Against this background, it is fair to argue that North Korea is in many respects getting closer to the status of former Eastern European cases of socialism, although the distance is still huge and will hardly ever be bridged. Nevertheless, we can learn a lot from the long-term effects of half-hearted reforms that were not able to achieve any solution of the elementary problems of socialist societies but managed to severely damage the legitimacy of the respective regimes. It would amount to reinventing the wheel if we ignored the vast literature on socialism and tried to understand North Korea exclusively from a particularist point of view. This is even more so since our access to North Korea is severely limited, whereas we can study socialism in Eastern Europe freely.[33]

As the example of European socialism has shown, a situation as described above can be remarkably sustainable, that is, a loss of legitimacy does not necessarily lead to an instant loss of power. An internally slowly decaying socialist society can look strong and sturdy from the outside until it is so hollowed out that it collapses. Ironically, this corresponds with Marx's idea of quantitative changes that keep accumulating without causing qualitative changes until a critical mass has been reached and a revolutionary situation emerges. In Europe, it was the sudden retraction of the cohesive might of the Soviet Union under Mikhail Gorbachev that disturbed the power equation within the satellite states and allowed the accumulated dissatisfaction to manifest itself in protests that became uncontrollable within weeks. The process of de-legitimization had been going on for decades but was often only measurable by the increasing investment of the socialist states into their internal security apparatuses.

Socialism is built on the premise of moral superiority. This can make it enormously strong despite severe hardships, as the "Arduous March" has demonstrated—as long as the state does not violate its own ideological principles. In North Korea, we see the additional feature of closely interconnecting socialism with nationalism, the latter being a powerful source of legitimacy. But ideological corruption has meanwhile taken place, and the accumulation of frustration has started. As we have seen in Eastern Europe, false claims of moral superiority can become a heavy liability. If the limit is reached and a spark ignites the fuse, strength suddenly turns into weakness.

There are indeed growing signs that the leaders in Pyongyang are about to lose the hearts of their people. It is therefore only logical that they decided to pull the emergency break and try to reverse a development that will lead right into transformation. With the hindsight of socialist experience in Europe, we would argue that the only option to maintain their grip on power is to move forward, ride the tiger and "own" the transformation process, following the example of the Communist Party in China. It remains to be seen whether the North Korean leaders recognize this, and whether the limitations of their political system leave them the necessary leeway for such a transformation.

Socialist Neoconservatism in Foreign Policy

Overall Trends

A core argument in this paper is that the foreign policy of North Korea should be understood to a significant degree as a function of domestic developments as described above. As tempting as it might be to interpret all of Kim Jong Il's moves in the international arena as a signal to the outside world (such as Washington) or as a reaction to external pressure, we should consider that, as in most countries, domestic considerations dominate. North Korea does care about its international image and attaches high importance to its foreign relations. However, it also regards Korea as a small country that has historically been threatened, plundered, subjugated, attacked, and exploited by its neighbors who are all much bigger and stronger in almost every respect. This leads to a certain attitude that ranges from distrust and paranoia to excessive demands for apologies and compensation.

If we agree that domestic developments influence and determine foreign policy, and if we understand that North Korea is going through a phase of socialist neoconservatism, then we should expect a reflection of this in the realm of foreign policy. Testing this hypothesis is the goal of this section.

The DPRK has since its existence been faced with the additional problem of the parallel existence of another Korea. At least since the late 1980s, this has been the "better" Korea in the eyes of most international observers. The peaceful democratic transition in South

Korea, coupled with the economic success of the *chaebŏl*, added heavy ideological pressure on North Korea. At the same time, China was reforming. With the dissolution of the Soviet Union and the collapse of Eastern European socialist countries, North Korea's world fell apart completely. The early 1990s have been characterized by desperate attempts to find new paradigms for foreign policy and for international economic exchanges. The famine of 1995–1997 provided the final proof that something had to be done quickly. The solution was a return to another old success model of the 1950: invite international aid and ensure that there is competition between the donors, and that they do not lose interest in donating. The nuclear program, the most internationally visible part of North Korea's foreign policy, has become a core part of this new approach.[34]

Along with the trend of returning to orthodox policies, the foreign relations of North Korea have continued to deteriorate and increasingly resemble the situation before 1994. This essentially means that South Korea, Japan, and the United States are seen and treated as enemies. It should be noted that the aforesaid countries are usually mentioned critically. The frequency of appearance of their names in KCNA articles not only indicates their importance in the eyes of the North Korean propagandists but also the degree to which North Korea regards them as a threat, or its use of them as scapegoats. We find that by 2008 the patterns of the period before the year 2000 have been reestablished, with the United States being mentioned most frequently, followed by South Korea, and Japan as a distant third. We also note that in the years 2000 and 2001 the North Korean propaganda apparatus has shown particular restraint.

Relations with South Korea

Although North Korea undertakes tremendous efforts to sideline and ignore South Korea in the Six-party Talks, its southern neighbor is without any doubt the major object of North Korea's foreign policy. Even the United States is only a means to an end, but South Korea is an end in itself, as unification is the final goal of North Korean foreign policy. South Korea is also the biggest threat to North Korean ideology. Geographic proximity, the same language, and the growing welfare gap make South Korea the preferred destination of tens of thousands of potential defectors. Their number so far is relatively low (a total of 17,000 since 1948, with 2,809 in 2008 alone),[35] but the example of Germany is well known in Pyongyang.

Graphs 1.3 and in particular 1.4 show how at the beginning there was only a muted change in the treatment of South Korea in North Korean media despite the onset of the neoconservative phase, most likely as a consequence of the Sunshine Policy of Presidents Kim Dae Jung and Roh Moo Hyun. However, we observe a dramatically decreased readiness in Pyongyang to cooperatively deal with the new Lee Myung Bak government, as if the latter's return to a *quid pro quo* policy was secretly welcomed by "socialist neocons" in Pyongyang.

By late 2008, the rhetoric had dropped all remaining caution that we could still observe in early 2008. Not only the terminology (fascist,[36] sycophant, puppet, traitor, lackey, running dog) but also the contents of the statements (demand for toppling the Lee Myung Bak government) suggest that North Korea has decided to wait for the next administration in Seoul and meanwhile will try to largely ignore the Republic of Korea (ROK). A return to old paradigms is also visible when South Korea and its leaders are accused of siding with the Japanese.

This combination of verbal abuse and support of political opposition has, with the exception of the aftermath of the Nixon Shock in the early 1970s, been the typical southern policy of North Korea until the collapse of the socialist system in Europe. Box 1 below provides a qualitative analysis and highlights the major issues of criticism of North Korean media against the South.

The attempts by the North to retract the dangerously close inter-Korean cooperation are exemplified by the treatment of the Kaesŏng Industrial Zone. Actual events reflect the conflict between the political necessity of socialist neoconservatism and the economic pragmatism that has spread in the past years. Kaesŏng is curtailed, but not closed, although in the worst case North Korea might indeed be ready to give up the income from the zone in exchange for restored internal stability. If compared to a record foreign trade turnover of US$3.8 billion in 2008 (+29.7 percent compared to 2007 and the highest since 1990, despite sanctions), it is obvious that the economic relevance of the Kaesŏng zone is not necessarily high enough to justify the growing political and ideological costs of this project. The externally financed trade deficit of North Korea in 2008 was the highest ever with over US$1.5 billion, more than five times the lowest amount in 1998.[37] The current strategy of North Korea is to end or at least curtail all "dangerous" cooperation projects and put the blame on South Korea. This does not mean that cooperation is being cancelled for good; however,

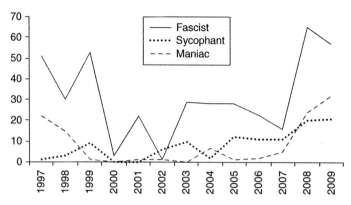

Graph 1.3   Change in the treatment of South Korea in North Korean media.

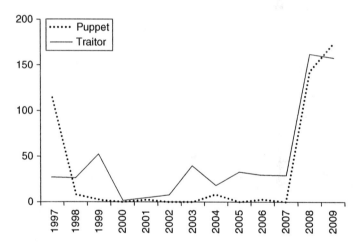

Graph 1.4   Return to old paradigms.

renewed contracts will very likely be more cautious regarding ideological "infection."

On January 30, 2009, the Committee for the Peaceful Reunification of Korea declared that it did not feel bound by the previous North-South agreements, especially referring to political and military confrontation; the Agreement on Reconciliation, Nonaggression, Cooperation, and Exchange between the North and the South; and the military boundary line in the West Sea. *Rodong Sinmun* on February 13th emphasized once more that "all the agreements adopted between the north and the

Box 1 Major issues of criticism against South Korea by KCNA in the period October–December 2008

Domestic issues:

- suppressing the democratic activities of its citizens, Hanch'ongryŏn (Korean Federation of University Student Councils), youth movements, media
- fascist suppression of women during demonstrations
- not abolishing the "fascist" National Security Law (NSL)
- revision of history textbooks and not fully uncovering past crimes in South Korean history
- attempting to establish a fascist dictatorial system
- banning books from libraries
- the law on part-time employment
- agricultural policy
- pushing the 2009 budget bill through the National Assembly

International relations:

- not abolishing the US-ROK Mutual Defense Treaty
- sycophancy towards the United States.
- the KORUS FTA
- military exercises
- favorable treatment of U.S. military forces
- revising OPLAN 5027–04
- sympathy with Japan

inter-Korean relations:

- faking alleged North Korean spying cases
- enlisting international support for reform and opening in North Korea
- aerial espionage
- psychological warfare against the DPRK including leaflets
- debasing and challenging the DPRK's ideology, system and its supreme dignity
- anti-unification policy and anti-reunification remarks
- putting the resolution of the nuclear issue ahead of improved inter-Korean relations
- war hysteria
- openly expressed the aim at unifying the country under its own system

south in the past have been reduced to dead documents after they were proved to be defunct."

Relations with Japan

Anti-Japanism has been a mainstay of North Korea's ideology and foreign policy ever since its foundation in 1948. As emphasized above, Kim Il Sung derived his legitimacy from his alleged leading role in the anti-Japanese liberation war; Japan was regarded as the arch enemy of the Korean people. However, the new pragmatism of the economic reform period opened the way to the long overdue normalization with

SOCIALIST NEOCONSERVATISM **25**

this eastern neighbor. A first attempt was made in 1984, when the first Joint Venture law aimed at increasing economic cooperation with Japan, although its target group was mostly ethnic Koreans. After many secret talks, by September 2002 Prime Minister Koizumi visited Pyongyang, held the first-ever summit with a North Korean leader, and achieved what can only be termed as highly unusual, showing the enormous readiness of North Korea to be pragmatic and risk-taking at that time. Kim Jong Il not only admitted that Japanese citizens had indeed been abducted in the 1970s but also allowed five survivors to return to Japan. Allegedly, this far-reaching concession was to be compensated by economic aid in the range of US$10 billion.[38] The reaction of the Japanese public was not as positive as expected, it was in fact the contrary, and the United States exerted heavy political pressure on Japan to stop their dovish approach at a time when the preemptive strike doctrine was being promoted in Washington.[39]

Accordingly, North Korea's relations with Japan froze and reached an all-time low, including decreasing foreign trade, while North Korea generated double-digit growth rates in trade with most other partners. Our analysis of North Korean media supports this picture. By 2009, the rhetoric had become even heavier than in the years before. The main arguments of the North Korean side can be summarized as follows: (1) Japan has no right to demand anything from North Korea (including clarification of the abduction issue) unless Japan shows sincere efforts to redress its own past, involving not only political steps such as apologies but also economic compensation following the German example; (2) Japan is the sworn enemy of the Korean people; (3) Japan prepares for a military attack and hence upgrades its military and sends its SDF forces outside its own territory.

Anti-Japanism thus returned as a major foreign policy line; note that it is particularly closely connected to nationalism, the mainstay of North Korean ideology and a crucial tool for maintaining the legitimacy of the leadership. In this context, it is interesting to note that Lee Myung Bak is particularly harshly attacked for his Japanese background (born in Japan), just as Kim Il Sung attacked Park Chung Hee (1961–1979) over the latter's military rank in the Japanese army. The use of the term anti-Japanese (usually referring to the heroic struggle of Koreans and in particular the Kim family) in KCNA articles analyzed yearly in the fourth quarter grew almost fourfold from 2002 to 2007.

In early 2009, *Rodong Sinmun* drew parallels with the situation around the 1919 uprising against the Japanese on March 1. As at that time, it

---

Box 2 Major issues of criticism against Japan by KCNA in the period October–
December 2008

International relations:
- military cooperation with the United States
- building a missile defense shield
- the intention of invading other nations
- contribution to peace-keeping activities, deployment of the SDF in the Middle East and
  ambitions to expand the operation of the SDF

Relations with Korea:
- claims of sovereignty over Tokdo
- preparing a reinvasion of Korea
  sanctions against North Korea
- crimes during the colonial period
- making economic cooperation dependent on the resolution of the abductee issue
- pushing the North Korean human rights issue at the UN
- suppressing the Korean minority
- plundering Korea's cultural heritage

Domestic issues:
- being a political pigmy
- Yasukuni Shrine visits of 48 Dietmen

---

argued, today there is a lot of pent-up resentment among Koreans. Now it is the U.S. imperialists who occupied South Korea in place of the Japanese imperialists, and who pursue the strategy for dominating Korea. Japan is accused of "whetting their sword for reinvasion" and trying to grab Tokdo instead of making an honest apology. In a rare disclosure of strategic objectives, *Rodong Sinmun* urges that the tripartite alliance between Washington, Tokyo, and Seoul must be prevented and checked.

On April 7, 2009, *Rodong Sinmun* called on all Koreans at home and abroad for a joint anti-Japanese struggle. Japan, it argued, was standing in the way of the Six-party Talks under the pretext of the abduction issue. Two weeks later, *Rodong Sinmun* commented on Japan's demands in the abduction issue. On April 20, 2009, it stated that "Japan is the arch abductor," referring to the "forcible drafting and abduction of Koreans committed by the Japanese imperialists." On April 28, *Minju Chosŏn* explained that Japan is responsible for the collapse of the Six-party Talks.

In connection with the satellite/missile launch, Japan was accused of hypocrisy since it has launched sixteen satellites of its own between 2004 and 2008. The wording of the related criticism is extremely heavy (shameless, brigandish, blackhearted, cunning, and crafty). It seems that the Japanese reaction to the North Korean missile launch has been used to raise the propaganda war against Tokyo to a higher level. In a reflection of nationalism, Parhae's influence[40] on the economy and culture of Japan is remembered. It "awakened the backward Japanese economy."[41]

Relations with the United States

North Korea's relations with the United States are enormously complex and would necessitate a separate chapter. In principle, it seems that North Korea has returned to its long-standing goal of having direct bilateral talks with the United States instead of a multilateral forum such as the Six-party Talks, thereby sidelining South Korea. The financial sanctions around Banco Delta Asia of Macao in late 2005 had also demonstrated that, without at least silent consent by the United States, North Korea would have no chance to actively and regularly participate in global economic exchange, including trade and access to finance.

If Japan is Pyongyang's arch enemy, then the United States is its nemesis. Most experts agree that North Korea's expressions of fear of the U.S. military power are real. Accordingly, there is indeed reason to believe that the nuclear program is in part motivated by a classical neorealist calculation of deterrence. North Korean leaders[42] perceive their situation as being constantly under surveillance by Washington, who is only waiting for a moment of weakness to strike. Accordingly, the aggressive policy since 2006, including the first nuclear test in October and all the way until the second nuclear test in 2009, corresponds with the logic as outlined below (see "Nuclear Issue" below), that is, that the deteriorating domestic situation has prompted North Korea to actively contain the risk of a U.S. intervention.

The absence of a strong initiative by the new Obama administration has added to the feeling of insecurity. The controversial arrest of two American journalists on March 2009, investigated by "a competent organ" (*haetang kikwan*) and liberated in August 2009 upon intervention by Bill Clinton, has added a new twist to the bilateral relationship. In particular, the release demonstrated that North Korea is willing to reach a deal with Washington.

The most frequently cited issue of criticism against the United States is the military presence in South Korea, including the upgrading of troops and equipment, military exercises, and so on. North Korean media also aggressively pushed the human rights question, stating that the United States is the biggest violator of human rights (Guantanamo) and hence has no right to criticize others. Indicating that this is a sensitive issue, reports by the United States on a serious situation of health care in North Korea and its consequences for North Korea's combat readiness were rejected as fabrications. Box 3 summarizes the major points of North Korean criticism of the United States.

There were a few times North Korean media referred to the case of Iraq, arguing that giving in to demands for disarmament will lead to destruction and hence cannot be accepted. This is not a new argument, as North Korea has repeatedly stated earlier that unilateral disarmament was short of committing suicide. However, a new turn in this regard was the statement of January 21, 2009, when KCNA declared, pointing at the Iraq experience, that the explicit attention that Washington was placing on the alleged DPRK missile threat had to be understood as a prelude for a preemptive attack by the United States.

On March 24, *Minju Chosŏn* stated that the U.S. troop relocation in the Asia-Pacific region (from Okinawa to Guam) was aimed at militarily containing China and Russia and being able to rapidly react to contingency on the Korean Peninsula and the Taiwan Strait. A few days later, *Rodong Sinmun* demanded the dismantlement of "the imperialists' overseas military bases." It is interesting to note how North Korea tries to involve China and Russia in its own policy against the United States.

On February 10, *Minju Chosŏn* criticized the United States over the modernization of its nuclear forces: The United States started the

---

Box 3   Major issues of criticism against the United States by KCNA in the period October–December 2008

International relations:
- establishing a global missile defense system
- setting up a new nuclear operation command in the Asia Pacific
- trying to put the Asian region under their control
- for raiding Syria and Pakistan
- moving more airplanes into the region
- modernization of its nuclear forces

Relations with North Korea:
- aerial espionage
- intending to launch a nuclear war on Korea
- its willingness to put Japan and South Korea under its nuclear umbrella
- applying double-standards to the nuclear activities of North Korea/Iran and Israel

nuclear arms race and forced other countries to join; North Korea, too, has been forced to spend "huge funds, manpower and a lot of time." It stresses that "it was none other than the U.S. that drove the DPRK to nuclear weaponization." This is an interesting remark since it hints at economic difficulties created by the focus on the military. It is unclear whether this is meant as an excuse meant for its own population, or as a hidden offer toward the United States.

Relations with China

Reports on China are much less detailed than we would expect, given the dominant role of the big neighbor for the economy and security of North Korea. In particular, a discussion of the Chinese reform policy is missing. However, our KCNA analysis shows a certain increase in the frequency of reporting about China, especially in the first years of the neoconservative reversal in 2004 and 2005. One of the few substantial comments found in the reports was made by the Chinese side on the occasion of the visit of a KWP delegation to China in late February 2009, when Jia Qinglin[43] emphasized that he warmly welcomed the visit by Kim Jong Il to China at any convenient time. This can be interpreted as the wish by the Chinese that the North Korean leader learns from their example. But when on March 17, 2009, Premier Kim Yong Il started his visit to China, North Korean readers learned little more than a few stations of his visit.

As a quantitative analysis of appearance in KCNA articles indicates, China and Russia are mentioned at about the same frequency. Since North Korean media are tools of propaganda, the discrepancy between the importance of these two countries for North Korea and their frequency of appearance in the media is not surprising. KCNA primarily publishes praise of North Korea or criticism of its enemies. Praise of friends, however, is rare.

Relations with Vietnam and Other Countries

After its bad experience with the Sino-Soviet split around 1960, North Korea had tried to reduce its dependency on big countries and focused on smaller, independent, and potentially friendly countries instead. This changed in the 1990s, but after years of dealing mainly with the members of the Six-party Talks and Korean Peninsula Energy Development Organization (KEDO),[44] we now see a certain return to such a policy, in particular in the context of the South-South relations (discussed below).

The case of Vietnam is particularly interesting. It is mentioned in a relatively large number of articles, which could be interpreted as part of the diversification policy in Pyongyang's international relations. On the other hand, the example of Vietnam also indicates that the neoconservative trend is what we described above—a not very promising *attempt* at turning back the wheel. It seems that the interest among North Korean leaders in alternative forms of socialism beyond the orthodoxy of around 1960 is still there. Vietnam is overshadowed by China but nevertheless has been another major example of successful socialist transformation in East Asia, demonstrating that China is not just the exception from the rule.[45] North Korea's relations with Vietnam and the official reporting thereof hence deserve special attention. A quantitative analysis of KCNA reporting shows that interest in this country shows a strong peak in 2007, when it increased sevenfold over the previous year, and still was twice as high as in the second-most intense period (1999).

On March 23, 2009, KCNA reported that a delegation of publicity and education officials of the Central Committee of the Communist Party of Vietnam headed by Nguyen Van Hoa had arrived. A delegation of political officers of the Korean People's Army (KPA) left to visit Vietnam on April 28th, and one day later a delegation of the Vietnam Union of Friendship Organizations arrived in Pyongyang. However, with the exception of 2007, we see a relatively stable interest. As in the case of China, this should be interpreted carefully, as a quantitative media analysis is by no means sufficient to track the actual intensity of bilateral relations. But it is worth noting that Vietnam is one of the few countries that are mentioned regularly in North Korean media.

South-South Relations and the New World Order

A glimpse at the official ranking of foreign countries in the eyes of Pyongyang is provided by the order in which they were mentioned as receivers of (Lunar) New Year's cards. Named representatives of the following countries were among the receivers, in the following order: PR China, Cuba, Russia, Laos, Vietnam, Lebanon, Maldives, Myanmar, Mongolia, Bangladesh, Syria, Cambodia, Thailand, Pakistan, Philippines, Tajikistan, Turkmenistan, Armenia, Jordan, Uzbekistan, Yemen, Monaco, Belarus, Croatia, Montenegro, Burkina Faso, Seychelles, Algeria, Ethiopia, Dominica, Trinidad and Tobago, and the Communist Party heads of Indonesia and India. Among other (unnamed) recipients of cards were the mayors of Moscow and Khabarovsk and the governors of Khabarovsk Territory and Maritime Territory. Note that Iran was not on this list, although the victory of the Islamic revolution in Iran was commemorated in a relatively long article on February 2, 2009. In addition to bilateral relations with its key adversaries and the major ally China, a major part of North Korea's foreign policy is the attempt at creating a multilateral alliance of anti-imperialist forces. This refers to the Nonaligned Movement (NAM, *ppŭllŏk pulgatam undong*) and in the past years increasingly also to the South-South cooperation (*namnam hyŏpcho*), a term that stands for the cooperation of developing countries and includes Iran as one of the most prominent partners. Collective self-reliance (*chiptanjŏk charyŏkkaengsaeng*) has been a principle stressed by North Korea for more than a decade.

Having attempted, with little success, to position itself as a leader of the NAM in the 1970s and 1980s, North Korea now returns to a policy that claims a major international role, thereby revealing another, rarely discussed rationale for the nuclear program. On February 23, 2009, *Rodong Sinmun* declared that the *sŏngun* politics of the Workers' Party of Korea under the leadership of Kim Jong Il has ensured peace and security in Northeast Asia so far. Peace could so far only be maintained "entirely thanks to the efforts exerted by the DPRK to bolster its military deterrent." Already it was argued in January that the North Korean nuclear program has prevented the outbreak of a nuclear war in the region.

According to North Korean media, a multipolar world is the trend of the times, and the unilateral leadership of the United States is about to end. It is claimed that North Korea has contributed strongly to the destruction of the "old" international order. The term "independence" has enjoyed increasing popularity since around 2005. Having been mentioned in about 150 KCNA articles up to the fourth quarter of 2002, it showed a steady increase to reach over 250 instances in the first quarter of 2009. On February 27, 2009, *Rodong Sinmun* demanded adherence to an anti-imperialist independent stand despite increased pressure. Cuba and Iraq were provided as examples of a successful and an unsuccessful policy. On January 27, *Rodong Sinmun* had pointed at Latin America and its successful defense of socialism from U.S. attacks.

Rodong Sinmun stressed on February 26 that all countries striving for independence should foil the "imperialists' ideological and cultural poisoning" with a revolutionary ideological offensive. Cultural exchange and the development of human civilization are criticized as Western attempts at destroying the ideological foundations of its adversaries.

It lamented that those who resist this ideological and cultural poisoning are berated as "closed societies" and "dictatorial states." The West advocates "freedom of thinking" and "theory of culture having no boundary" in order to force these countries to open their doors. We could interpret this stern warning as another indicator of serious problems regarding domestic ideological stability.

The theoretical rationale for the post-1956 policy of peaceful coexistence as promoted by Moscow and a core ideological element of socialist foreign policy has been the assumption that time is on the side of socialism. According to Marx, capitalism would at first be progressive but eventually reach its limits, take on the form of aggressive imperialism, and then collapse.[46] On February 24, 2009, *Rodong Sinmun* argued along these lines, declaring that the ongoing economic crisis was particularly severe and pushed capitalism to the verge of collapse. In full accord with classical socialist foreign policy views, it warned that in times of crisis imperialists resort to aggression and that it has to be expected that the United States will start an aggression against "North Korea, Asia and the world."

Nuclear Weapons

We do not intend to discuss the North Korean nuclear program in all its details and regarding its motivations; this will be done elsewhere in this book. The aim of this short section is to show how the nuclear program is reflected in state media publications, and to connect this to the domestic, in particular the ideological, developments we have outlined above in the context of the socialist neoconservative trend.

We would argue that, despite the obvious relevance of nuclear weapons for defense, the main purpose of the program must be sought in domestic motives, albeit the latter are not free of influence by foreign policy goals and developments. Domestic motives include the poor leadership record of Kim Jong Il. Ever since he took power, North Korea experienced one catastrophe after the other, beginning with the famine, natural disasters, and a failed economic reform policy. The successful development of nuclear devices is about the only success Kim Jong Il can present to his people. If we consider the high status of independence and nationalism in North Korea, this is a powerful argument to bolster his legitimacy not only among the ordinary people but also among the much more crucial elite. In the absence of any signs of broad public unrest, the only short-term scenario of sudden change in North Korea involves a coup by the educated, well-informed, and powerful North Korean "*nomenklatura*," regardless how realistic such a coup is. Accordingly, we are pessimistic that true and full denuclearization is a realistic option under the current conditions.

The official DPRK position on denuclearization is, however, quite different. The core element is the alleged last will of Kim Il Sung to denuclearize the Korean Peninsula. On second glance, this is a very flexible statement. As the Unites States has aircraft carriers and nuclear submarines, and since its long-range missiles can reach North Korea, it will always be easy for Pyongyang to argue that the peninsula is not free of a nuclear threat and hence it cannot give up its only deterrent.

Foreign policy goals of the nuclear program are clearly economic, on one hand, as every step of dismantlement is to be accompanied by economic compensation. They are also of a much more substantial political and diplomatic nature, as they include normalization of diplomatic relations with the Unites States and the conclusion of a peace treaty, and, most importantly, the acknowledgement that North Korea as a nuclear power enjoys equal rights as the Unites States, China, Russia, the United Kingdom, France, India, and so on. It takes little imagination to anticipate all kinds of demands based on this rationale that at some point will become unacceptable for the West and will serve as an excuse for North Korea to maintain its nuclear deterrent. Alas, the existence of the program is the only reason for the disproportionally high international interest in this small and underdeveloped country; so why give this up?

As our quantitative analysis indicates, the nuclear issue and socialist neoconservatism are interrelated. Graph 1.5 shows that there was a dramatic increase in the use of the term "nuclear" in the last quarter of 2002 (a whopping 1,550 percent over 2001). Obviously, this is the time after the visit to Pyongyang by Assistant Secretary of State James Kelly and the public revelation that North Korea had "confessed" to running a clandestine nuclear program on October 15, 2002. It is also, however, the time when, one year after 9/11, the Unites States was intensifying its War on Terror, and Bush's National Security Strategy (including the right to preemptive attacks) was published on September 4, 2002. In the first quarter of 2003, that is, the time of the attack on Iraq (March 20), the number of KCNA articles with the term "nuclear" rose to almost 300 (!).

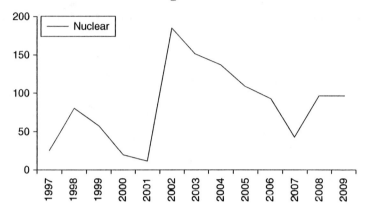

Graph 1.5   The term "nuclear" alone does not properly reflect rising tension.

This sudden prominence of the nuclear issue coincides with the failed cash-for-abductees deal between Kim Jong Il and Prime Minister Koizumi of Japan in September of 2002 and the resultant jeopardized economic reform measures of July 2002.[47] Assuming that it took the North Korean leadership a while to understand what was happening and how serious the American threats had to be taken, we see how substantially the situation had changed for the "reformers"[48] by 2003. The risk assessment of North Korea's top leadership was also modified. With regime survival being the highest priority, the double threat of weakening legitimacy as a consequence of economic reforms and the specter of being the next member of the "Axis of Evil" to be forcibly "liberated" has dramatically increased the perceived costs of continuing reforms and prompted the return to orthodox positions. Although we do not know for sure whether the train blast in Ryongch'ŏn of late April 2004 was indeed a terrorist attack or just an accident, the former would add to this picture of growing insecurity and socialist neo-conservatism as the response to it.

The decreasing prominence of the term "nuclear" in Graph 1.5 is somewhat astounding; however, we know that things need not be called directly by their name to be discussed. Graph 1.6 illustrates how ideology reacted with a certain time lag; the propaganda machine creating the traditional picture of being under "siege"[49] in order to rally North Koreans "around the flag" (a consequence

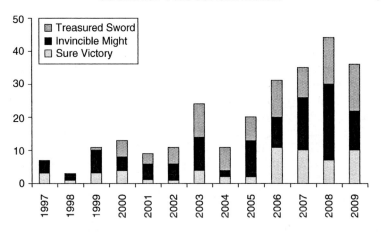

Graph 1.6 Ideological code words illustrate an increasingly militant stance.

of sanctions)[50] has been running at full speed since 2006 (the year of the first nuclear test), "treasured sword" (*wiryŏkhan pogŏm*) and "invincible might" (*paeksŭngŭi wiryŏk*) being euphemisms for nuclear weapons. In terms of rhetoric, we are back in the pre-2000 era of menace. On January 23, 2009, a spokesman for the National Peace Committee of Korea stated that the outbreak of a nuclear war on the Korean peninsula is a matter of time. Aggression would be answered with aggression. A week later, an army spokesman emphasized that North Korea will never give up its nuclear weapons unless the United States rolls back its hostile policy toward the DPRK and the complete removal of the nuclear threat by the Unites States. He specifically mentioned nuclear shells (for artillery). He insisted on verification in South Korea, that is, access for North Korean teams to all the territory and all facilities.

Conclusion

We set out with the goal of shedding some light on recent North Korean foreign policy behavior, especially against the background of domestic developments and the ideological foundation of legitimacy. In particular, we identified a socialist neoconservative trend, a return to hard-line and inflexible socialist values that has increasingly been replacing the pragmatic policy of the reform era. We combined a qualitative assessment of the situation with a quantitative analysis of North Korean media and applied this method to domestic policy and foreign affairs.

We have found that since around 2004–2005, and even more so since 2008, North Korea is returning to orthodoxy as it was created in the late 1950s and early 1960s, resembling a strongly Koreanized version of the Stalinist Soviet model. This refers to an emphasis on classical socialism with a strong nationalist component, values such as collectivism and self-sacrifice, militarism, political repression, xenophobia, and the prospect of a rosy future in exchange for enduring the temporary hardships of leading a front-line life.

In terms of economic policy, this socialist neoconservatism is reflected in a renewed emphasis on heavy industry and chemical industry at the expense of light industry, and the production of industrial goods versus consumer goods. The most visible sign of the neoorthodox trend in the economy is the resuscitation of the North Korean version of the Great Leap Forward. This campaign is officially termed the "great revolutionary upsurge," although we would rather call it Ch'ŏllima-2, after the original of 1958. The rediscovery of speed-battles adds to this impression.

External economic relations, too, are returning to orthodox positions. International economic cooperation is regarded as a necessary evil again, with grave consequences for politically risky projects such as the Kaesŏng Industrial Complex and inter-Korean tourism. The Six-party Talks are pushed into the background in favor of bilateral talks with Washington, probably under the silent participation of Beijing. However, we also argued that it would be unrealistic to expect a complete end to all international economic exchanges. Rather, we have to expect a redefinition and adjustment to the more risk-averse (in terms of ideological infection and preservation of independence) neoconservative policy.

This trend has been reflected in the North Korean state media's view on their external affairs. The radically changed position *vis-à-vis* the Lee Myung Bak government, the renewed emphasis on anti-Japanism, and the new interest in the Nonaligned movement all support this view. The emphasis on South-South cooperation adds to the new old strategy of diversification in foreign policy, as opposed to dealing with just a few major partners in the context of the Six-party Talks or KEDO.

With regard to the Unites States, the North Korean goals are to engage in bilateral talks to establish diplomatic relations, negotiate the denuclearization of the Korean peninsula, and to alleviate the military threat. Access to the world economy is seen as depending on U.S. consent. However, there is no trust. North Korea suspects that Washington's strategy is first disarmament followed by an attack on a defenseless enemy, along the line of Iraq, prepared by attempts at destabilizing the regime economically and ideologically.

The nuclear weapons program is presented, against this background, as the only available counterstrategy. It is now harder than ever to find signs of readiness on the part of North Korea to give up this program any time soon, although an exit is still kept open by referring to a complete denuclearization of the peninsula on the basis of equal rights between North Korea and the Unites States. The Six-party Talks in this context are reduced to a forum of confrontation, something that their very structure suggested from the outset. It is very unlikely that they will produce any tangible result, neither regarding denuclearization of North Korea nor forming an alliance between the other five parties. They might, however, serve as a fig leaf to hide their engagement in bilateral talks. We also stressed the key role of the nuclear program for bolstering Kim Jong Il's tattered legitimacy that had suffered from a string of failures; nuclear weapons are the only success he can present to his people and, more importantly, to the elite.

The economic reform period of the early twenty-first century seems to be over, at least for now. We stick to our argument that the potential of the reforms was enormous, and that they could have led to transformation. However, North Korea's leaders lacked the resoluteness to push the changes far enough, and the external situation affected the risk assessment negatively. Hence, in Kornai's terminology, in the end this was only a perfection measure, an attempt at making the system work, like many similar efforts we have seen in Europe. Therefore, the return to socialist conservatism is not as surprising as the reform experiment itself. We still do not fully understand what had triggered the reforms of July 2002, who the promoters and masterminds were, what the original plans and calculations have been. It is hence difficult to fully comprehend why exactly the reforms were ended and a new era of socialist neoconservatism has begun.

We have identified a few possible reasons, including a deteriorating domestic situation due to a changed societal contract in the wake of marketization, which raised the ideological and political costs of the reforms beyond the economic benefits. The equation was further disturbed by the increased security threat as perceived by North Korea in the context of the War on Terror, the "Axis of Evil" logic, and the Preemptive Strike doctrine. The domestic situation has become even tenser. Since August–September 2008, and probably even before, the North Korean leader experienced serious health problems. Without a leader, the political system built by Kim Il Sung cannot function. We are convinced that this system can, and will, be transformed so that it is headed by an organ of collective leadership. However, such a transformation is difficult and, above all, needs time. Time might be running out, however, for North Korea. If the notoriously unfounded rumors about an heir to North Korean leadership turn out to be correct this time, if Kim Jong Il has indeed chosen one of his sons as the next leader, then we must interpret this as a sign of desperation, as a backup option. The succession issue as such is not the subject of this chapter; however, we have argued elsewhere that existing reality in North Korea will most likely not allow such a hereditary transfer of power to be successful and sustainable.[51]

New opportunities have led to a diversification of North Korea's society that has left no village unaffected. Individuals tend to value their own situation not against absolute criteria but in relation to the situation of others. The results, as seen in other socialist countries, are growing dissatisfaction among those who find themselves to be the underprivileged and considered among the "true believers" of the system, who are concerned that everything they built with hard work during the past decades is crumbling to dust, and that their ideals are being betrayed. In this respect, North Korea more than ever has started resembling European socialism, although a wide gap still remains. Dissatisfaction will not lead to immediate results, but frustration accumulates and legitimacy weakens, thus preparing the ground for a sudden change, as was observed in Europe in 1989. If oxygen and gasoline come together, all it takes is a spark.

The regime has to react either by moving ahead and increasing the pace, scale, and scope of reforms, as it happened in China and Vietnam, or by trying to reverse the course and return to orthodoxy. For the moment, the North Korean leadership has chosen the path of socialist neoconservatism, for the reasons mentioned above. But all that we know about (socialist) economies tells us that, eventually, measures such as Ch'ŏllima-2 will inevitably fail. North Korea will have to rethink its neoconservative socialist economic policy, and foreign policy will follow suit. Concerned parties should be ready to seize that opportunity and offer a way out beyond the continuation of the game of nuclear blackmail. There are reasons to believe that the first reform effort failed partly because South Korea's Sunshine Policy was overshadowed by Washington's hard-line stance.

The outlook for the future thus depends heavily on the reaction of the international community. Pressure, sanctions, and military actions in the context of the Proliferation Security Initiative (PSI) are certainly justified by moral standards and legally backed by United Nations Security Council (UNSC) resolutions. They will, however, push North Korea further toward the conservative end of its policy spectrum, prolong the duration of the neoconservative phase, and increase the risk of conflict. The other wiser option for dealing with North Korea, as we would argue, is the attempt to recreate a climate that will keep the door open for a return to international cooperation and economic reform.

Notes

1. David Beetham, *The Legitimation of Power* (London: Macmillan, 1991).
2. Janos Kornai, *The Socialist System: The Political Economy of Communism* (Princeton: Princeton University Press, 1992).
3. Kim Jong Il, *Giving Priority to Ideological Work is Essential for Accomplishing Socialism* (Pyongyang, Korea: Foreign Languages Publishing House, 1995), http://www.korea-dpr.com/library/101.pdf.
4. Janos Kornai, *The Socialist System: The Political Economy of Communism*.
5. Suh Dae-Sook, *Kim Il Sung: The North Korean Leader* (New York: Columbia University Press, 1988); and Adrian Buzo, *The Guerilla Dynasty: Politics and Leadership in North Korea* (Boulder: Westview, 1999).
6. See Robert C. Tucker, ed., *Stalinism: Essays in Historical Interpretation* (New York and London: W.W. Norton, 1977).
7. For archival evidence, see Rüdiger Frank, *The GDR and North Korea: The Reconstruction of Hamhŭng 1954–1962* (Aachen: Shaker, 1996).
8. See Dieter Segert, ed., *Postsocialism. Remains of State Socialism and New Capitalisms in Europe* (Vienna: Braunmueller, 2007).
9. Such campaigns, and their failure, are typical for socialist systems. On an abstract level, they try to achieve in a centrally coordinated way what higher wages or fear of losing one's job do automatically in market economies: an increase in productivity, that is, in output per working hour. The difference is that instead of being work-harder-campaigns, in fact, they were work-longer-campaigns. Rather than increasing productivity, they increased the input of labor. Paul Krugman has argued famously that a similar logic was behind the East Asian Miracle, and that such a strategy is not sustainable. The same is true for socialism: continuously asking, and later forcing, people to work longer will eventually stop increasing production; productivity will in fact decrease as people get exhausted and decide to withhold performance. Paul Krugman, "The Myth of Asia's Miracle," *Foreign Affairs* 73, 6 (Nov–Dec 1994): 62–78.
10. Although, interestingly, the New Village Movement (*saemaŭl undong*) in South Korea in the early 1970s shows striking resemblance with Mao's Cultural Revolution.

11. See Brian Myers, "The Watershed that Wasn't: Re-Evaluating Kim Il Sung's 'Juche Speech' of 1955," *Acta Koreana* 9, 1 (January 2006): 89–115.
12. See Karl Marx and Frederick Engels, "The Manifesto of the Communist Party (originally printed as Karl Marx and Frederick Engels, *Manifest der Kommunistischen Partei* (London, 1848))," *Marx/Engels Selected Works, Volume One* (Moscow: Progress Publishers, 1969), 98–137. Marx-Engels Archive, http://www.marxists.org/archive/marx/works/1848/communist-manifesto.
13. Janos Kornai, *The Socialist System: The Political Economy of Communism*.
14. Ian Adams, *Political Ideology Today* (Manchester: Manchester University Press, 1993), 109–147; and Chris M. Hann, ed., *Postsocialism: Ideals, Ideologies, and Practices in Eurasia* (London and New York: Routledge, 2002).
15. John Jorganson, "Tan'gun and the Legitimization of a Threatened Dynasty: North Korea's Rediscovery of Tan'gun," *Korea Observer* 27 (1996): 282.
16. Rodong Sinmun (2003c), Sòn'gun Chòngch'inùn Minjokùi Chajusòngùl Wihan P'ilsùngùi Pogòm (Military-First Policy is a Precious Sword of Sure Victory for the Sovereignty of the Nation), April 3, 2003, http://www.kcna.co.jp/calendar/2003/04/04–04/2003–04–04–003.html, accessed May 1, 2003.
17. See Janos Kornai, *The Socialist System: The Political Economy of Communism*.
18. See Rüdiger Frank, "Economic Reforms in North Korea (1998–2004): Systemic Restrictions, Quantitative Analysis, Ideological Background," *Journal of the Asia Pacific Economy* 10, 3 (2005): 278–311.
19. Kim Jong Il, "21 Seginǔn Kǒch'anghan Chǒnbyǒnǔi Segi, Ch'angjoǔi Segiida [The 21st Century is a Century of Great Change and Creation]," *Rodong Sinmun*, January 2004, 2.
20. *Rodong Sinmun*, March 12, 2009.
21. *chosǒn chungang t'ongsinsa*, http://www.kcna.co.jp.
22. For a related discussion, see Rüdiger Frank, "The End of Socialism and a Wedding Gift for the Groom? The True Meaning of the Military First Policy," *NAPSNET Special Report* and *DPRK Briefing Book (Transition)*, December 11, 2003, http://www.nautilus.org/DPRKBriefingBook/transition/Ruediger_Socialism.html.
23. Rüdiger Frank, *The GDR and North Korea: The Reconstruction of Hamhǔng 1954–1962*, 97.
24. During the semireligious nationalist *Tonghak* movement of the late nineteenth century, the principle of "People are Heaven," or more literally, "Man and God are One" (*innaech'ǒn*) had been used widely, and today it is a key concept of the *Ch'ǒndokyo* religion that is also practiced in South Korea.
25. The People's Republic of China, too, introduced *Qingming* as an official holiday for the first time in 2008, lasting for two days (4–5 April).
26. On a side note, even East Germany had started a rethinking of its own traditions a few years before its collapse, including a positive reinterpretation of Prussian military tradition.
27. See Stephan Haggard and Marcus Noland, *Famine in North Korea: Markets, Aid, and Reform* (New York: Columbia University Press, 2007).
28. See Rüdiger Frank, "North Korea: Domestic Politics and Economy," in Rüdiger Frank, Jim Hoare, Patrick Köllner and Susan Pares, eds., *Korea 2008: Politics, Economy, and Society*. (Leiden and Boston: Brill, 2009), 27–44.
29. Kim, Jong Il, *Giving Priority to Ideological Work is Essential for Accomplishing Socialism*, (Pyongyang, Korea: Foreign Languages Publishing House, 1995), http:// www.korea-dpr.com/library/101.pdf.
30. Korean Central News Agency (KCNA), December 30, 2008.
31. Chaesung Chun, "Moving From a North Korean Nuclear Problem to the Problem of North Korea," *NAPSNET Policy Forum Online 09–047*, June 11, 2009, http://www.nautilus.org/fora/security/09047Chun.pdf.
32. Janos Kornai, *The Socialist System: The Political Economy of Communism*.

33. See Rüdiger Frank and Sabine Burghart, eds., *Transformation of State Socialism: North Korea and the Experience of Europe and East Asia* (Vienna: Praesens, 2009).
34. See Rüdiger Frank, "Lessons from the Past: The First Wave of Developmental Assistance to North Korea and the German Reconstruction of Hamhŭng," *Pacific Focus* XXIII, 1 (April 2008): 46–74.
35. Source: Yonhap News Agency.
36. We should note that the term "fascist" (as in fascist dictatorship, *p'assyo tokjae*) is not reserved to South Korea but is occasionally also applied to Japan. "Puppet," "sycophant," and "traitor" refer exclusively to Seoul.
37. KOTRA, *2008 Puhanŭi taewoemuyŏk tonghyang* [Trends in North Korea's foreign trade 2008] (Seoul: Korea Trade and Investment Promotion Agency, 2009), KOTRA 09–020.
38. Mark Manyin, "North Korea-Japan Relations: The Normalization Talks and the Compensation/Reparations Issue," *CRS Report for Congress RS20526*, (2001): 4, http://www.fcnl.org/pdfs/01june13_nkjapan.pdf.
39. *Rodong Sinmun*, September 4, 2002.
40. Parhae, also known as Bohai, was founded by remnants of the Koguryŏ elite after the fall of their kingdom in the seventh century. It occupied roughly what today is Manchuria and part of Russia's Far East. Today, Korean ultranationalists base their claim to these territories on ancient Koguryŏ and Parhae rule. The mentioning of Parhae is therefore not only a direct hit at the face of Japan but also an indirect one directed at China.
41. *Rodong Sinmun*, February 20, 2009.
42. Based on personal conversation of the author with North Korean cadres in Pyongyang and abroad, including embassy staff, government and party officials.
43. Jia Qinglin, a high ranking member of the Standing Committee of the Politburo of the Communist Party of China.
44. This includes the United States, China, Russia, Japan, South Korea, and the European Union.
45. See Ari Kokko, "Vietnam: 20 Years of Doi Moi," Rüdiger Frank and Sabine Burghart, eds., *North Korea, East Asia, and the Transformation of Socialist Systems: Institutional Frameworks and the European Experience* (Vienna: Praesens, 2009); Adam Fforde and Stefan De Vylder *From Plan To Market: The Economic Transition in Vietnam* (Boulder, San Francisco, and Oxford: Westview Press, 1996); Melanie Beresford and Dang Phong, *Economic Transition in Vietnam: Trade and Aid in the Demise of a Centrally Planned Economy* (London: Edward Elgar, 2001); and Duncan McCargo, ed., *Rethinking Vietnam* (London and New York: Routledge Curzon, 2004).
46. Karl Marx and Frederick Engels, "The Manifesto of the Communist Party."
47. Rüdiger Frank, "Economic Reforms in North Korea (1998–2004): Systemic Restrictions, Quantitative Analysis, Ideological Background," *Journal of the Asia Pacific Economy* 10, 3 (2005): 278–311; and Rüdiger Frank, "Dreaming an Impossible Dream? Opening, Reform, and the Future of the North Korean Economy," *Global Asia* 4, 2 (Summer 2009): 18–23.
48. It is not yet clear whether identifying such a group within the North Korean leadership is justified, at least not as a well defined entity or faction.
49. Selig Harrison, *Korean Endgame: A Strategy for Reunification and U.S. Disengagement* (Princeton: Princeton University Press, 2000).
50. David Cortright and George A. Lopez, eds., *Economic Sanctions: Panacea or Peacebuilding in a Post-Cold War World* (Boulder: Westview Press, 1995); and Rüdiger Frank, "The Political Economy of Sanctions against North Korea," *Asian Perspective* 30, 3 (2006); (Seoul: Institute for Far Eastern Studies, Kyungnam University, and Portland State University), 5–36.
51. Rüdiger Frank, "The Future of Political Leadership in North Korea," *Napsnet Policy Forum Online 08-072A*, September 23, 2008, http://www.nautilus.org/fora/security/08072.Frank.html.

CHAPTER TWO

People's Exit, Regime Stability, and North Korean Diplomacy

KYUNG-AE PARK

For nearly two decades, the North Korean government has been suffering from a chronic economic downturn. The persistent economic crisis has led to a virtual malfunctioning of the economic sector and the state-controlled distribution system. The state economy was unable to pay workers their regular wages and provide food through the Public Distribution System (PDS), to which only a small fraction of the population had access. Such vast changes in the overall spectrum of the national economy drove many North Koreans to exit from their country. Since the mid-1990s, when famine spread throughout the state, cross-border traffic has grown rapidly. The North Korean border-crossers began to enter China, South Korea, and other neighboring countries in large numbers.

As suggested in a growing literature that securitizes the phenomenon of refugee migration and analyzes it as a national as well as a regional security issue, the growing cross-border flows of North Koreans have far-reaching political implications for both Pyongyang and the international community. Many recent studies depart from the traditional view that refugee migration is the unintended consequences of military violence, emphasizing that it is a root cause of regional insecurity and instability.[1] They argue that it is a new transnational issue reshaping security environment by creating transborder conflicts and thus aggravating already precarious regional stability. Also viewing it as a national security issue, many observers regard people's exit phenomenon as a sign of collapse of the home regime, and as a "threat" to regime legitimacy and internal stability.[2] Others similarly argue that refugees could play a key role for regime change in their homeland. As one scholar observed, they could contribute significantly to democratic change in their native country by assisting and actively participating in the struggle of the domestic opposition, contesting the regime's international legitimacy, and obstructing friendly relations with the receiving countries through effective lobbies.[3] Some advocate exploiting refugee flows for the purpose of politically destabilizing the home regime.[4] According to them, refugees bring with them both useful intelligence and a wealth of general information regarding their native society, and thus the international community should encourage people's exit and work together to deal with the challenges posed by the refugees. This is particularly valuable when their home country is a closed and authoritarian system. Furthermore, they argue that the exit of high ranking government officials and professionals might be an indication of a power struggle within the home country, which could create opportunities that host countries could seize in order to empower the opposition groups in the home country.

Critics of this view argue that a massive refugee exit would not necessarily lead to regime collapse and regime transition but rather to a harsher crackdown on the refugees. In addition, considering the likely chaotic aftermath of a sudden instability or collapse of the home regime, where the security of the region and the safety of people's lives would be directly threatened, they view it as something to be avoided, not to be provoked. Accordingly, refugees should not be regarded as an agency fuelling regime breakdown in their homeland.

Much of the North Korean refugee research has focused on the human rights issues faced by the refugees, the political and economic status of the refugees in receiving countries, especially, in China and South Korea, their resettlement process, and regional conflicts caused by the refugees.[5] A largely unexplored area in the refugee research concerns the political consequences of the refugee flight for the current regime in Pyongyang. While some studies have examined the political and economic effects of North Korean people's exit on receiving countries,[6] few have examined its political effects on the North Korean regime. By analyzing whether North Korean refugees are expected to play a role of political opposition in exile, this chapter examines the phenomenon of North Korean people's exit and its implications for the stability of the Pyongyang regime, as well as its foreign policy toward the receiving countries of the refugees. The chapter will first examine the trends and patterns of people's exit from North Korea. Then it will evaluate whether refugees could become a resourceful critical mass that could challenge the current North Korean regime. Finally, it will analyze the impact of the exit phenomenon on Pyongyang's foreign policy.

The Exit Phenomenon

North Korean border-crossers began entering China and its neighboring countries in large numbers in the mid-1990s, as the Public Distribution System (PDS) began to grow increasingly ineffective and food security became a daily struggle for a large portion of the population. Although it is difficult to obtain reliable information on the number of North Koreans living in China, partly because many of them stay in hiding and some are moving back and forth across the border, most observers cite a figure of 100,000 to 300,000. The estimate by the U.S. State Department is much lower at approximately 30,000 to 50,000,[7] and the 2008 Amnesty International Report cited a ballpark figure of close to 50,000.[8] North Koreans seek refuge in China where they can receive the support and protection of local ethnic Korean communities, including those in the Yanbian Korean Autonomous Prefecture in Jilin Province, as well as those in Heilongjiang and Liaoning provinces. The Korean community in China has been offering protection to refugees for more than a decade. Although certain "aid fatigue" and the tightening grip of the Chinese authorities have impacted the eagerness with which Korean communities accept refugees, the memory of the North Korean hospitality and offers of food and shelter during the Cultural Revolution remains strong. One survey of North Korean refugees in China found that an overwhelming majority of 88 percent received help from the Korean ethnic community directly and more than three-quarters were living with Korean-Chinese.[9] Most refugees in China, however, live under a constant fear of arrest and, each year, on average, about 10 percent of them are repatriated forcibly.[10] According to the same survey, a majority of them, 64 percent, preferred to go to South Korea, followed by, surprisingly, the United States, to which 19 percent showed preference, and only 14 percent were satisfied to stay in China, possibly due to its harsh crackdown on refugees.[11] North Korean refugees enter China and then seek refuge in foreign embassies or make their way to third countries such as Vietnam, Thailand, Burma, Cambodia, Laos, and Mongolia, with the goal to resettle in South Korea.

South Korea, as the final destination of a vast majority of North Koreans, accepts them as Korean citizens and provides resettlement programs, which include financial aid and training. Most refugees who arrived in South Korea before the 1990s[12] were male political elites or military officers fleeing for political or ideological reasons, or individuals who had committed state crimes. However, the refugee community formed over the past decade reveals a different pattern of composition. In 2008, the number of refugees entering the South topped 15,000 (see Table 2.1). One of the most striking characteristics of this new refugee community is the ever-increasing proportion of women. In the late 1990s, most refugees were young single men; however, since 2002, women have surpassed men in numbers. In fact, in 2008, women accounted for 78 percent of refugees, up from 55 percent in 2002. Another noteworthy trend is the increase of the so-called "chain" defection. Unlike in the 1990s, many refugees today stay in touch with their families back home or in China and pave the way for their exit through smugglers or brokers, who charge the refugees for facilitating passage of their family members. Many refugees use the resettlement funds provided by the South Korean government to pay for their family's reunion, which further aggravates the financial problems they face during the resettlement process. Those who arrived in South Korea as "chain" refugees accounted for 20 percent of the total refugee population as of 2004.[13]

For the overwhelming majority of North Korean refugees in South Korea, the primary motivation for leaving their homeland is a desire to survive and generally improve their living conditions. While most refugees left for mere survival in the 1990s, with the food crisis ameliorating, recently more and more North Koreans are leaving in search of better jobs and economic betterment. It is observed that the pattern of exit has changed from survival to voluntary types. For this reason, some define today's refugees as "migrating laborers" rather than refugees, not different from the labor migrants of other countries.[14] To them, the borders they cross are not political barriers, but economic opportunities.[15] It is clear that economic difficulty is the prime reason for the exit of North Koreans. Many of them come from the North Hamgyong province, one of the poorest provinces and worst hit by famine, which is located in the northeastern region near the Chinese border.

Most refugees had no jobs or had worked as manual laborers in the North before fleeing to the South. As of January 2009, about 87 percent of the 15,271 refugees had been either unemployed back home or

Table 2.1 North Korean refugees entering South Korea

	Before 1989	1990–1994	1995	1996	1997	1998	1999	2000
Male	562	80	35	43	56	53	90	179
Female	45	6	6	13	30	18	58	133
Total	607	86	41	56	86	71	148	312

	2001	2002	2003	2004	2005	2006	2007	2008	2009, February	Total
Male	294	506	469	626	423	509	570	612	158	5,265
Female	289	632	812	1268	960	1,509	1,974	2,197	435	10,385
Total	583	1,138	1,281	1894	1,383	2,018	2,544	2,809	593	15,650

Source: "Statistics on Saeteomin," Ministry of Unification, Seoul, Korea, 2009.

Table 2.2   Occupation in North Korea (January 2009)

	Unemployed	Laborers	Office workers	Professionals	Sports and Arts	Service workers	Military	Total
N	7,102	6,206	356	336	150	586	535	15,271
%	47	40	2	2	1	4	4	100

Source: Ministry of Unification, Seoul, Korea, 2009.

Table 2.3   Educational Level of Refugees (January 2009)

	Preschool	Kinder garden	Elementary	Middle and High school	College	University	Other	Total
N	424	126	926	10,669	1,334	1,194	598	15,271
%	3	1	6	70	8	8	4	100

Source: Ministry of Unification, Seoul, Korea, 2009.

Table 2.4   Age of Refugees (January 2009)

Age	0–9	10–19	20–29	30–39	40–49	50–59	60	Total
Total	575	1,833	4,251	5,050	2,183	661	718	15,271
%	4	12	28	33	14	4	5	100

Source: Ministry of Unification, Seoul, Korea, 2009.

manual laborers (see Table 2.2). Soldiers accounted for 4 percent and office workers and professionals occupied only 2 percent, respectively. As the educational attainment data in Table 2.3 suggest, 70 percent of refugees attended middle or high school. Those with completed college or university education accounted for only 8 percent. The data suggests that only a very small number of refugees belonged to the elite or even the middle class. A vast majority of refugees, 75 percent, were in their twenties to forties when fleeing from the North. Many of the refugees as of 2009 were in their thirties, amounting to 33 percent of the total, with 28 percent in their twenties, and 14 percent in their forties (see Table 2.4). In sum, the typical refugee of the recent years is an impoverished, undereducated, young manual worker or an unemployed individual from a remote rural area, and is mostly female.

There have been reports about difficulties that the resettled North Koreans experience during their integration in the South. For instance, in the case of refugee youth, their middle and high school attendance rates are quite low, as shown in one survey: In 2005, the rates were merely 58.4 and 10.4 percent, respectively, and their drop-out rate, 13.7 percent, was about ten times higher than that of South Korean students.[16] Another survey revealed that about one-third of the refugee children and youth thought they were still North Koreans, although they were physically living in the South, and missed their days in North Korea.[17] What is more surprising is that only 10 percent of them hoped to become like South Koreans when they grew up. Facing difficulty in adapting to the capitalist way of life in South Korea, many refugees were found to suffer from posttraumatic stress disorder and some even wanted to return to North Korea or resettle elsewhere.[18]

Recently, some refugees have chosen to go beyond South Korea and China, even to the West, searching for better living conditions. Since the U.S. Human Rights Act went into effect in September 2004, the United States has accommodated about ninety North Korean refugees.[19] Great Britain admitted about 850 refugees by mid-2008, some 130 in 2007 alone, although many were found later to have already acquired South Korean citizenship.[20] Norway is North Korean refugees' favored destination in Europe due to its well-established social welfare system, but, out of the 72 asylum seekers, only seven were admitted, as most of them already held South Korean or Chinese citizenship.[21] According to one survey, 69 out of 100 refugees interviewed in South Korea preferred to proceed to a Western country.[22] If people's exit from North Korea continues to increase in the future, more people are likely to seek refugee status in the West.

Implications of People's Exit for Regime Stability in North Korea

In democratic regimes, grassroots organizations such as political parties, professional associations, and labor unions can play influential roles as internal allies for a dissident movement that threatens regime stability. However, allies of any mass movement in authoritarian regimes need to be external, such as transnational social movements, foreign governments,[23] or overseas dissident groups. Some value the political significance of refugees as likely members of overseas dissident groups and view them as an agency of fuelling the momentum for a gradual emergence of mass resistance in their home country. In addition, according to Weiner, refugees can serve as an instrument of threat against the home country, when the receiving countries attempt to pursue foreign policy objectives against that country.[24] As such, refugees are often perceived to influence directly the survival chances of the regime back home. Can North Korean refugees play a political role similar to that of overseas dissident groups, providing organizational basis for challenging the North Korean regime? Can they be expected to become an opposition in exile and play a major role in promoting regime instability and eventually regime change in North Korea? The chapter will attempt to analyze the issue by examining the following four questions.

Are North Korean Refugees Political Dissidents?

As alluded to earlier, people's exit from North Korea has been spurred mainly by economic, rather than political, considerations. Only 9 percent of the North Koreans in the South listed a political reason, or dissatisfaction with the regime, as the motive for their exit, while 55 percent of them listed economic difficulties. Those who came for a humanitarian reason as chain refugees striving to reunite with their families accounted for 20 percent. As noted above, the refugee community is dominated by those from the North and South Hamgyong provinces, who account for about three-quarters of the total refugees.[25] These provinces are close to the border and were the hardest hit by the food shortages. If people choose to exit for political reasons, refugees would not be so skewed toward these provinces. In addition, as is the case with South Korea-based refugees, the overwhelming majority of refugees in China came from impoverished backgrounds, as manual laborers and farmers. In 2005, they occupied 87 percent of a total of 1,346 refugees interviewed, with 62 percent laborers and 35 percent farmers.[26] As such, the overwhelming majority of North Koreans who crossed the border cannot be perceived as political dissenters whose exit could threaten the stability of the North Korean regime.

Furthermore, as noted earlier, women comprise almost 80 percent of the total number of North Korean refugees. What precipitated the women's exit from the country? As the economy began to deteriorate, women were the first victims of layoffs. However, at the same time, they had to assume the duty of family breadwinners in lieu of men who were still bound to the official economic sectors, often without receiving any regular wages. In order to find an alternative means for feeding themselves and their families, many women began to cross the border, as famine became pervasive. In one survey, more than 80 percent of women cited hunger as the reason for crossing the border.[27] The Refugees International also found that only two women among the sixty-five interviewed in 2003 and 2004 left the country for political reasons.[28] The concerns of these two women were their "hostile" class family backgrounds in North Korea, which they did not want to pass down to their children. As primary breadwinners in their families, women are forced to exit the country for economic survival. Also, North Korean men who are still tied to the place of their official employment are considerably less mobile.

Another possible reason could be the higher value ascribed to women as targets for arranged marriages, forced labor, and even entertainment in various sex industries. The Trafficking in Persons Report of the U.S. Department of State has placed North Korea in the lowest tier for five consecutive years, classifying it as a major source country of commercial sexual exploitation. Almost 80 to 90 percent of North Korean women in China were found to be victims of trafficking.[29] One important pulling factor stimulating trafficking of women to China is the gender imbalance caused by China's one-child policy, and parents' general preference for male offspring. Also fueling this gender gap is China's modernization, which sees more and more women leave their native countryside in search of better-paid jobs in the urban industrial sector. In the rural Yanbian area, for example, the gender ratio between males and females among the unmarried age group is a staggering 14 to 1, suggesting a high demand for women.[30] The Chinese State Council also estimates that 38 million bachelors in its rural provinces have difficulty finding a spouse.[31] Desperate to find a marital partner, Chinese bachelors resort to entering the North Korean bride market, thus aggravating the issue of women's trafficking. Unfortunately, some North Korean women are desperate enough to voluntarily enter this market, since they perceive a "live-in" arrangement as a guarantee of some financial security and reduced risk of getting arrested by the police for staying illegally in China. Some of these women are not only married to Chinese men but also to their North Korean spouses, and often have children back home. By entering into a second marriage in China, they are trying to alleviate their North Korean families' poverty.

Economic disarray caused an increase also in family breakdowns in North Korea, resulting in higher divorce rates. The high rate of North

Korean marriage failures is the result of women's frequent absences from home when searching for food, trading in distant places or peddling across the country, as well as their selling of sex for survival both in and out of North Korea. Family breakdowns, in turn, contribute to an increase in trafficking of teenage girls whose parents can no longer accept their custody. In addition, female refugees' testimonies reveal that economic hardships aggravated domestic violence against women.

In North Korea, the breakdown of the national economy forced women into involvement in private market ventures, such as private production and trading, as viable venues of income generation. Almost 70 percent of women who were not employed in the formal state sector became involved in trading activities.[32] Once women turned into the leading force of North Korea's marketization, they became also more resourceful and financially independent. Men, on the other hand, experienced a certain loss of identity, with their traditional economic roles shrinking, which made them more vulnerable to substance abuse. Many women reported that they fled North Korea to simply escape their husbands' physical, mental, and verbal abuse.[33] A study found that almost 20 percent of women defectors who reached South Korea after 1994 had left their husbands behind, a substantial increase from 6.9 percent prior to 1994.[34] Leaving the abusive relationship and their husband behind was the only solution for many female refugees who settled in South Korea with their children. Economic difficulties had a profound impact on women border-crossers.

As such, the trend in women's exit proves that economic consideration should be viewed as the most relevant push factor. Women are increasingly more responsible for securing economic livelihood for their families, and thus are forced to cross the border. Forming an overwhelming majority of the refugees, these women do not share an identity of political exiles. One woman living in South Korea remarked, "I agonize over whether I should reveal my sadness over Kim Jong Il's health...He is still our Dear Leader. It is the people who work with him and give him false reports who are bad. When I hear about his on-the-spot guidance and eating humble meals, I believe he cares for the people."[35] A July 2008 survey of refugees living in Seoul revealed that about 75 percent of them did not show any negative sentiment toward Kim Jong Il's leadership.[36] Moreover, a growing number of refugees were found remitting money to their families back home. Out of some 15,000 refugees settled in the South as of early 2009, over 6,000 were sending money to North Korea.[37] With family members back home, a fear of possible repercussions against those relatives would make it even more difficult for refugees to engage in a dissident movement against the North Korean regime.

Are North Korean Refugees a Resourceful Critical Mass?

According to the resource mobilization theory, poor people with grievances but no resources to fight for their rights are unable to initiate any organized protest. Only those who have "economic basis, social standing, organizational network and political connections" possess the "capability to press their claims in the political arena" and can instigate some collective action.[38] In particular, the economic power of refugees has been considered a critical factor in supporting democratic political movement inside homelands.[39] Without any doubt, the North Korean refugee community in the South forms an economically marginal group without much social standing. A survey revealed that a majority, 57.3 percent, considered themselves as lower class in South Korea and another 27.5 percent as living in abject poverty, while only 5 percent self-identified as middle class.[40] Another recent survey found that refugees earned less than one million won on average per month and that more than 60 percent of them were not satisfied with their income.[41] In addition, the unemployment rate among refugees, which is estimated at about 30 percent, is overwhelmingly higher than South Korea's average rate, and a majority of refugees, about 70 percent, are employed as part-time or irregular employees.[42]

The North Korean refugee community not only lacks economic and social assets but also political resources. As Hirschman observed, new immigrants "tend to be, at least initially, relatively un-vociferous members of society."[43] As such, they would hardly have the means to establish political connections and organizational network indispensable for a critical mass in a dissident movement. North Koreans in the South do not seem to be an exception. There are some 46 organizations formed by them in South Korea. Most of these, however, are social groups established with the aim of promoting a bond amongst North Koreans, as shown in Table 2.5, and only four of them were started with an explicit political goal, that is, to engage in anti-North Korean activities. Among them, The Democracy Network Against North Korean Gulag was founded in 2003 by former political prisoners striving to promote the need to dismantle North Korea's concentration camps. The North Korea Freedom Campaign was set up in 2008 for a similar reason of

Table 2.5   Refugee Organizations

Group	Political	Social and resettlement	Academic	Cultural	Media	Religious	Total
Number	4	20	5	7	4	6	46

Source: Collected and classified by the author.

putting an end to the existence of political prisons. The Committee for the Democratization of North Korea, represented by Hwang Jang Yop, the highest-ranked North Korean official who ever defected, was established in 2000 under the banner of an anti-Kim Jong Il movement. The Fighters for Free North Korea established in 2008 is also an anti-Kim group that is most active in sending leaflets into the North. It has helped a group of refugees fly leaflets critical of Kim's regime, urging the party cadres of the North to "oppose and topple" the regime. On some occasions, they even attached local currency as an incentive for North Koreans to pick up the propaganda.

However, even politically driven organizations are hardly resourceful enough politically, economically, and socially to become a critical mass. When refugees struggle for their own survival and resettlement in the South, participation in an organized dissident movement is not a top priority for them. Despite the recent formation of new refugee opposition groups in South Korea, the dissent might not possess the power to bring a breakthrough in sparking regime instability in the North. In addition, according to Paul Tabori, overseas dissident activities can rarely survive more than one generation.[44] The refugee community in the South cannot be seen as capable of forming a resourceful critical mass; to become such a mass, they would need to be equipped with organizational expertise, financial capability, and leadership in order to take collective action and to pose a serious threat to the regime in the North.

Does Exit Always Lead to Regime Instability?

According to Albert Hirschman, there are two types of reactions to discontent with organizational systems: to "voice" one's complaints in the hopes that matters will improve, or to "exit" by taking business elsewhere.[45] Since the food crisis, many North Koreans have been forced to choose the latter, and their mass exit from the country has been viewed as a prelude to the regime's imminent instability. In the case of people's exit, Hirschman argues that the state may react to the loss by taking measures to improve its performance. However, at the same time, he points out that mass exit can reduce social protest: the exit can function as an outlet for dissatisfied groups, and people will less likely resort to voice, especially when voice is more costly than exit. The role of voice would decrease as the opportunities for exit increase. Due to the seesaw relationship between the two, people's exit alleviates a number of economic and political problems for the state.[46] Allowing potential dissidents to exit can deflect internal pressures, which otherwise might result in an explosion, and thus can contain social protest. Therefore, according to Hirschman, exit might not necessarily pose a threat to the regime, but rather could bring a positive political effect of venting people's frustration. If exit tends to drive out voice, it could lead authoritarian regimes to even deliberately turn the exit valve to hold down the opposition voice. In this line of thinking, the available option for North Koreans to exit, albeit a risky one, to China, South Korea, and other countries can undermine the consolidation of a "voice" opposition. The presence of the exit option in North Korea can thus bring a political effect of the containment of social protest, preventing the regime's political stability from facing any serious threats. Given this reasoning, it would be unrealistic to perceive people's exit as an element of a political threat to North Korea, one that could seriously damage the regime's stability.

Would China and South Korea Encourage Refugee Influx and Exile Politics Against North Korea?

Receiving countries can view refugees as an instrumental agency of threat against the sending country and can tap into the refugee source in order to pursue policies against their home country. Often, pro-exile policies reflect the host countries' animosity toward the home regime, and refugee groups receive assistance "in recognition of their use as foreign policy instruments in related international rivalries."[47] As the two major receiving countries of North Korean refugees, if China and South Korea were to support refugee flight from Pyongyang and any dissident movement in exile, their goal for the refugee communities would ultimately be to repudiate the Pyongyang regime and trigger its instability. However, North Korean regime's instability is not in the best interests of either China or South Korea, as it could threaten their own security, as well as the security of the entire region. It could also be detrimental to the growth of their economy and could create a massive humanitarian and social crisis. As Pyongyang's collapse either through implosion or explosion is a potential time bomb for both countries, they are forced to attach much importance to ensuring the survival of the North Korean regime. Ironically, North Korea's vulnerability works as a great strength for Pyongyang, since it carries a potential threat to both its neighbors. It is China's and South Korea's hope, therefore, to avoid an exodus of refugees. North Korean refugees seeking resettlement in China and the South already pose some serious diplomatic and security concerns for both governments. For this reason, the receiving countries would be reluctant to encourage any refugee dissident movement, which would further complicate their situations. In particular, in China, such movement could threaten to boomerang against Beijing by triggering its own domestic dissident movement.

Unlike in Eastern Europe, where vibrant exile communities played a major role in promoting changes back home, in the case of North Korea, any overseas dissident group that could provide an impetus for a challenge to the North Korean government is virtually nonexistent. Reportedly, some 300 North Korean refugees have established an anti-Kim Jong Il group in China. It is claimed that its leaders are mostly former high-level officials of the Kim Il Sung government, who have been receiving the Chinese government's protection for several decades, in spite of Pyongyang's demand for their repatriation.[48] However, this group is unlikely to create any major political space due to China's fear of triggering instability in North Korea. Even the conservative South Korean government is not in a position to strongly encourage the refugees' anti-Kim Jong Il activities, as shown in its recent calls for restraint to some refugee organizations that floated leaflets, denouncing Kim Jong Il and calling for his ouster, into North Korea. The Seoul government made calls to halt the "freedom" leaflets campaign, warning that perpetrators could face imprisonment. Both South Korea and China, who do not want to see a sudden collapse of the North Korean regime, cannot be expected to encourage a refugees' dissident movement aimed at toppling the incumbent North Korean regime.

As such, the refugee community does not currently represent a critical mass that could trigger instability of the Pyongyang regime. This is contrary to the perception that people's exit is a sign of North Korea's regime collapse and a prelude to future overseas dissident movements against the Pyongyang government. North Korean regime stability does not seem to be threatened by the current refugee situation, although the potential of refugees becoming a critical threat should not be discounted should people's exit ever reach the point of developing into an uncontrollable mass exodus.

Implications of People's Exit for North Korean Diplomacy

Although the North Korean refugee community might be considered politically insignificant by the North Korean leadership due to its unthreatening nature, could it be a working force that North Korea should factor into the making of its foreign policy? In the past, the refugee issue was at the center of the legitimacy war between the two Koreas as they engaged in a fierce competition over their status on the Korean peninsula and attempted to undercut each other in every possible way. Refugees, who were considered political capital, then represented a symbolic victory and a certain superiority claim for either of the receiving Korean states. For this reason, political refugees on either side were granted special rewards and treatment, and were praised for their "brave act of defection." As the number of refugees increased, however, North Korean refugees began to be perceived as a liability rather than an asset by Seoul and other receiving countries, as too many of them could pose an economic strain. South Korea received only about 15,000 refugees in the past decade and a half, and China keeps tightening its grip on them. The worst fear for both countries is a massive flight of refugees across the border in the case of the fall of the Kim Jong Il regime. The United States has so far allowed merely seventy North Koreans to claim refugee status, even after the passage of the North Korean Human Rights Act in 2004. The cautious refugee policy of these countries has prevented serious diplomatic confrontations with Pyongyang. In fact, for North Korea, refugees are not always a liability in its foreign policy. In its efforts to solicit support from other countries, Pyongyang can play its mass exodus card to exploit neighboring countries' need to prevent possible instability in the region resulting from a sudden collapse of North Korea. It also can exploit the fact that an inflow of refugees might threaten domestic stability of receiving countries. On a few occasions, the refugee issue challenged Pyongyang's foreign policy when a large number of refugees were allowed to settle in South Korea through "planned defections" staged by South Korean nongovernmental organizations (NGOs). However, the refugee issue has not taken a priority in North Korea's foreign policy.

Nevertheless, Pyongyang cannot turn a deaf ear to the refugee issue. The continuous flow of refugees into China, South Korea, and other neighboring countries can increasingly cause diplomatic conflict and international attention-raising human rights concerns. Over the years, North Korea has already become a target of strong criticism from international human rights groups for its prohibition of unauthorized exit from the country and punishment for repatriated refugees. Pyongyang's penal code mandates labor reeducation of more than three years for illegal border-crossing, and more serious violations, such as making contact with South Koreans, religious organizations, or other foreigners, can result in five to ten years of imprisonment in reeducation camps or even greater consequences, including the death penalty. In order to deflect the international criticism of such severe punishment, notwithstanding that it does not acknowledge the existence of human rights abuses or recognize transnational trafficking, Pyongyang indeed eased the severity of punishment in the early 2000s. It made a distinction between political refugees and economic ones, who crossed the border simply in search of food. Pyongyang began to treat the punishment of these refugees in separate ways, and this dual penalty system makes it difficult for the international community to claim all border-crossers as refugees.[49] By revising its human rights legal provisions, North Korea attempted to better address refugees' human rights and to reduce its vulnerability to international challenges. In an effort to further avoid arousing international human rights concerns, Pyongyang recently decreased the number of public executions.[50] The refugee issue alone has already called for changes in Pyongyang's attitude toward the international community, and the North Korean government has shown to some degree its desire to deflect international criticism.

North Korea most often refrains from publicly responding to refugee issues raised by the international community; however, it did not hesitate to challenge other countries diplomatically when several mass-scale defections, planned ahead of time, occurred. After the South Korean government flew a total of 486 refugees from Vietnam in July 2004 for resettlement in Seoul, North Korea reacted harshly by condemning the planned large-scale defection and demanding the refugees' return. North Korea called the incident "premeditated allurement, abduction and terrorism committed by the South Korean authorities against people in the North in broad daylight."[51] Pyongyang perceived it as a politically motivated action intended to attack its human rights situation and to instigate the regime's collapse.

North Korea, consequently, cut off all dialogue with Seoul, and this incident became a decisive factor in the freezing of inter-Korean relations for almost a year. North Korea also recalled its ambassador to Vietnam, causing a severe diplomatic friction with the country. Although North Korean refugees, as argued above, are considered politically insignificant by the Pyongyang leadership, they could trigger continuing diplomatic conflicts for the leadership and invite intensified human rights criticism from the international community.

North Korea has been able to avoid, thus far, serious frictions with China on refugee issues, as China has made every effort to keep the issue bilateral in order to avoid international attention. It has kept the stance that it would settle the refugee issue in accordance with its domestic law and its agreements with North Korea. China does not recognize North Korean border-crossers as refugees but regards them as unauthorized economic migrants who must be repatriated to North Korea. Both countries have agreed in 1986 to "mutually cooperate on the work of preventing illegal border crossing of residents."[52] Although China has been a signatory to the United Nations (UN) Refugee Convention since 1982, it continues to repatriate North Koreans back to their homeland. For China, to recognize North Korean refugees as such would be tantamount to creating a new pulling factor for North Koreans to enter the country en masse. The Chinese government would face grave consequences and endless trouble. Also, it would certainly undermine China's relationship with Pyongyang. For these reasons, China is only reluctantly dealing with the North Korean refugee issue. In an effort to discourage North Korean refugees from crossing the border, Beijing offers rewards of around US$500 to those who turn them in. At the same time, the government fines those who assist refugees by up to US$3,600, especially targeting South Korean missionaries and NGO workers. China demands all foreign organizations to stop accommodating North Korean refugees and helping them enter diplomatic missions to seek asylum. It arrested some South Korean missionary groups that smuggled refugees into Seoul. Since the 2008 Beijing Olympics, China has further tightened the control over its border with North Korea. By taking all these measures, Beijing is trying to block the development of the "underground railroad" in China. Furthermore, China has denied access for the UN High Commissioner for Refugees (UNHCR) to North Koreans residing within its territory. Not being allowed to seek assistance from the Beijing office of the UNHCR, North Koreans often choose to seek refuge in foreign diplomatic compounds and schools, or travel to a third country, such as Thailand, where they have access to UNHCR, who determines their refugee status. It is in China's best interests to discourage North Koreans from crossing the border, and Pyongyang has been able to take advantage of this fact in its policy toward Beijing.

However, the increasing influx of North Korean refugees and the pressure on China from the international human rights community could create a situation that would leave China in an awkward position and strain its relations with other countries. The U.S. Congress passed a resolution in 2007 calling on the Chinese government to stop repatriating North Korean refugees and instead help them seek asylum. If China keeps turning a blind eye to the calls from outside, it will continue to generate disapproval from other countries. If China clamps down too hard on refugees, its actions could result in NGOs' efforts to orchestrate some high-profile asylum cases at foreign embassies and consulates, which would certainly provoke diplomatic disputes with the governments involved. In fact, South Korea once summoned a Chinese envoy to protest the arrest of North Korean refugees rushed into its international school in Beijing and the use of force against its diplomats who tried to intervene. Several other incidents involving North Koreans dashing into a Japanese Consulate compound, followed by a subsequent forced entry by the Chinese police, led to a diplomatic discord with Japan, which in turn ended up blaming Beijing for violating the right of diplomatic missions to provide sanctuary. On one hand, China is reluctant to antagonize its ally, North Korea, and it wants to avoid destabilizing the Pyongyang government. The refugee issue is also linked to China's own human rights problems. Therefore, China will continue to deal with the issue as quietly as possible, so that it does not aggravate the problem any further. On the other hand, China will try to avoid diplomatic frictions with other involved countries, including South Korea and the United States. In particular, since China's position now clashes with the Obama administration's and Seoul's Lee Myung Bak government's renewed emphasis on human rights, its refugee policy would incur serious concern and criticism from the international community. Thus,

China will try to demonstrate to the international community that it respects its commitment to international norms and human rights and honors its obligations under the UN Convention relating to the status of refugees. Most recently, in 2008, Beijing, in a rare move, allowed over forty refugees taking shelter in foreign missions to depart to the United States and South Korea. As China is kept under pressure, it is forced to seek compromise and balance its policy in order to avert an intensifying standoff with the international community, and this will challenge the Pyongyang-Beijing bilateral ties.

In Pyongyang's foreign policy toward Seoul's decadelong liberal governments, its refugees did not form a core contending issue, as South Korea was not proactive in promoting the outflow of North Koreans. Seoul did not actively emphasize the refugee concern so as to avoid unnecessary diplomatic frictions with North Korea as well as China. The basic premise was that its active diplomatic intervention in refugee issues could be detrimental to an improvement in bilateral relations with both countries. It also realized that an exodus of refugees to South Korea would cause too high a cost for its government and, at the same time, its active intervention could potentially aggravate the plight of refugees who would likely suffer from a bloody crackdown by the Chinese and North Korean authorities. In order to better accommodate and arrange settlement of refugees, Seoul established *Hanawon*, a three-month camp where they would be housed and educated, with an optional job-training course afterward. South Korea has also provided financial aid to North Korean refugees. As the number of refugees increased, however, Seoul had to slash financial subsidies by two-thirds in 2004 and strengthen the screening of asylum seekers, which seemingly discouraged the North Korean refugees' desire to settle in Seoul. South Korea also took a reserved stance during the UNHCR meetings by either not participating in, or abstaining from, voting on a UN resolution calling for improvement in human rights in North Korea. Out of its desire to maintain an engagement policy and not to further alienate Pyongyang from the international community, Seoul conducted a quiet, soft diplomacy on the issue of refugees.

However, Pyongyang's foreign policy toward Seoul on refugee issues is facing a tough challenge from the new conservative Lee government. In approaching the refugee issue, the Lee government, unlike South Korea's previous two liberal governments, has taken a tougher stance on violations of refugees' human rights. Shortly after the government came to power, it consulted with several receiving countries, including

Thailand and Mongolia, on the potential of establishing refugee camps in those regions. It also cast a positive vote in the March 2008 UN Human Rights Council on the extension of the term of the UN special rapporteur on North Korean human rights, adopting a stronger stance after a decade of near silence from the two previous governments. In November 2008, Seoul went still further by cosponsoring a resolution at the UN General Assembly criticizing Pyongyang's dire human rights situation, the first time it has done so. It has proactively raised the issue of human rights in the North and did not hesitate to cosponsor with the European Union another UN resolution condemning Pyongyang's human rights abuses, when it was submitted to the 10th session of the UN Human Rights Council in March 2009. North Korea countered Seoul by saying that there can be "neither dialogue nor the normalization of the inter-Korean relations as long as the Lee [Myung Bak] group kicks up the 'human rights' ruckus against the DPRK."[53] The South Korean government's increasing willingness to accept more refugees and to refocus on their human rights would contribute to precipitating the already adversarial relationship between the two countries. North Korea's foreign policy toward the South will face a tougher challenge on the refugee issue, which could easily spark another political confrontation.

In dealing with the refugee issue, North Korea has been facing more challenges from the United States than from China or South Korea. The United States has labeled North Korea one of the world's worst human rights violators and, in 2004, enacted the North Korean Human Rights Act. The Act authorized an annual fund of up to US$24 million to promote human rights of North Koreans by providing them with humanitarian assistance, protecting North Korean refugees by means of humanitarian and legal assistance, and supporting them in obtaining political asylum in the United States.[54] In response to this legislation, North Korea broke off from its previous quiet diplomacy approach on refugee issues and lashed out at the Act, calling it a "declaration of war" that would threaten any future dialogue attempting to resolve the nuclear issue. Citing remarks made by a U.S. Senator before the Act's passage in the Senate, that the downfall of the North Korean government was not far off, Pyongyang vehemently denounced the Act as an instrument to topple its regime.[55] North Korea also noted public statements made by Jay *Lefkowitz*, George Bush's Special Envoy on North Korean Human Rights, who characterized Pyongyang as "a government that inflicts on its citizens repression reminiscent of the most cruel totalitarian rulers of the 20th century..."[56] The United

States has disavowed any interest to bring down the regime, but North Korea perceived the legislation as a pretext motivated by Washington's desire for its regime change. Since Seoul's bringing of a large group of refugees from Vietnam in July 2004 also coincided with the passage of the Act, Pyongyang publicly accused the United States of working with South Korea with the ultimate goal of forcing its regime collapse. Despite North Korea's denouncement, the U.S. Congress in late September 2008 extended the Act to finance another four years of efforts to help North Korean refugees.

Although the human rights issue of North Korean refugees has strained U.S.-North Korea bilateral relations, Washington has not proactively searched for refugees and offered them asylum. In fact, when two North Korean refugees rushed into the U.S. Consulate in Shenyang in 2002, pleading for an approval of their entry into the United States, the Bush administration rejected their request. Washington has thus far accepted only about ninety refugees and has not promoted liberal resettlement policies, primarily out of fear that such actions might foster escape routes, the "underground railroad" system, for refugees into the United States. According to a Congressional report, encouraging North Korean refugees "to seek asylum at American diplomatic posts...could act as a magnet for drawing larger numbers of North Koreans over the border."[57] Washington has also refrained from pressing the issue of human rights of refugees, as it seeks a breakthrough in its nuclear negotiations with Pyongyang. The approach the United States has chosen, not to raise the profile of Pyongyang's human rights abuses, has assisted North Korea in managing refugee issues without incurring a serious standoff with the United States.

Washington's relatively passive stance, however, evoked some criticism within the policy community that advocated the use of refugee flows for the political purpose of weakening the Pyongyang regime. Amid their concerns that Washington has taken a step backward in trying to relieve the refugee problems, top nuclear negotiators of the new Obama administration met with a group of defectors and family members of North Korean abductees. Following the meeting, the State Department announced that the government has "not forgotten and will never forget the suffering of the abductees and their families."[58] In addition, the Obama administration's emphasis on U.S. leadership for promoting human rights worldwide will certainly challenge Pyongyang's foreign policy toward the United States. President Obama has made repeated references to human rights and stressed that he would exert bilateral and multilateral pressure on North Korea to improve its human rights record. Given this emphasis, refugee issues can come to the fore in future bilateral relations. Pyongyang's arrest in March 2009 of two American journalists, who were collecting information on the plight of refugees along North Korea's border with China, has already raised the profile of refugee and human rights issues. In the middle of unprecedented confrontational bilateral relations, the journalists had been convicted of illegal entry and "grave crimes against the Korean nation" before the former president, Clinton, secured their release. The North Korean refugee issue could be the cause of possible incidents of this kind in the future and could become a serious diplomatic concern straining Pyongyang's foreign policy.

As examined above, in contrast to the argument that people's exit could spark regime instability and eventual regime breakdown, North Korean people's exit is not expected to trigger any political threat to the regime. Most of the North Korean refugees are not political dissidents, nor have they organized into any resourceful critical mass capable of generating a threat to its home country. In addition, people's exit does not necessarily destabilize the regime as it can sometimes yield a positive political effect, by driving out dissidents' voice. Furthermore, several of the receiving countries, in particular China and South Korea, would not encourage exile dissident movement against North Korea for fear of Pyongyang's collapse.

In Pyongyang's foreign policy arena, the refugee issue has not been considered a priority agenda. However, given the changing diplomatic environment surrounding North Korea, the issue is expected to become one of the major contentions that could strain Pyongyang's policy toward China, South Korea, and the United States. With the increasing flow of refugees into these countries, the stakes of these governments on the refugee issue could come into conflict with those of North Korea, straining North Korea's relationships with its neighboring nations. In the currently unsettling and fluid diplomatic environment in the region, the refugee issue could emerge as a core challenge for Pyongyang in its foreign policy arena.

Notes

1. See, for example, Melissa Curley and Wong Siu-Lun, *Security and Migration in Asia: The Dynamics of Securitisation* (New York: Routledge, 2008). Alan Dupont, *East Asia Imperiled: Transnational Challenges to Security* (Cambridge: Cambridge University Press, 2001).

2. Andreas Schloehardt, "Migrant Trafficking and Regional Security," *Forum for Applied Research and Public Policy* 16, 2 (Summer 2001). Also see Harald Kleinschmidt, "Migration, Regional Integration and Human Security: An Overview of Research Developments," in Harald Kleinschmidt, ed., *Migration, Regional Integration and Human Security: The Formation and Maintenance of Transnational Spaces* (Hampshire, England: Ashgate Publishing Ltd., 2006), 110.

3. Yossi Shain, "Ethnic Diasporas and U.S. Foreign Policy," *Political Science Quarterly* 109, 5 (Winter 1994–1995): 811–841.

4. For an analysis of how refugees can be viewed as an instrumental agency of threat against the sending country, see Aristide Zolberg, Astri Suhrke, and Sergio Aguayo, "International Factors in the Formation of Refugee Movement," *International Migration Review* 20 (1986).

5. Rhoda Margesson, Emma Chanlett-Avery, and Andorra Bruno, "North Korean Refugees in China and Human Rights Issues: International Response and US Policy Options," *Congressional Research Service Report for Congress*, September 26, 2007; Stephan Haggard and Marcus Noland, *The North Korean Refugee Crisis: Human Rights and International Response* (Washington, DC: U.S. Committee for Human Rights in North Korea, 2006); Hazel Smith, "North Koreans in China: Sorting Fact from Fiction," in Tsuneo Akaha and Anna Vassilieva, eds., *Crossing National Borders: Human Migration Issues in Northeast Asia* (New York: United Nations University Press, 2005); Byung-Ho Chung, "Between Defector and Migrant: Identities and Strategies of North Koreans in South Korea," *Korean Studies* 32 (2009); Ihn Hyuck Kim, "Bukhan Inkwon kwa Talbukja Munje [Human Rights and the Problem of North Korean Refugees]," *Tongil Junryak* 5, 2 (December 2005); Jooshin Jung, ed., *Hyundai Talbukja Moonjeeui Ihae [Understanding of Contemporary North Korean Refugee Problems]* (Seoul, Korea: Prima Books, 2009); and Suyeol Oh and Jusam Kim, "Talbuk Sataerul Dulrossan Dongbuka Giyookeui Galdeungkwa Hyupruk [Conflicts and Cooperation on North Korean Refugee Issues in Northeast Asia]," *Tongil Junryak* 6, 1 (August 2006).

6. For example, Ming Liu, "China and the North Korean Crisis: Facing Test and Transition," *Pacific Affairs* 76, 3 (Fall 2003); and Andrei Lankov, "North Korean Refugees in Northeast China," *Asian Survey* 44, 6 (2004).

7. Rhoda Margesson, Emma Chanlett-Avery, and Andorra Bruno, "North Korean Refugees in China and Human Rights Issues," 4.

8. *Amnesty International Report*, 2008, 180.

9. Yoonok Chang, "North Korean Refugees in China: Evidence from a Survey," in Stephan Haggard and Marcus Noland, eds, *The North Korean Refugee Crisis*, 21.

10. James Seymour, "China: Background Paper on the Situation of North Koreas in China," commissioned by the UN High Commissioner for Refugees, *Protection Information Section*, January 2005, 26. According to Amnesty International, about 150 to 300 of North Koreans who crossed the border were forcefully repatriated each week. See *Amnesty International Report*, 2007, 159.

11. Yoonok Chang, "North Korean Refugees in China: Evidence from a Survey," 21.

12. A total of 607 between 1949–1989. See "Statistics on Saeteomin," *Ministry of Unification, Seoul, Korea*, 2009.

13. "Motives of Defection," *Social-Cultural Affairs Bureau, Ministry of Unification, Seoul, Korea*, June 2004.

14. Jung A Kim, "Buk Chulsin Ijuja, Geudeul eun Nugui myeu Mueutei Munjeinga? [Who Are the Migrants from the North and What Are the Problems?]," paper delivered at the *Workshop on North Korean Human Rights: Alternative Approaches to North Korean Human Rights*, sponsored by Dasan Human Rights Center, Seoul, Korea, November 30, 2005.

15. See Byung-Ho Chung, "Between Defector and Migrant: Identities and Strategies of North Koreans in South Korea," 20.

16. *2005 Nyeon Kukjunggamsa Jechuljaryo IV [2005 Documents for Parliamentary Inspection of National Affairs]* (Seoul, Korea: Ministry of Unification), 87 and 73.

17. Hong Jung Kyu, "One-third of North Korean Refugee Youths Miss Their Lives in North Korea," *Hankyoreh Sinmun* [*Hankyoreh Daily*], February 9, 2007, cited in Jih-Un Kim and Dong-Jin Jang, "Aliens among Brothers?: The Status and Perception of North Korean Refugees in South Korea," *Asian Perspective* 31, 2 (2007): 17.

18. See, for example, *Amnesty International Report*, 2008, 181; Ihn Hyuck Kim, "Bukhan Inkwon kwa Talbukja Munje [Human Rights and the Problem of North Korean Refugees]," 101–104; Jeon Woo Taek, "Issues and Problems of Adaptation of North Korean Defectors to South Korean Society: An In-depth Interview Study with 32 Defectors," *Yonsei Medical Journal* 41, 3 (2000); and Roland Bleiker, "Identity, Difference, and the Dilemmas of Inter-Korean Relations: Insights from Northern Defectors and the German Precedent," *Asian Perspective* 28, 2 (Summer 2004).

19. The figure is as of mid-2009.

20. Kim Sung-Jin, "Actual Conditions of North Korean Defectors," *Vantage Point* 31, 11 (November 2008): 18.

21. Ibid.

22. *Taipei Times*, November 22, 2004, cited in James Seymour, "The Exodus: North Korea's Out-Migration," in John Feffer, ed., *The Future of U.S.-Korean Relations* (New York: Routledge, 2006), 150.

23. Kurt Schock, "People Power and Political Opportunities: Social Movement Mobilization and Outcomes in the Philippines and Burma," *Social Problems* 46, 3 (August 1999): 361.

24. Myron Weiner, *The Global Migration Crisis: Challenge to States and to Human Rights* (New York: Harper Collins College Publishers, 1995), 137.

25. Yoonok Chang, "North Korean Refugees in China: Evidence from a Survey," 17.

26. Ibid., 16.

27. Moon Sookjae, et. al., "Bukhan Yeosongduleui Talbuk Dongkiawa Sangwhal Siltae [Motives of Defection of North Korean Women and the Status of Their Daily Lives]," *Daehan Gajonghakwheoji* 38, 5 (2000): 145, quoted in Im Sunhee, *Siklyangnan kwa Bukhan Yeoseongeui Yeokhal mit Euisik Byeonhwa* [*Food Crisis and Changes in the Role and Consciousness of North Korean Women*] (Seoul, Korea: KINU, 2004), 57.

28. Joel Charny, "Acts of Betrayal," *Refugees International*, April 2005, 7. The interviews were conducted in 2003 and 2004.

29. Rhoda Margesson, Emma Chanlett-Avery, and Andorra Bruno, *North Korean Refugees in China and Human Rights Issues*, 5.

30. Byung-Ho Chung, "Living Dangerously in Two Worlds: The Risks and Tactics of North Korean Refugee Children in China," *Korea Journal* 43, 3 (Autumn 2003): 198.

31. Sung Jin Lee, "Tragedy is Inherited for Refugees," *The Daily NK*, May 23, 2009.

32. Choi Myungsook, "90nyundai eiwho Josun Yeosongdeuleui Gajungaeseoui Samae Kwanhaeyeo [North Korean Women's Family Life after the 1990s]," in *Life of Women in North and South Korea and Korean-Chinese Women* (Seoul, Korea: Korean Women's Institute, Ewha Womans University, 1999), 10.

33. See Citizens' Alliance for North Korean Human Rights, *Class and Gender Discrimination in North Korea*, July 2005, 20; and *White Paper on Human Rights in North Korea*, 2003, 172.

34. Park Hyun-Sun, *Hyundai Bukhaneui Gajok Jedoei Gwanhan Yeonku* [*Research on Contemporary Family System in North Korea*] (Seoul, Korea: Ph.D. Dissertation, Ewha Womans University, 1999), quoted in Kyungja Jung and Bronwen Dalton, "Rhetoric Versus Reality for the Women of North Korea: Mothers of the Revolution," *Asian Survey* XLVI, 5 (September–October 2006): 755.

35. Cited in Andrew Salmon, "North Koreans Escape to Freedom but still Holds Kim Jong Il Dear," *The Times*, May 29, 2009.

36. *Survey on 297 North Korean Defectors* (Seoul, Korea: Institute for Peace and Unification Studies, Seoul National University), July 24, 2008.

37. *Chosun Ilbo*, February 9, 2009.

38. Rod Aya, "Popular Intervention in Revolutionary Situations," in Charles Bright and Susan Harding, eds., *Statemaking and Social Movements* (Ann Arbor: University of Michigan Press, 1984), 330–331.

39. Yossi Shain, "Mexican-American Diaspora's Impact on Mexico," *Political Science Quarterly* 114, 4 (Winter 1999–2000): 661–691.

40. Database Center for North Korean Human Rights, "2005 Nyeondo Saeteomin Jeongchaksiltae Yeongu [2005 Research Report on the Status of the Saeteomin Resettlement]," 158–159.

41. A survey conducted in March 2009 by the Ministry of Unification. See Kim Sue-young, "N. Korean Defectors Earn Less than W1 Mil. Per Month," *Korea Times*, March 24, 2009.

42. Yoon Yeo-Sang, "Guknae Bukhan Ital Jumindului Jeukeung mit Jogi Jongchak Bangan [Adaptation and Early Settlement Plans for the North Korean Escapees in South Korea]," *Database Center for North Korean Human Rights*, 2007. In 2006, their unemployment rate was between 14.7 and 36.5 percent, which stood in sharp contrast to South Korea's average rate of 3.5 percent. See "2006 Nyeon Kukjunggamsa Jechuljaryo [2006 Documents for Parliamentary Inspection of National Affairs]," *Ministry of Unification*, cited in Jih-Un Kim and Dong-Jin Jang, "Aliens Among Brothers?" 9–10. In 2005, about 52 percent of the refugees were daily workers and 17 percent were temporary workers, in comparison to the overall average of 9.7 percent and 22 percent, respectively, for the whole nation. See Ibid.

43. Albert Hirschman, "Exit, Voice, and the State," *World Politics* 31, 1 (October 1978): 102.

44. Paul Tabori, *The Anatomy of Exile* (London: Harrap, 1972), 38.

45. Albert Hirschman, "Exit, Voice, and the State," 90. Also see his book, *Exit, Voice, and Loyalty: Responses to Decline in Firms, Organizations, and States* (Cambridge, MA: Harvard University Press, 1970).

46. Ibid., 101–102.

47. Aristide Zolberg, Astri Suhrke, and Sergio Aguayo, "International Factors in the Formation of Refugee Movement," *International Migration Review*, 166.

48. *Weolgan Joongang* [*Joongang Monthly*] 351 (February 2005).

49. See, for example, Kum Soon Lee, "Talbukja Munje Haegeul Bangan [The Ways to Solve the Defector Problem]," *Research Reports, Korean Institute for National Unification*, December 1999, 99–102.

50. "White Paper on Human Rights in North Korea, 2009," *Korea Institute for National Unification*.

51. Korean Central News Agency, quoted in "North Korea: Harsher Policies against Border-Crossers," *Human Rights Watch*, 1 (March 2007): 1.

52. It is stipulated in Article 4 of the 1986 Mutual Cooperation Protocol for the Work of Maintaining National Security and Social Order in the Border Areas between China and North Korea.

53. "N. Korea says Dialogue Impossible until Human Rights Issue Dropped," *North Korea Newsletter*, 47 (March 26, 2009).

54. The U.S. Freedom House, financed by the money allocated under this Act, sponsored in December 2005 the largest-ever North Korean human rights conference in Seoul. The U.S. Special Envoy on North Korean Human Rights, Jay Lefkowitz, gave a speech demanding an improvement of the human rights situation in North Korea.

55. *Rodong Sinmun* [*Korean Workers' Party Newspaper*], October 18, 2004.

56. Jay Lefkowitz, "Freedom for All North Koreans," *Wall Street Journal*, April 28, 2006.

57. "North Korean Refugees in China and Human Rights Issues: International Response and U.S. Policy Options," *Congressional Research Service Report*, RL34189, January 18, 2008, 23.

58. Stephen Bosworth and Sung Kim met with them. *Associated Press*, April 29, 2009.

CHAPTER THREE

Food Crisis and North Korea's Aid Diplomacy: Seeking the Path of Least Resistance

MARK MANYIN

It has been nearly a decade and a half since North Korea, then in the grips of a devastating famine, opened itself to the international community for food and development assistance. Since that time, much has changed in both North Korea's internal and external environments. This chapter seeks to analyze North Korean behavior during this time by examining data on food aid as well as on inflows of aid and commercial imports from China.[1]

Data Challenges

A major challenge of identifying and assessing North Korea's aid diplomacy is gathering data. North Korean data are sporadic and questionable, and gaining access to reliable North Korean statistics is problematic, to say the least. This leaves the researcher reliant upon mirror statistics from aid donors and trade partners, as well as interviews with aid workers. It also means that the researcher has to infer North Korean policy from the behavior and impressions of outsiders, leading to a "blind men and the elephant" problem of trying to stitch together a coherent picture based upon sporadic and often unconnected pieces of data. Also, the on-again, off-again nature of North Korea's commercial imports and occasionally its aid inflows can make it difficult to distinguish patterns from statistical noise in the data.

The data problem is complicated by the opacity of North Korea's two largest benefactors, South Korea and China. Comprehensive South Korean figures in the latter Roh years became increasingly difficult to obtain. Whether by accident or design, the Ministry of Unification's and Korean Export-Import Bank's publication of statistics became less and less transparent over time. This problem seems to have been rectified under the Lee Myung Bak government and because Seoul's aid flows to North Korea have fallen precipitously with the overall deterioration in North-South Korean relations following Lee's inauguration in February 2008. However, given the highly politicized nature of Seoul's policy toward Pyongyang, aid data on the Roh years that is retroactively published must be sifted with a fine sieve.

The results of digging through the data on aid to North Korea is a kaleidoscope of images that occasionally coalesce into insights but also often produce mysteries, particularly in the case of China. The Chinese government does not publish or release its data on aid to North Korea, except to report to the World Food Program's International Food Aid Information System (INTERFAIS) database. However, the manner of such reporting makes it impossible to distinguish between China's aid and commercial exports, to say nothing of the extent to which commercial exports are being sent at "friendship" prices to North Korea. As discussed below, there is some evidence that Chinese exporters have been charging a premium to North Korea for some items, particularly on fuel since the mid-2000s. However, this leads to a second puzzle: are the North Koreans actually paying for these items? As is discussed below, one of North Korea's largest sources of aid may be an implicit subsidy from China, which has allowed North Korea to run persistently higher bilateral trade deficits. This reduces the utility of China's customs data on prices.

With these caveats in mind, the chapter proceeds as follows: first is an examination of North Korea's food aid diplomacy, with a focus on five elements of North Korea's opportunistic strategy of ensuring a stable supply of food on the most favorable terms possible. The food assistance section is followed by a look at the data on inflows from China, North Korea's largest provider of aid. Chinese commercial exports of food and fuel are examined, including the subjects of friendship prices and China's presumed balance of payments support to North Korea. In general, the chapter does not deal with assistance from nongovernmental organizations (NGOs), which in some areas and at some times has been significant.

Food Aid

Food assistance is perhaps the largest form of aid North Korea receives. The DPRK's food gap generally is estimated to be in the range of one million metric tons (MT) per year. According to Noland and Haggard, nearly 70 percent of the assistance North Korea had received through 2005 took the form of food aid.[2] The Noland/Haggard analysis does not include food aid from China, which the World Food Program (WFP) reports has been the second-largest donor to North Korea.[3] The importance of food aid is also shown in South Korean outlays under its Democratic Republic of Korea (DPRK) Support Fund: food and related aid (i.e., fertilizer and funds given to South Korean NGOs for humanitarian work) have constituted well over half of the US$3.3 billion spent under the fund. And, by value, food aid comprises more than half the aid provided by the United States and virtually all of Japanese assistance.[4] The data on food aid reveal a number of characteristics of North Korea's food aid diplomacy.

Ensuring a Floor of Food Inflows

Figure 3.1 shows estimates of the total volume of food assistance flowing into North Korea, based on the WFP's INTERFAIS database.

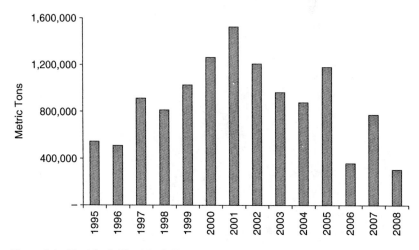

Figure 3.1   Total food aid to North Korea, 1995–2008.

The figure shows that, since 1997, by which time North Korean authorities presumably had adapted to the new food environment and consolidated their food aid diplomacy, North Korea had ensured a rather stable inflow of food. While it is true that food inflows vary significantly, this obscures the larger point that in all but two years— 2006 and 2008—over 650,000 MT of food was brought into the country either gratis or on concessional terms. In other words, North Korea's aid diplomacy has been rather successful in ensuring a stable supply.

Opportunism

North Korea has been adept at maintaining this inflow of food by opportunistically turning from one donor to another[5] (see Figure 3.2). In 1995, when North Korea first sought outside help to alleviate its famine, Japan and South Korea were the first to respond with large aid packages. In the years immediately following, European countries and the United States gave large pledges through the WFP, and China began to resume the shipments that had largely halted after the death of Kim Il Sung. Subsequently, in the late 1990s and early 2000s, Chinese and especially U.S. food aid rose steadily, more than offsetting the gradual reduction in European and South Korean aid. Japan, acting

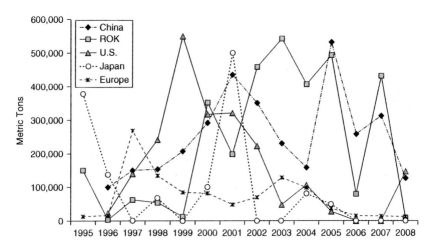

Figure 3.2 Annual food aid by major donors, 1995–2008.

on Prime Minister Junichiro Koizumi's drive to normalize relations with North Korea, came forward with a massive food package in 2001. But Japanese aid dropped to zero the following year when normalization talks foundered over the issue of Japanese citizens abducted in the 1970s and 1980s. This pattern repeated itself on a smaller scale in 2004–2005.

Meanwhile, South Korea reemerged as a major food donor following the first-ever inter-Korean summit in June 2000 between Kim Dae Jung and Kim Jong Il. In the period of 2002–2004, Seoul was the largest recorded provider of food aid to Pyongyang. Except for a dip in 2006, South Korea generally provided between 400,000 and 500,000 MT a year.[6] During that time period, donor fatigue set in among the Western countries, which began to react negatively to a number of developments: North Korea's tightening of restrictions in 2004 and 2005 on the WFP's access around the country and ability to monitor shipments; the eruption of the second nuclear crisis in 2002; and the realization that the North Korean regime effectively had chosen to remain dependent on food aid because it was not expending foreign exchange on imports of food.[7] By 2005, China and South Korea were virtually the only donors to North Korea, including in the months after severe floods in 2007 contributed to an exceptionally poor harvest that year.

In early 2008, however, North Korea reacted negatively when the new Lee Myung Bak government in Seoul announced that it would only provide food and fertilizer if requested by Pyongyang.[8] (The Kim Dae Jung and Roh Moo Hyun governments apparently had not waited for a request from North Korea.) Instead, North Korea turned to the United States, which agreed to provide 500,000 MT after Pyongyang agreed to loosen its restrictions on access and monitoring. Ultimately, however, the working relationship between the United States and the DPRK broke down; only about 170,000 MT of the assistance was provided.

Not only has North Korea donor-shopped among its major food providers, but it has also opportunistically obtained one-off donations from other countries. The largest example is Syria, which donated 140,000 MT in 1996 and 42,000 MT in 1999. An analysis of WFP's INTERFAIS data reveals that these one-off appeals were particularly important in the mid- to late 1990s. In 1996, food aid from outside the top five donors represented 45 percent of the total, a share that steadily declined in subsequent years. By 2000, however, donors outside the top five accounted for less than 10 percent of the total, a feature that has persisted ever since.[9]

Prioritizing Bilateral Donations

A third feature of the North Korean aid regime is that bilateral donations have been more important than those made through the WFP, the dominant multilateral actor in food assistance. The channel of delivery—multilateral or bilateral—is significant because bilateral contributions are given as a result of direct negotiations between North Korea and the donor country. They therefore are a useful proxy for North Korean aid diplomacy.

In the initial famine years, according to INTERFAIS, over 75 percent of the donations were bilateral in nature, as donors scrambled to provide food any way they could in response to North Korea's urgent appeals. From 1997 to 1999, the multilateral channel dominated. By this time, the WFP operation and its donor appeals had become somewhat routine, European aid (which has consistently been sent through the WFP) was at its peak, and South Korean and Japanese food donations were being sent through the WFP rather than bilaterally. Additionally, China's contributions—always sent bilaterally—were still modest, in the 150,000 MT range.

By the early 2000s, the importance of bilateral donations had grown in importance. The WFP, through the INTERFAIS database, reports that the bilateral route accounted for over 60 percent of total contributions for all years after 2001. In the period of 2005–2007, bilateral donations—essentially those from China and South Korea—comprised over 80 percent of the food donated to North Korea. The WFP became virtually irrelevant from the period 2006–2007, the period when North Korean authorities pushed the WFP to scale back to a skeletal operation. The WFP's importance temporarily resumed in 2008, when it became clear that Seoul's typical 400,000–500,000 provision of food aid would not be forthcoming from the new Lee Myung Bak government, North Korea then negotiated a new protocol with the United States. About 400,000 MT, or 80 percent, of the ensuing 500,000 MT U.S. pledge in food aid was to be sent through the WFP, which under the agreement was to have greater freedom to monitor its shipments. The remaining 100,000 MT was to be channeled through a consortium of U.S. nongovernmental organizations (NGOs).

Even the percentages mentioned in the previous paragraph understate the importance of political factors in the donations. In 1999, 2000, and 2001, donations through the WFP exceeded those given directly to North Korea, and featured large, politically driven donations from the United States and Japan. This was the peak period of U.S. aid, which, as Marc Noland and Stephan Haggard have documented, took place when the Clinton Administration acted at least in part in response to North Korean actions on political matters, such as participating in the Four-party Talks, missile talks, and opening up suspected missile sites.[10] They also were years when Japan, which has always explicitly linked food donations to diplomatic gains, turned up its aid spigot by sending over 600,000 MT in conjunction with the reopening of Japan–North Korea normalization talks. So, despite the WFP's twelve years of operating in North Korea, a sizeable portion of Pyongyang's food assistance has been received as a result of direct negotiations with its aid partners.

Simplifying Food Aid Diplomacy

A look at the WFP data reveals that North Korea's food aid diplomacy has targeted four players—China, South Korea, the United States, and Japan. These four accounted for over 80 percent of total food aid provided to North Korea in 1995–2007. Moreover, the importance of the "Big Four" have been even more after the Europeans ceased to be major food donors since 1998, as they began to prioritize development

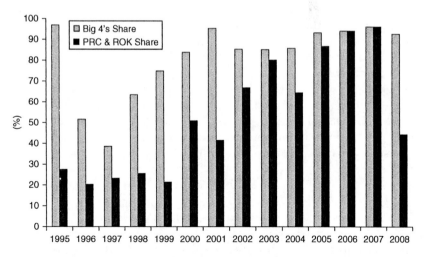

Figure 3.3 "Big 4" (ROK, PRC, United States, Japan) share of food aid contributions.

assistance (see Figure 3.3). Also, the number and size of anomalous one-off large donations, such as the aforementioned 140,000 contribution by Syria, fell off significantly. By 2000, the four contributed over 80 percent, and in most years over 90 percent, of all the food given to North Korea.

The implication is that, in the worst famine years of the mid-1990s, North Korea scrambled to obtain food from whatever sources it could find. By 1999 and 2000, donors had essentially been reduced to four countries, presumably making North Korea's aid diplomacy much easier to carry out.

In the period 2002–2007, North Korea simplified its food aid diplomacy further by effectively shrinking the list of donors to two, China and South Korea. In the period 2002–2004, China and South Korea alone provided well over half of the donations. By 2005, these two countries were virtually the only ones donating food. This was the case until South Korean food aid ceased at the beginning of the Lee Administration and North Korea turned to the United States to try to make up the shortfall.

Minimizing Conditionality

North Korean authorities preferred Chinese and South Korean food aid since these shipments were provided with little to no monitoring. There is no evidence that China has attempted to track, monitor, or impose any other humanitarian conditions on its food assistance to North Korea. As for South Korea, South Korean monitoring visits did increase over the course of the decade. For instance, South Korean officials conducted twenty monitoring trips in 2005, up from one in 2000. However, the visits were relatively few in number, conducted by nonresident officials, and were largely confined to major food distribution centers. By way of comparison, in 2005, the WFP had a much more intrusive presence in North Korea, with over forty expatriate staff and six offices around the country conducting thousands of monitoring trips every year.

Pushing Back during Times of Plenty

Another feature of North Korea's food aid behavior shows wide shifts in the central authorities' attitudes toward the WFP. In general, North

Korea has used times of plenty to push back against the WFP, particularly since 2004. The following year, North Korea had its best harvest in a decade. By then, Pyongyang could count on large, and largely unconditional, food aid from South Korea and China. These two situations allowed Pyongyang to demand that the WFP switch to development assistance and reduce its intrusiveness inside North Korea.[11] In the years prior to this move, the WFP had steadily increased the number of counties in North Korea it could reach and the ability of its field offices to monitor aid shipments, notwithstanding tightened restrictions that the North Korean authorities' imposed in the fall of 2004.[12]

Weeks of negotiations ensued, resulting in a 2006 agreement by which the WFP drastically scaled down its program and designed it to feed only 1.9 million people, which was less than a third of the 6.4 million people the WFP previously had targeted. In the deal, the WFP expatriate staff was cut by 75 percent, to ten people, all of whom were based in Pyongyang.[13]

Softening during Times of Hardship

In contrast, times of worsened shortages often have coincided with more permissive attitudes. In 1997, during the height of the famine, WFP official Tun Myat used the threat of withdrawal to successfully pressure Pyongyang to open the northeastern provinces.[14] Likewise, the May 2008 North Korea-U.S. agreement to provide 500,000 MT of food with fewer restrictions came after it was clear that North Korea would not be receiving any food or fertilizer aid from South Korea.

However, a better-than-average harvest in the fall of 2008 was followed by the breakdown of a June 2008 North Korea-WFP agreement that had enabled the WFP to return in full force to North Korea. As a result, the WFP program was reduced to a skeletal presence. Later, in March 2009, North Korea asked the U.S. NGOs to shut down their portion of the U.S. government food aid program three months early. Many speculated that North Korea had closed the program in part due to the overall deterioration in relations with the United States and South Korea in 2009. Notably, North Korean authorities shut down neither the relief and development programs run privately by many of the same U.S. NGOs nor the low-profile, US$4 million U.S. government program to aid rural hospitals.[15]

In August 2009, North Korea reversed months of belligerent rhetoric and actions, and began making overtures toward the United States and South Korea. Some have speculated that Pyongyang may have been partly motivated to soften its stance by a desire for increased food donations due to ongoing shortages. Other contributing factors may have been Kim Jong Il's apparent reemergence after a prolonged illness, and the effects of U.N. Security Council sanctions imposed after the May 2009 nuclear test.

Chinese Assistance

Despite the widespread assumption that China is North Korea's most important benefactor, the least is known about Beijing's aid to Pyongyang. Information about Chinese assistance therefore is often anecdotal and partial. From the data that is available, three features stand out. First, the relative importance of Chinese aid has risen markedly over the past few years. Second, most of the reporting on Chinese aid emphasizes that such assistance has become increasingly decentralized, particularly since the mid-2000s. Third, since the late 1990s, North Korea always seems to have been able to count on Chinese aid, though that assistance has changed in form over time. True, there have been times when China has withheld assistance, such as in the 1993–1994 period following Kim Il Sung's death. But in the end, however reluctantly, China has returned to its role as North Korea's main patron. No doubt, planners in Pyongyang have been able to operate under the assumption that Beijing will not be willing to risk the collapse of the North Korean regime, which could trigger a flood of refugees across the North Korea-China border and lead to South Korean and American intervention north of the demilitarized zone.

Chinese assistance to North Korea is divided into four types: construction of factories and other facilities; provision of food; provision of fuel; and, perhaps most importantly, implicit balance of payments subsidies. Of the first kind, large-scale demonstration projects that Chinese construction firms build at little or no cost to Pyongyang are characteristic of Chinese assistance around the globe.[16] An example of this type of aid is the glass factory that reportedly was built after Chinese parliamentary chief Wu Bangguo visited Pyongyang in 2003 in an effort to persuade North Korea to join the nuclear talks. However, the fragmented and often secretive nature of Chinese assistance program has meant it is nearly impossible to gather data and other information about these projects. Researchers therefore must rely on news reports. Thus, least is known about this form of assistance.

Inflows of Chinese Food

The second type of Chinese assistance has taken the form of food shipments. As mentioned above, according to the World Food Programme statistics, China has been the second-largest provider of food aid, primarily corn and then rice, to North Korea since 1995.[17] According to some sources, the unconditional nature of Chinese food assistance has allowed Chinese food assistance to be used for the military and the elite. According to International Crisis Group (ICG) interviews with WFP officials, for instance, the WFP's in-house monitoring throughout North Korea in 2005 revealed no knowledge of Chinese-donated food, despite estimates that China gave over 400,000 MT of aid that year.[18]

However, calculating Chinese food aid is problematic; the opaque way the Chinese government reports its food aid to the WFP makes it impossible for the WFP to distinguish between aid and commercial exports.[19] As Figure 3.4 shows, North Korean imports of cereals from

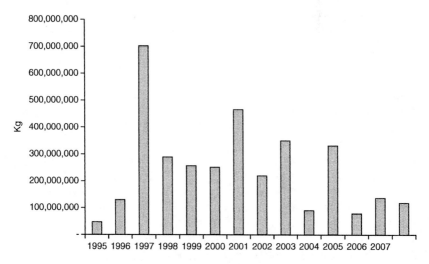

Figure 3.4   China's export of cereals to North Korea.

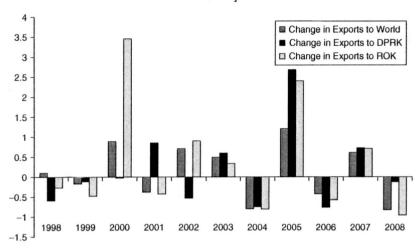

Figure 3.5   Year-on-Year percentage change in PRC cereals exports.

China have been substantial, particularly in the 1997–2003 period. Aside from 2004 and 2006, the inflow of grains from China has always exceeded 100,000 MT. Chinese exports of cereals since 2005 appear to have undergone a secular shift downward. Between 2005 and 2006, shipments of corn and rice fell by a factor of four, from around 330,000 MT in 2005 to under 80,000 MT the following year. Although exports nearly doubled in 2007, following flooding and a poor harvest, they have yet to reach the same level as had been the case in the past.

Moreover, as Figure 3.5 shows, Chinese cereal exports to North Korea appear to be only occasionally tethered to trends in Chinese shipments of these products to the world and to South Korea. The tightest correlation appears to be in 2003–2007, when Chinese grain exports to North Korea rose or fell by roughly the same percentage as Chinese exports to South Korea and its other trading partners. During the other years, Chinese shipments to North Korea bucked more general trends in Chinese grain exports, perhaps indicating that events particular to North Korea—be it increased North Korean demand and/or political considerations in Pyongyang—were driving Chinese bilateral exports. For instance, it is interesting that in 2008, when global and national food shortages and rising prices led to restrictions on Chinese food exports, Chinese grain shipments to North Korea fell by only 13 percent, against 82 percent and 96 percent declines in shipments to the world and to South Korea, respectively.

Inflows of Chinese Fuel

Fuel is also widely considered to be a component of Chinese assistance to North Korea. Figure 3.6 shows Chinese shipments of crude oil, coal, and other petroleum products in 1995–2008. After dropping sharply during the famine years, energy inflows stabilized somewhat around 2000–2002. Strikingly, since 2005, fuel imports have been virtually unchanged. During this same period, North Korean imports of Chinese cereals has dropped, indicating that fuel may be assuming a larger component of Chinese economic patronage.

Friendship Prices?

It is widely believed that substantial portions of Chinese exports of food and fuel have been provided on friendship prices, or at least were so provided until market forces began assuming a larger role in the

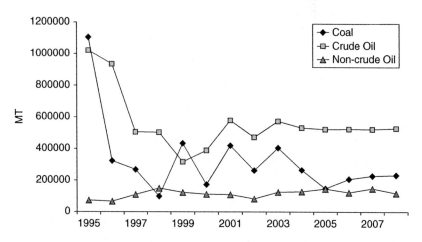

Figure 3.6   Chinese energy shipments to North Korea, 1995–2008

mid-2000s.[20] The shift downward in Chinese cereals exports after 2005 may be an indication of this change. However, Chinese customs data contradict this point, throwing the analysis into some confusion. According to Chinese customs, aside from three years—1995, 1996, and 2008—North Korean importers generally paid a slight *premium* to bring in grains from China.

Chinese customs data also report that North Korea also has been paying a premium on oil and coal imports, particularly since the middle of the decade. If accurate, this data would seem to confirm the many anecdotal reports that the era of friendship prices has passed.

Export Credits and China's Implicit Balance of Payments Aid

However, the information on prices that is reported by Chinese Customs may be largely irrelevant, as it is unclear what prices North Korean importers at the end of the day are actually paying. According to a number of sources, China has allowed North Korea to run up large—and growing—trade deficits. This is perhaps the most important source of Chinese assistance, particularly over the past seven years.

Noland and Haggard estimate that the cumulative value of North Korea's chronic trade deficit with China (China to North Korea) from the mid-1980s through 2006 was nearly US$7 billion.[21] Since 2002, although North Korean exports to China have nearly doubled, imports from China have risen more than fourfold, leading to a cumulative trade deficit since 2002 of nearly US$4 billion. As Figure 3.7 shows, North Korea's trade deficit with China has grown over the past decade, particularly since 2005, when imports from China began to take off. In 2008 alone, North Korea is estimated to have run a US$1.2 billion gap with China.

While increased Chinese foreign direct investment in North Korea since 2005 as well as remittances from North Koreans in China undoubtedly have helped finance this bilateral trade deficit, press reports and other research indicates that the central government in Beijing provides at least partial credits to Chinese exporters who receive orders from North Korea.[22] If these reports are accurate, it may indicate that the system may be a hybrid market/command one, such that the orders for Chinese products are driven by demand from North Korean customers.

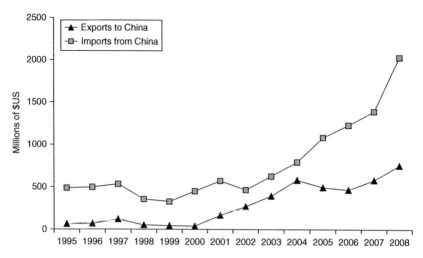

Figure 3.7   North Korea-China trade, 1995–2008

The exporters then approach Chinese central authorities to determine the portion of the order that will be subsidized.[23]

In this context, it is worth noting that China's relative economic importance to North Korea has risen markedly since earlier in the decade. Table 3.1, reprinted from Dick Nanto's work on the North Korean economy, shows North Korea's major trading partners since 2000. The table demonstrates the growing dominance of China and South Korea, who by 2007 provided around 75 percent of North Korean imports and exports (see also Table 3.2).

China's rise is particularly striking. In 2000, it accounted for 3 percent of North Korea's total estimated exports and 24 percent of imports. By 2007, these numbers had jumped to 31 percent and 43 percent, respectively. According to some reports, the 41 percent jump in bilateral trade in 2008, combined with a fall in DPRK-ROK trade after the election of President Lee Myung Bak, led China to account for nearly three-quarters of North Korean trade.[24]

Conclusion

The foregoing analysis leads to a number of conclusions about North Korea's aid diplomacy, none of which should come as a

Table 3.1   Estimated North Korean Trade by Selected Trading Partner, 2000–2008 (US$ in millions)

North Korean Exports

	2000	2001	2002	2003	2004	2005	2006	2007	2008
World	1,307	1,148	1,278	1,251	1,524	1,683	2,048	1,854	n.a.
China	37	167	271	395	586	499	468	584	754
Japan	257	226	235	174	164	132	78	0	0
S. Korea	152	176	272	289	258	340	520	765	930
Russia	8	17	11	3	5	7	20	34	14
India*	20	3	5	1	4	8	9	41	n.a.
Thailand	19	24	45	57	91	133	148	34	29
Germany	25	23	29	24	22	45	17	16	21

North Korean Imports

	2000	2001	2002	2003	2004	2005	2006	2007	2008
World	1,859	3,083	1,970	2,049	2,615	3,093	2,962	3,242	n.a.
China	451	573	468	628	799	1,081	1,232	1,393	2,033
Japan	207	1,066	133	92	89	62	44	9	8
S. Korea	273	227	370	435	439	715	830	1,032	890
Russia	38	62	69	111	205	206	190	126	97
India	173	162	182	157	121	55	105	660	n.a.
Thailand	189	106	172	204	239	207	216	184	48
Germany	53	80	139	71	68	63	63	34	31
Balance of Trade	−552	−1,935	−692	−799	−1,090	−1,410	−914	−1,388	n.a.

Source: Reprinted from Dick Nanto, CRS Report RL32493, North Korea: Economic Leverage and Policy Analysis. S. Korean data from S. Korea, Unification Ministry. World trade data from U.N. COMTRADE Database, accessed via U.S. Department of Commerce, Trade Policy Information System, August 2008. Country data from Global Trade Atlas and U.N. COMTRADE Database. World trade totals mirror data derived from U.N. reported country trade with North Korea plus inter-Korean trade reported by South Korea and adjusted Indian data for 2006 and 2007.
*Data for Indian imports from North Korea seem in error. (Items such as electrical machinery and parts, in particular, likely actually were imported from South Korea.) After comparing reported Indian data with that for China, 2006 imports by India from North Korea of $475 million were reduced to $9 million, and 2007 imports of $173 million were reduced to $41 million.
n.a. = not available.

surprise to those who follow North Korean behavior closely. North Korean officials have been highly opportunistic over the past fourteen years, turning from one benefactor to another in accordance with their needs. This is shown most prominently in North Korea's pursuit of food aid. Through such steps, North Korean aid diplomacy has been effective in assuring a significant supply of food and fuel. In contrast, though this is not discussed in this chapter, the DPRK has been largely unsuccessful in reaching its stated goal of transitioning from humanitarian to developmental assistance. North Korea has sought international donors that impose minimum conditions on their assistance. Whether as part of a deliberate policy or the outcome of steps taken in other areas, in 2003–2007, North Korea essentially had narrowed its aid providers to South Korea and China. Both countries provided their assistance with no or minimal humanitarian conditions. Meanwhile, the United States, European countries, Japan, and United Nations organizations largely withdrew from the field due to political factors, most prominently the emergence of the second nuclear crisis and the breakdown of normalization talks between Pyongyang and Tokyo over the abduction issue.

When harvests and the economy improved, North Korean central authorities generally have been less accommodating in their relations with food aid donors. This behavior was on prominent display in the spring of 2008, when Pyongyang reacted to the stoppage of food aid from South Korea by turning to the United States and consenting to long-standing U.S. demands for fewer restrictions on monitoring. One related factor that is not explored in the chapter, but which is worth noting, is that the experience of international aid providers, particularly NGOs, reveals that local North Korean officials tend to be much more accommodating and flexible than their central government intermediaries.

Since the early 2000s, North Korea has successfully kept an often reluctant China as its most consistent and reliable aid partner. Chinese customs data indicate commercial food inflows from China fell significantly after 2005 and have not yet recovered, fuel imports have been remarkably constant, and food and fuel imports are no longer provided on friendship prices. However, any evidence of premiums reportedly paid by North Korean importers may be offset by what is perhaps the largest and most important form of Chinese assistance, balance of payments support for North Korea's chronic bilateral trade deficit.

Overall, the chapter reveals how strikingly little has fundamentally changed in the behavior of the central government in Pyongyang since 1995, despite remarkable changes both inside North Korea and in the external environment it confronts.

Appendix: Data Table

Table 3.2 South Korean Government expenditures on North-South relations

| Year | Total | Humanitarian Aid | | | | | Road & Rail | Kumgang Tours | Aid to ROK Business | Kaesong Industrial Complex | Family Reunions | others | Exch. Rate |
| | Total | Total Humanitarian | Food Aid | | Fertilizer | | Humanit Aid to NGOs | | | | | | | |
	$ mil	$ mil	$ mil	Metric Tons	$ mil	Metric Tons	$ mil	$ mil	$ mil	$ mil	$ mil	$ mil	$ mil	(won/$)
1991	3.0	–	–	–	–		–	–	–	–	–	–	3.0	733.8
1992	0.7	–	–	–	–		–	–	–	–	–	0.7	–	781.1
1995	236.6	–	236.6	150,000	–		–	–	–	–	–	–	–	770.9
1996	9.8	–	3.8	–	–		3.1	–	–	–	–	–	6.1	805.1
1997	0.0	–	–	–	–		20.1	–	–	–	–	–	–	953.6
1998	0.0	–	–	–	–		14.3	–	–	–	–	0.0	0.0	1,395.0
1999	28.9	–	–	–	28.5		–	–	–	–	–	0.4	–	1,188.7
2000	178.0	163.1	76.7	500,000	83.4	155,000	3.0	12.9	–	0.4	–	2.8	1.8	1,131.1
2001	170.7	90.3	14.7	–	49.5	300,000	26.1	69.6	34.9	0.8	–	1.2	0.1	1,291.0
2002	254.6	175.4	84.6	400,000	66.6	200,000	24.1	53.5	26.7	2.2	–	20.6	0.4	1,250.7
2003	343.3	256.9	159.2	400,000	70.1	300,000	27.6	94.1	5.0	10.7	–	3.5	0.7	1,191.9
2004	326.8	196.3	98.3	400,000	84.5	300,000	13.6	96.6	6.2	27.8	6.0	3.7	3.8	1,143.7
2005	596.4	357.3	193.8	500,000	123.4	300,000	40.0	193.2	0.0	28.5	25.7	16.7	15.0	1,024.1
2006	393.5	226.7	10.7	100,000	125.7	350,000	90.3	93.1	1.3	50.2	80.8	15.9	16.0	955.1
2007	635.4	395.7	157.3	400,000	103.5	350,000	134.9	68.3	0.5	61.0	82.9	30.8	131.1	929.2
2008	159.4	54.1	3.9	n.a.	0.0	0	50.2	14.4	1.5	9.8	52.2	19.0	58.5	1,103.4
Total $mil	3,337.0	2,222.0	1,039.5		735.2		447.3	695.6	76.1	191.5	247.5	115.1	236.6	

Source: ROK EXIM Bank's "DPRK Support Fund," via Ministry of Unification.

Notes

1. The author would like to thank Marcus Noland and Stephan Haggard, on whose works this analysis relies heavily.
2. Stephan Haggard and Marcus Noland, *Famine in North Korea. Markets, Aid, and Reform* (New York: Columbia University Press, 2007).
3. Derived from data obtained from INTERFAIS on May 20, 2009 (for 1995–2007) and August 6, 2009 (for 2008).
4. For details on U.S. assistance to North Korea, see Mark Manyin and Mary Beth Nikitin, "CRS Report 40095: Assistance to North Korea," *Congressional Research Service.*
5. For more, see Haggard and Noland, *Famine in North Korea*, ch. 6.
6. For a time, South Korea suspended humanitarian assistance following North Korea's missile and nuclear tests in July and October 2006, respectively.
7. For evidence of this last point, see Marcus Noland and Stephan Haggard, "Statement for April 28, 2005 House International Relations Committee Hearing."
8. During and after the 2007 Presidential campaign, Lee Myung Bak had stated that while other forms of aid would be linked to progress in denuclearizing North Korea, his government would continue providing humanitarian assistance.
9. Analysis of INTERFAIS data searched on May 20, 2009.
10. For details, see Haggard and Noland, *Famine in North Korea*, tables 6.2 and 6.3.
11. North Korean authorities also banned sales of grain in private markets, attempted to revive the state-run public distribution system, and asked all foreigners working for foreign NGOs to leave the country. The latter decision was largely reversed later. See Noland and Haggard, *Famine in North Korea*, 104–107, for a useful description of this period.
12. By the spring of 2005, many of these restrictions were partially relaxed. See Mark Manyin, "CRS Report RL31785: U.S. Assistance to North Korea (Updated April 26, 2005)," *Congressional Research Service*, 11–15. For a description of the progress the WFP had made in earlier years, see Hazel Smith, "Overcoming Humanitarian Dilemmas in the DPRK (North Korea)," *United States Institute of Peace Special Report 90* (July 2002).
13. WFP Press Release, "WFP Set to Resume Operations in North Korea," May 11, 2006; undated WFP document, "Projected 2007 Needs for WFP Projects and Operations, Korea, DPR."
14. Andrew Natsios, *The Great North Korean Famine* (Washington, DC: U.S. Institute of Peace, 2001), 175–177.
15. For more, see Mark Manyin and Mary Beth Nikitin, "CRS Report 40095: Assistance to North Korea," *Congressional Research Service*, May 20, 2009.
16. See Thomas Lum, Hannah Fisher, Julissa Gomez-Granger, and Anne Leland, "CRS Report R40361: Chinese Foreign Aid Activities in Africa, Latin America, and Southeast Asia," *Congressional Research Service*, February 25, 2009.
17. According to WFP officials, soon-to-be-released data will state that China sent no food aid to North Korea in 2008. June 2009 correspondence with INTERFAIS official.
18. "Asia Report No. 112 –1: China And North Korea: Comrades Forever?," International Crisis Group (February 2006), 3.
19. 2005 and 2009 Interviews with WFP and INTERFAIS officials.
20. For instance, Nick Eberstadt, among others, has posited that falling PRC exports of grain in 1994–1996, followed by sharp spike in 1996 and 1997, appear to be on track with reports of growing dissatisfaction with North Korea following Kim Il Sung's death. This reportedly was followed by restoration of friendship terms after the May 1996 Li Peng/ Hong Song Nam meeting, in which China reportedly agreed to provide food aid and return to friendship prices for commerce. Haggard and Noland, *Famine in North Korea*, 155–160.

21. Stephan Haggard and Marcus Noland, "North Korea's External Economic Relations,"
    Peterson Institute for International Economics Working Paper Series, WP 07–7, August 2007.
    http://www.iie.com/publications/wp/wp07–7.pdf.
22. See, for instance, Robert J. Saiget, "China, NKorea Trade Booming Despite Rocket
    Tensions," *Agence France Presse*, April 5, 2009.
23. I am indebted to Marc Noland and Stephan Haggard for this insight.
24. "North's Trade Hits Record $3.8 Billion," *JoongAng Ilb*, May 18, 2009.

CHAPTER FOUR

Military-First (Songun) Politics: Implications for External Policies

HAN S. PARK

A country's foreign policy is always affected by its ideological stance. But nowhere is this the case more pronouncedly than in the Democratic People's Republic of Korea (DPRK). Since the inception of the political system in 1948, and especially following the Korean War (1950–1953), Pyongyang's foreign policy has closely and directly reflected its ruling political ideology. The purpose of this chapter is to ascertain the way in which the official ideology of *Juche* has decisively influenced how the government has chosen to conduct its foreign and diplomatic policy. The core tool by which the North Korean leadership establishes its basis of regime legitimacy has always been, and will continue to be, ideology. There are two significant reasons for this. First, the mere presence of a powerful and threatening South Korea (with twice the North Korean population, an enormously affluent economy, and a strong military capability that includes a long-standing security alliance with the United States) has forced the North to compete for legitimacy in the eyes and minds of its own people. Second, even as it has had to continue this competition, North Korea lost its entire support system from around the world as the Communist bloc disappeared practically overnight. This means that it suddenly became imperative for the North Korean leadership to find a way of ensuring its sustenance without "comrade" states with whom it had maintained security alliances, economic interactions, and ideologically shared values. The evolution of *Juche*, which has extended to the doctrine of the Military-First (*Songun*) Politics, the official state ideology, must be viewed and examined in the context of its role and place in helping the political system create and maintain comparative and competitive legitimacy for its rightful existence. As this process has unfolded, the system's patterns of external policy conduct have been created; viewed in this way, the country's foreign policy may be seen as an extension of its internal legitimating ideology. This chapter will examine this process, and suggest that the DPRK's policy strategies and tactics have been "rationally" and carefully chosen to serve its policy and system objectives in the particular national and geopolitical context in which it has had to operate.

The Basis of Legitimacy and the Advancement of *Juche*

Even before the establishment of government both North and South of the 38th Parallel in 1948, there were ideologically divergent groups and factions throughout the peninsula that eventually culminated into the two regimes that have been known as the Democratic Republic of Korea in the North and the Republic of Korea in the South.[1] Since their respective inceptions of government, the two have regarded and defined their territorial jurisdiction, legally or politically, as being the entire peninsula, creating a confrontational situation in which each claims sole legitimacy over the divided territory. Thus, each system has employed theories of legitimation in order to gain leverage with which to claim the right to govern the entire peninsula with a comparative advantage.

Theories of legitimacy suggest that there are two analytically distinct bases upon which a regime may claim its legitimacy for power. The first of these is the performance of the regime in satisfying the basic needs of the people, as well as its continuing ability to meet rising public demands for material affluence. If a regime is capable of performing effectively in these regards, then the regime and its ruling elite may claim the right to govern. But the performance function of the state alone is not sufficient. It needs to be complemented by psychological and emotional support for the regime by the governed, the people. This non-tangible basis of legitimacy is facilitated by ideology. In fact, this psychological support may be critically important to legitimacy. Carl Friedrich, among others, conceptualizes legitimacy in terms of "belief" of the governed; Sternberger and Merelman observes that legitimacy means "recognition" by the governed of government's right to govern, and "oughtness" perceived by the public to be morally proper for a society.[2] The dual bases of legitimacy, performance and ideology, work together for all kinds of political systems but never with the same degree of significance. Some systems rely more heavily on performance and others more on ideology, depending on the stage of development and the immediate challenge faced by the political system.[3]

It is fair to say that the DPRK has used ideology as the primary basis of regime legitimacy, while South Korea has based its justification of ruling on performance. This contrast has become progressively distinct as the economic performance has accorded the comparative advantage to the South. In the eyes of North Korea, the South has compromised its national sovereignty and independence for the sake of pursuing economic growth, and thus the system lacks legitimacy. This prompted the Pyongyang government to advance and develop an ideology that is almost entirely predicated on nationalism. In fact, Kim Il Sung's rise to power was itself facilitated by the belief that he was a guerrilla fighter against Japanese colonial rule (1910–1945). The nationalist ideology has paved a way for the now infamous ideology of *Juche*. As we examine the evolution of this ideology over the years, one will be struck by the fact that it has adjusted itself to changing international, inter-Korea, and domestic needs and conditions. One might also discern that the Military-First Politics (*Songun Jongchi*) is to be seen as an extension of the *Juche* ideology itself. We will examine this process below.

The Evolution of *Juche*: Toward the Birth of *Songun*

The word "*juche*" is a common word in the Korean language and often used in a variety of contexts. It simply means "self-supporting," "self-reliance," "non-interference by others," and "independence." But when Kim Il Sung used this concept in early 1950s, or even earlier, the meaning became charged with a political connotation of "sovereignty" or independence from foreign involvement. In this initial stage of the ideological evolution, North Korea could not afford looking beyond its immediate and comfortable ideological allies such as the Soviet Union and the Eastern European states, the People's Republic of China, and Vietnam.[4]

Following the Korean War (1950–1953), North Korea found a new enemy who helped South Korea and destroyed much of the northern half of the country with massive air strikes; this new enemy was the

United States of America. In the war, the city of Pyongyang was practically leveled to the ground, leaving no physical structures standing and millions of people killed or wounded.[5] Ever since the War, there has been a genuine fear among North Korean residents that American forces might renew hostility.[6] The fact that U.S. forces have been stationed continuously in the South, with routine military exercises conducted jointly with South Korean armed forces, has always made North Korea uneasy and apprehensive. Since the adoption of the armistice agreement in 1953, Pyongyang has persistently demanded the withdrawal of U.S. troops from the Korean peninsula. North Koreans were particularly resentful of the hegemonic expansion of U.S. military influence.

Coupled with the presence of the United States in Korea, the growing Sino-Soviet dispute in 1960, which drove the two Communist giants to the brink of war, and Soviet involvement in Eastern Europe and Vietnam were instrumental in the growth of anti-hegemonism in the North Korean political and diplomatic orientation. Pyongyang was put in a precarious position between the two super powers of the communist bloc, as it did not wish to antagonize either of them by maintaining intimate relations with one at the expense of the other. This forced the Pyongyang government to declare a path of equidistance and, thus, "self-reliance." But it was the Soviet Union that became a more convenient target of North Korean criticism due to Moscow's expansionist policy. By contrast, China provided a role model of sorts by indulging in the massive indigenization of Marxism-Leninism during the fanatic phase of the Great Proletariat Cultural Revolution in the late 1960s. While North Korea did not express great enthusiasm for the Cultural Revolution, it restrained itself from publicly denouncing the Chinese campaign for creating a personality cult for Mao Zedong. In fact, North Korea followed the footsteps of Mao in instigating concerted efforts to develop an indigenous ideology and in creating a charismatic leadership for Kim Il Sung himself. Just as Mao criticized Moscow for its hegemonic policies, Kim expressed displeasure with the Soviet Union's interventionist policies. As pointed out in the preceding discussion, this doctrine of anti-hegemonism was further reinforced by Pyongyang's interest in denouncing the American influence in South Korea. In short, the ideological insistence of political sovereignty under *Juche* became reinforced by the political reality surrounding the peninsula.

While Pyongyang was forced to reinforce its "self-reliance" posture, it quickly became arrested by its own ideology with regard to expanding its economic activities beyond its handful of socialist allies.

Politically, though, by the end of the 1960s, North Korea had become a stable regime devoid of any immediate source of opposition against Kim's authority. His leadership could not be challenged, for it was steadily gaining a charismatic quality. By this time, as pointed out above, almost all political enemies had been eliminated from the leadership circles. Furthermore, the economy had fully recovered from the shambles of the Korean War. It may sound unbelievable, but the North Korean economy in this period was superior to that of South Korea.

What Pyongyang needed at this historical juncture was a persuasive ideology with which to legitimize Kim's charismatic leadership and to demonstrate ideological superiority to the South. It may be generalized that once a regime is established and stability is secured, the next step taken by the regime is to expand its legitimacy through political education. This stage of development may be termed political integration, during which the ruling elite attempts to further the basis of regime legitimacy through the introduction of an official political ideology. Many newly independent countries have consistently shown the flowering of nationalism as their official ideology. North Korea is not an exception.

It is this transition of circumstances that prompted the accentuation of nationalism as the cornerstone of *Juche*. The fact that South Korea was led by Syngman Rhee, who was educated in the United States and had been a long-term resident of that country, indicated a strong American influence on the Rhee regime, thereby providing Kim Il Sung with the necessary ammunition to condemn the South for being shamelessly antinationalistic and pathetically subjected to foreign domination. In contrast with the southern situation, the North was in a position to declare a policy of equidistance to its communist allies and join the nonaligned movement. Pyongyang managed to establish *Juche* institutes in several nonaligned countries, such as India. This political climate proved to be an ideal situation for Pyongyang to adopt ultranationalism as the foundation of *Juche* ideology.

Nationalism in the mid-1960s was still primarily anti-foreignism without a coherent philosophical structure. But as the ideology was further refined in the late 1960s and much of the 1970s, it was able to identify a set of goals and strategies to implement nationalism. Specifically, *Juche* was defined in terms of three analytically distinct objectives: political sovereignty, economic subsistence, and military self-defense. Political sovereignty forced the regime to limit its political and diplomatic ties to those countries with which Pyongyang was ideologically compatible, thus limiting foreign relations continuously to only a handful of socialist countries. It is in this period that North Korea campaigned against the South for superiority in legitimacy. Overwhelmed by nationalist sentiment, Pyongyang believed that the Seoul regime could be overthrown by its own masses on the grounds that the South lacked nationalist solidarity and, thus, political legitimacy. The North Korean government believed that the people in the South could be induced to participate in an anti-regime mass movement, all they had to do was only to pull the trigger to disturb the precarious stability. The infiltration of the Blue House, the presidential residence in Seoul, by a North Korean commando unit in 1968 could be interpreted as the expression of Pyongyang's determination to disturb political stability in hopes of inciting mass uprisings against the Park Chung Hee regime.[7]

The policies of economic self-reliance eventually deterred economic growth, forcing North Korea to fall further behind its neighboring countries, especially South Korea. This period happened to coincide with the high-growth years for the Newly Industrializing Countries (NICs) and the "Asian tigers," which included South Korea. All of these countries employed the export-led strategy toward economic growth. Instead of promoting a balanced growth, as was the case in North Korea, the NICs concentrated their efforts on the production of export goods that could be competitive in the international market. But North Korea alienated itself from world economic activities in order to establish a *Juche* economy. One should not forget that at this time there was growing sentiment among Third World countries for the *dependencia* movement whereby economic and cultural independence was proclaimed to be the only way of avoiding certain subjugation to the industrialized hegemonic countries.[8]

What has been economically most detrimental is the principle of military self-reliance. Kim Il Sung's opinion on the importance of military power was unambiguously demonstrated in his early years when he was campaigning for national independence. In his Manchuria days, his group was known for its employment of militant means, for which weapons had been secured at all costs. He criticized Kim Koo, Yo Woon Yong, and Ahn Chang Ho, who had a broad base of support for their patriotism and reliance on the nonmilitary/nonviolence principle. According to Kim, a nonviolent revolution would not work in the fight against colonialism and expansionism.[9] In fact, military self-reliance was viewed as a necessary condition for political sovereignty. To this extent, no amount of resources devoted to building military strength was considered too large; North Korea has consistently invested an inordinate proportion of its national wealth in the weapons industry. Kim also witnessed the dramatic event that the Japanese imperial forces, which were so formidable as to be able to invade East and Southeast Asia, Russia, and eventually the Hawaiian islands, were forced to unconditionally surrender to the power of American atomic bombs. Given this, it is not surprising for Kim to have been engulfed by his own obsessive desire for weapons, specifically atomic bombs.

Although the military principle may have deterred economic growth in general, one should not underestimate the fact that North Korea's primary source of foreign currency earnings has been the export of weapons that include a wide range of arsenals, ranging from conventional weapons to sophisticated missiles. There seems to be no shortage of demand for North Korean weapons in the international market, especially in the Arab world. The controversy surrounding North Korea's nuclear weapons production must be seen in the greater context of North Korea's ideological doctrine of military self-reliance.

In short, the policies designed to adhere to the principles of political, economic, and military self-reliance may not be designed to attain maximal material payoff. In fact, they have been largely counterproductive for the development of industry and often detrimental to the welfare of the society as a whole. Nevertheless, the principles were intended to promote nationalism among the masses and to demonstrate a position of superiority for regime legitimacy over the southern counterpart. As suggested above, it was in this period that North Korea is believed to have increased the sales of weapons, including short range missiles, to selected Middle Eastern states.[10]

It did not take long before the ideology incorporated the concept of "paternalist" socialism. As the ideology became intimately tied to the regime as an instrument of legitimatization of power, the leadership articulated a new theoretical dimension in which the leadership itself was sanctified as the generator and embodiment of the ideology. This process not only coincided with a quantum leap in the charismatization of the Great Leader but also with the regime's need for the official promotion of Kim Jong Il's leadership caliber, which began in conjunction with the Sixth Party Congress in 1980. Kim Il Sung saw a great flaw of the socialist system as seen in the Soviet Union, Vietnam, and China in the almost universal inability of the ruling elite to resolve the succession issue. It was not accidental for North Korea to choose the hereditary approach as the succession mechanism. The North Korean people had never seen a popularly elected leadership in their entire history. The dynastic systems of early modern Korea were replaced abruptly by the Japanese colonial power. Kim Il Sung was quickly and naturally seen as a royal leader of sorts. Thus, deification of the leader's family was not deviant, as seen from the age-old Oriental despotic cultural perspective.[11] A significant implication of paternalism is that it is not only the "father" himself but the whole family that is destined to rule. This will naturally sanctify the hereditary succession of power by the son. As the father attained a charisma as the paternalist leader, the son was naturally expected to be included in the charisma of the family. At *Mankyongdae*, the birthplace of Kim Il Sung, a family museum was erected in the early 1980s, in which the Kim clan is heralded as the center of the independence movement. The historical documentation ends with the young Kim having demonstrated unusual leadership quality and unparalleled patriotism.

As this was a period when the North Korean leadership needed to inculcate effective political orientation of the masses, it was desirable for the system to keep the people shielded from the external world, especially South Korea and the West. This further isolated the country's economy from the world market, reinforcing the self-reliant economy contained within the system.

By the end of the 1980s, *Juche* evolved into a legitimate *Weltanschauung* with a philosophical structure. As discussed earlier, the articulation of the structure of human nature and the theory of the "political-social life" are relatively recent developments. It does not suggest that *Juche* represents a unique and complete worldview, but it is a worldview nonetheless, with some coherent structure as opposed to a mere political slogan.

The idea that man is the center of the universe is by no means a new perspective, nor is the doctrine of political sovereignty or self-determination. Furthermore, nothing is new about *Juche*'s emphasis on human consciousness as the determinant of human behavior. What is original, however, is that the Confucian concepts of human centeredness and human determinism have been integrated into a ruling political ideology.

As will be discussed more fully later, human nature inherently longs for being in "the center of the universe," whereby man's relationship with nature and society is clearly prescribed. Nature exists solely for the sake of human beings; as such, man is fully entitled to explore natural resources. Yet, man also has the obligation to manage and "control" the global physical environment. According to *Juche*, science is a tool designed to utilize as well as rehabilitate nature for the advancement of human well-being for both the present and future. According to this perspective, no person should be subjected to another person's capricious control, nor should he be submitted to institutional manipulation. Institutions, as in the case of science, are designed to serve human beings rather than be served by them. Even ideologies themselves are regarded as institutional means to human well-being. Another component of human nature is faculty that makes value judgment possible. Humans are endowed with the natural right and capability to make behavioral choices through free consciousness. Yet another component of human nature allows one to keep oneself from the enslavement by instruments of life, such as material resources and social institutions.

The above elements of human nature, however, are to be cultivated and developed through socialization and political education. It is for this reason that ideological education becomes an integral part of human development, and such an education should be continuous throughout one's life. The practice of "education through work" in the form of a "factory college" should be seen in this vein. A "factory college" refers to the practice whereby classes at the college level are offered at dormitory sites of factories offering degree and certification programs in a variety of specialized fields. College professors from regular institutions of high education, such as Kim Il Sung University and Kim Chaek University, are mobilized as instructors. Classes routinely begin with rituals that are intended to glorify the two Kims' works and their legacy. The ideology basically adheres to the claims of the *dependencia* school of thought that views the world essentially as an exploitive system as long as nations are unable to sustain the self-sufficiency of basic needs and military self-defense. Here, *Juche* is faced with the formidable task of discrediting the achievements of the Newly Industrializing Countries, especially South Korea, because the NICs have shown that international division of labor and export-led economies could be prosperous, thus challenging the very premises of the *dependencia* school. For this reason, North Korea was always sympathetic with the nonaligned movement and maintained close ties with the Group of 77. Furthermore, the epidemic breakdown of socialist systems in Eastern Europe and the Soviet Union itself, as well as the development of a reform-oriented China, forced North Korea to dissociate itself from this global trend. The very need for dissociation from other socialist countries has been instrumental to the rapid transition of *Juche* itself as a unique ideological system under the banner of "socialism in our style" (*urisik sahoejuii*). This ideological position may sound similar to other forms of nationalized socialism, as evidenced by China under Deng Xiaoping and Yugoslavia under Tito. But what is radically unique about North Korea is that *Juche* in its advanced version is a completely different breed of ideology, as opposed to a variation of socialism.

As observed above, in an effort to address the issue of political consolidation and to wage the "war" for legitimacy *vis-à-vis* the South and to shield the population from unwanted influences from the West, North Korea has opted to develop and continuously refine the ideology of *Juche*. In this process, its foreign and diplomatic activities have been severely restricted, especially in the economic arena. One should remember that it was in this period that North Korea lost all the support system from the Communist bloc. To further exacerbate the situation, the DPRK also came under a successive string of economic and political "sanctions" from the West for its nuclear programs.

Over its long process of evolution, *Juche* has finally incorporated a premise that the military is the heart, the brain, and the body of the political system. This ultimate accentuation of the military as an institution has occurred since the adoption of the 1998 constitution. What was conceived in the Constitution was the seed of the Military-First (*Songun*) doctrine, but it has blown fully into a comprehensive ideological and philosophical system in the ten years following its mention, and the most recent new Constitution that was adopted in April 2009 clearly documents it. This new Constitution elevates the Military Commission to the level of supreme leadership, and its chairman, currently Kim Jong Il, as the "supreme leader" with virtually omnipotent power in the system. One might say, without a proper understanding of *Juche*, Kim Il Sung's North Korea cannot be comprehended, one might also say that a proper understanding of Kim Jong Il's North Korea is possible only with a proper comprehension of *Songun*.

The *Songun* theoreticians claim that *Songun* has advanced *Juche* to a higher plane by providing it with a realistic perspective of history and of the politics of the world. Just as in the case of *Juche*, this *Songun* is alleged to be in a constant process of evolving toward its perfection. At present, there are limited written sources regarding *Songun* for a researcher to discern its definitive picture. Yet, consulting available publications from North Korea and a series of personal interviews with scholars who are the leading promoters and theoreticians of this system of ideas, one might be able to portray the essence of its philosophical and theoretical attributes. It is hoped that the following pages may be of some help to North Korea observers in explaining the system characteristics and policy behaviors of the DPRK under Kim Jong Il. For this important reason, one must investigate further the conceptual and philosophical underpinnings of *Songun*.

SONGUN: An Anatomy

If one understands *Songun* Politics as just a doctrine that provides the military absolute power, and the rest of the political system as secondary and subservient to that institution, one's comprehension would be fatally flawed. Using limited sources of documents and publications from Pyongyang, combined with this author's personal contacts, the following functions of the military may be ascertained that are consistent with the *Songun* principle.[12]

The Military is the "Center" of the Political System

Since the death of Kim Il Sung in 1994, the concept of the "center" (of the Party)—*Dang Jungang*—has been used in North Korea to refer specifically to refer to Kim Jong Il. The "center" in this context means more than the locus of power. It means the central nervous system (of the body). The military is the guardian for the brain, which must be protected and never be made vulnerable. When the military is theorized to be the center, it carries the same connotation. In this sense, the military is not just an institution designed to perform the function of defending the country from external hostility. Rather, it provides all other institutions of the government with legitimacy. All policy goals are articulated by the military and they are disseminated to other organizations with specific strategic and tactical recommendations for implementations. Once policies are implemented, their effectiveness will be evaluated by the military. In this way, the military serves the system as the "brain" of the nervous system of the body politic.

The Military is the Provider and Problem Solver

To North Koreans, the military is not an abstract authority but a practical performer. It responds directly and effectively to people's needs and wants. It delivers in a way that no others can; it provides services and goods to the people, as well as protects their security. When I visited farm villages in 2009, I asked a group of farmers about their understanding of the *Songun* doctrine, they concurred that it is the military that makes farming possible, as the soldiers come to the village to work on a whole range of farm work, from tilling soil to seeding, irrigating, and harvesting. It is a widespread belief that the military not only protects the people's lives from foreign hostility but also delivers food and services. It is common to notice in the streets of North Korea soldiers carrying bags of grain to civilian homes. In fact, the concern commonly expressed by the foreign providers of food, that the military may snatch the food aid away from the civilians, is rather speculative. The reality is that the military has food and other necessities in relatively ample supply due to the practice of the Independent Accounting System, whereby the military retains the revenues it generates from exporting military equipment, including missiles and conventional weapons. In this way, the military is in a position of being able to share resources with the public. It may also be possible that the military can actually perform the service of delivering foreign aid food to the civilians throughout the remote villages. Moreover, the delivery and provision functions of the military are not limited to services and food—they include virtually all kinds of other commodities and goods.

Not only is the military regarded as the embodiment of the legitimate power and authority, it is also considered the most able in practically all spheres of people's life as the problem solver. Each unit of dwellers (defined as a *ban*) is assigned to a military post that is responsible for looking after all types of needs of the people, ranging from technical assistance for repairing household electrical appliances to fixing faucets and sewage systems. Under the *Songun* society, people are supposed to have faith that the military is equipped with the resources, knowledge, and skills to solve the problems of people's daily lives. In this way, the doctrine calls for complete dependence of the people on the military. The popular belief being promoted under the banner of *Songun* is that "no problem is too big or too small for the military to solve." In this way, it is promoted that people cannot sustain and continue to exist without the military.

The Military is the Engine for Social Engineering

The military is also the leader with the prime opinion. People trust that soldiers are well educated and possess ideological preparedness. In fact, military education always gives top priority to the schooling in ideology and politics. They are the ones who will then teach the common villagers. When they are on leave from military barracks, they are normally sent to their home towns and to the villagers for the purpose of training and educating the commoners to carry on the "revolution" without interruption. In my numerous trips to North Korea, I have consistently been amazed by the ability of soldiers to spell out in most specific terms their mission as soldiers and as leaders of the "revolutionary struggle." It might be appropriate to characterize the mission of the military in North Korea today as the role of "social engineer." The concept of social engineering is one of future orientation. Social engineering requires architecting the society for the future, and driving the course of social change toward desired goals. People are expected to look up to the military for its visionary leadership, and they only need to follow the guidance of the military. The norms and values desirable for the society will be created by the military, and it is the military that is designated to disseminate them to the people. In this sense, the military is the greatest educator. At the heart of military education is the Military University. This institution is central to developing the ideology of *Songun* and training military officers, as well as disseminating *Songun* philosophy throughout the educational institutions in the country.

The Military is the Creator and Advancer of a New Culture

Cultural change occurs in every society, and North Korea is no exception. Unlike the common expectation, that as society becomes modernized the youth become disillusioned with the establishment and get attracted to a consumerist life style, there seems to be no appreciable generation gap in the country. There also seems to be little discrepancy between the rural and urban areas in this regard. The country has maintained a remarkable degree of uniformity in its cultural orientation. This uniformity has been made largely through the institution of the military. With a ten year compulsory military service and a large contingent of the military population (in excess of one million), virtually every family has at least one soldier in uniform. As pointed out above, the military performs an extensive role in the civilian villages, and this is coupled with the fact that practically all physically able citizens in the country are mobilized in the People's Militia. In fact, there is hardly any separation between the military and civilian sectors. In this context, it is not surprising that the military culture is the North Korean culture. The cultural traits include uniformity, a clear definition of a common enemy, and resolve and determination as the highest virtues. The *Songun* doctrine has created a belief system in which the public must follow the military, as the latter is always right. It is no longer the Party (the Korean Workers' Party) that leads the way, nor is it the government that assumes the role of leadership. One intriguing feature of the North Korean culture is the pervasive sense of equality, in that the participation of the rank-and-file people in decision-making processes provides a

significant sense of self-worth and moral boost to them. Everyone is supposed to be equal in the sense that all are involved in making decisions
that affect everyone. Therefore, the life in North Korea is one of successive meetings and deliberations at all levels of the society, including
the military itself. These meetings typically begin with self-criticisms
(confessions) by every participant, and conclude with remedial recommendation for any wrongdoing on any member regardless of his or her
standing in the social and political strata. The principle of "One for All,
and All for One" is not just a slogan any more. It works and is felt in the
country. This doctrine epitomizes the "military way." Thus, the same
practice is emulated in the civilian life. Every administrative unit, the
ban, convenes a regular meeting every week for the purpose of information dissemination from the Center (the Supreme Leadership) and to
stage the process of self-criticism. Thus, a drastically unconventional
value system has emerged in conjunction with the new Constitution of
2009, and it is the notion that the single yardstick of "universal virtue"
is one's orientation toward *Suryong*.[13]

The Military is the Synthesizer of the Body-Mind-Spirit (BMS)

Unlike the idea of *Juche*'s self-defense, *Songun* is a more comprehensive
doctrine; its task is not limited to the physical and material aspects but
includes just as importantly the psychological and spiritual domains. In
this way, *Songun* has become a source of political and social philosophy,
just as *Juche* was during the Kim Il Sung era. One should remember
that the doctrine of *Juche* reached its height as it advanced the philosophical outlook of the Political-Social Body (PSB) in the late 1980s.
The PSB attempted to articulate the theory of human development
(maturation) by providing a progressive theory of personal development, that is, one becomes a Social Body as s/he undergoes the process
of transformation from essentially a biological being to a social being.
The biological being is one full of instinctive desires for physical com-
fort. The social being, however, is charged with social and political
consciousness (*eusiksong*). The concept of human development, thus,
became an important feature of the *Juche* philosophy. Now, the philosophy of *Songun* is attempting to integrate the three components of
human existence, the mind-body-spirit. Here, the notion of an ideal
personhood is being created: one becomes ideally developed through
the attainment of a physical skill such as martial art (body), education and training in arts and sciences of one form or another (mind),
and of devotion to a sense of mission for life (spirit). The curriculum

in education, both in the military and civilian sectors, is designed to promote all three.

The Military as the Exemplar

During my frequent travels in North Korea, my favorite question to a single woman or girl is to ask what kind of man she would wish to marry. Of late, I have noticed that the common answer is "a soldier." One has to appreciate this in the context that the military institution houses the best manifestations of all the three above: the military artists are revered, as they include the most accomplished artists in the country; the military houses the best scientists, as demonstrated by the advancement of nuclear physics and the engineering of the bomb; and, of course, the military shows the resolve and unwavering loyalty to the cause of fighting the "most powerful enemy" in the world, the United States.

Even a cursory view of *Songun*, as discussed above, clearly suggests that it is a peculiar system of ideas that are not commonly found in world politics. The birth and evolution of *Songun* reflect closely the international political environment led by the American Administrations, especially during the Bush era, that was regarded to be particularly hostile and threatening by North Korea.

SONGUN and Foreign Policy

Clearly, *Songun* has been solidly established as a political theory of sorts that has affected every aspect of people's life and political culture throughout the country. Then in what way has the doctrine influenced the foreign and inter-Korea policy orientations and behaviors? The notion that nuclear weaponry is the only "guarantor" for national security and a reliable means of deterrence against military provocation from hostile governments is a direct product of *Songun* politics. The two rounds of underground nuclear tests in 2006 and 2009 and numerous missile launches were all designed and conducted by the military on the principle of *Songun* politics. Given this, Pyongyang's foreign and inter-Korea policies are expected to be closely dictated by the same principle of self-defense. However, Pyongyang has experienced that national security and economic prosperity are often mutually contradictory, especially in the context of the nuclear controversy. The pursuit of nuclear weapons on the part of North Korea has been costly in terms of exploring economic opportunities abroad. Repeated sanctions by the United Nations (UN) and its key members have denied Pyongyang the opportunity to become a legitimate actor in the global market; this has reached a point where they had to depend on primary economic and food aid from the South over the course of ten years under Kim Dae Jung and Roh Moo Hyun presidencies. The Lee government did not waste time to criticize the previous governments for being overly conciliatory toward North Korea. It even called the decade of Kim-Roh Administrations as a "lost decade." The virtual absence of economic and humanitarian aid from the Lee government has forced Pyongyang to more aggressively seek economic opportunities elsewhere in the global community and further refine its foreign and economic policies.

One such newly emphasized front is the Nordic countries of Europe. Unlike other Western countries, the Scandinavian countries established diplomatic relations with North Korea in the 1970s, but actual interaction in terms of trade and investment has been virtually restricted by the absence of U.S. consent. Of late, however, North Korea has shown heightened activity in the area of green energy and sustainable development, and the Nordic countries have responded positively, especially since the inception of the Obama Administration in Washington.[14] North Korea is especially interested in renewable energy and green technology, partly because it, as a latecomer, can induce a "correct" and futuristic course of development.[15] On the United States front, Pyongyang is not expected to compromise its nuclear preparedness as long as the current security environment prevails, but it has shown willingness to work with Washington in the economic and social-political areas by not resorting to an ideologically inflexible stance. In the past, Pyongyang has consistently resisted a certain kind of businesses from the West that carry the stigma of what it called "businesses of economic imperialism," such as associated with Coca-Cola or McDonald's, but this approach appears to have changed recently in 2010. It seems to be prepared to work with almost any company or product.[16] This does not necessarily mean that those foreign companies will rush into North Korea, but what is unconventional is that Pyongyang is far more aggressive in reaching out to businesses in the West.

The "China rising" syndrome has gradually affected the bilateral relationship between China and North Korea. What has changed is China's greater self-assertion in its foreign policy conduct. With the enormous economic capability and leverage that it enjoys, China now can afford to be less sensitive in framing its foreign policies to fit the

Western orientations toward North Korea. Despite the adoption of UN Security Council Resolution 1874 in April 2009 as a measure against North Korea, Chinese Premier Wen Jiabao made a visit to Pyongyang in October that year for a meeting with Kim Jong Il. In this meeting, China made a considerable amount of commitment to economic aid. Much to the dislike of the United States and the Western world, China extended an invitation to Kim Jong Il, who is expected to visit Beijing early this year. These are indications that China will make its own policy toward Pyongyang strictly based on its own interest. At the same time, North Korea has evidently adopted a policy of economic development patterned after the Chinese model, of inducing foreign investments while maintaining a monolithic political system under the Chinese Communist Party. Scholars and political observers around the world have shown skepticism over this curious mixture of economic capitalism and political communism that the post-Mao leadership has assumed. They thought that the precarious combination of the two theoretically incompatible practices would be short-lived and ineffective. But if what has been happening in China over the past thirty years, especially in its economy, is any indication, China has clearly succeeded in promoting economic development without pluralist democracy. All the explosive economic growth was initiated by the policy of attracting foreign investment into the selected Special Economic Zones in the late 1970s and early 1980s. Deng Xiaoping as the father of China Rising has instilled in the Chinese leadership the sense that capitalism should not be feared as long as it is adapted to China's special characteristics. The North Korean leadership has been intrigued by the Chinese experience, and seemingly has decided to apply the same model. Thus, we are likely to see a dualistic approach in which economic policy is separated from politics. As alluded to earlier, this will allow Pyongyang to be aggressive in attracting foreign enterprises and investments regardless of ideological or stigmatic ramifications associated with foreign economic presence. However, the huge political cloud cast by the nuclear controversy will continue to plague North Korea's economic ventures. In order to deal with this cloud, Pyongyang is continuously reminded of the importance of improving relations with the United States.

With the virtual opening of a bilateral channel when U.S. Special Envoy Steve Bosworth visited Pyongyang in December 2009, North Korea seems to view Washington in a new light. It is evident that the *Songun* leadership, with Kim Jong Il at the helm, has now seen a new possibility of drastically reversing its relationship with the United States by offering a "partnership" in the global denuclearization, which has been known to have captivated President Obama's interest. In this, one might see a quantum leap and radical shift in DPRK's policy toward the United States, and possibly in the bilateral relationship itself. However, Pyongyang is not expected to revise its position, for it is so firmly locked in by *Songun* politics that it will not relinquish its security preparedness (nuclear weapons) for any amount of economic incentives.

At the same time, Pyongyang is likely to honor its agreement to work systematically toward dismantling the nuclear program and even the weapons themselves if reciprocal actions are taken by the United States for alleviating its security concern. Pyongyang sees denuclearization as a process, rather than a single action, and has insisted on a solution based on the principle of "words for words, action for action," which guided the actual agreement signed by Kim Gae Kwan and Christopher Hill at the last round of Beijing's Six-party Talks in 2007. Pyongyang is of the opinion that the Beijing multilateral talks have completed their task and there is no need for further meetings.

The Obama Administration, in contrast with the Lee Myung Bak government in Seoul, does not appear to require North Korea to first denuclearize before any negotiation for economic or political issues can take place. As long as Washington is willing to carry on bilateral direct talks and to adopt incremental steps in the process of the denuclearization of North Korea, the prospect for a rapid improvement in their relationship is promising.

What about Pyongyang's policy toward Seoul? For the first time in a long while, North Korea appears to show confusing and nonuniform signals in its policy conduct toward the South. On one hand, the *Songun* leadership regards the Lee government to be hostile and incompatible with it. The very inception of the Lee leadership was founded on the premise that the Sunshine Policy of Kim-Roh governments (1998–2007) was misguided. In fact, President Lee's northern policy was widely seen as similar to President George W. Bush's hawkish North Korea policy, and Lee was referred to as a "Little Bush." Pyongyang did not expect any change in Lee's policy posture, and there was none, at least in the first few months. But Pyongyang surprised the world by sending a formidable delegation to Seoul for the funeral ceremony of late president Kim Dae Jung in August 2009. What is surprising was that the delegation requested a visit with President Lee, with the rationalization that it is natural to visit the head of the state on the occasion of a "state funeral" ceremony. But this was an unexpectedly conciliatory gesture on the part of Pyongyang. Since then it was reported that there were other occasions in 2009 in which North Korean delegations met with their southern counterparts, including one in Singapore where the agenda was the convening of a summit meeting. How can one interpret these apparent policy overtures that are not consistent with the official declaration that the Lee government is hostile? One might conjecture that the Obama Administration might have expressed the desire to North Korea for Pyongyang's better relationship with Seoul as a condition conducive to U.S.-DPRK rapprochement. If Pyongyang's softened policy toward the South is due to its intense desire to better its ties with Washington, this represents a departure in its inter-Korea policy from the long-held principle that inter-Korea relations cannot be interfered with by any foreign power. If this be so, it would indeed be interesting to see how Pyongyang's relations with other governments affect its policy toward the South. This will border on a paradigm shift in inter-Korea relations from national self-determination to the internationalization of inter-Korea relations. The Lee government appears to have already adopted such a paradigm shift. In the final analysis, Pyongyang's foreign policy and inter-Korea policy may be intertwined, showing an infinitely complex arena of policymaking within and around the DPRK.

Concluding Remarks

This chapter has examined the nature of the belief systems embedded in the ideology of *Juche*. It has been observed that the ideology is consistent with the salient cultural condition of Confucianism and that *Juche* has shown an evolution that culminated in the current Military-First Politics (*Songun*). This process of evolution shows that the ideology has adapted itself to changing international, inter-Korea, and domestic conditions. Despite all the continuity and consistency about the ideology of *Juche*, one distinct impact of this "self reliance" doctrine is that it has been detrimental to the promotion of economic growth. However, *Juche* politics has been the conscious choice by the North Korean leadership, who also sees the merits of this ideology in vying with the South on the legitimacy issue and boosting the morale of the people in the face of economic difficulties. The *Juche* ideology and *Songun* politics may have been instrumental in equipping the state with the nuclear capability, which clearly has provided the system with a status in the international arena and a bargaining leverage. The question today is: Will the North Korean state "bargain the nuke away"

108 Han S. Park

for security and development advances? This question is beyond the scope of this chapter, but a simple answer has to be in the affirmative, which will involve a complex dynamics of negotiations through multiple channels and forums in the years ahead. The *Juche* ideology and its extension to *Songun* ideology might have been a liability for North Korea's foreign policy, and they have certainly restricted North Korea's diplomatic strategies and maneuverings. But, as we discussed in this chapter, if Pyongyang achieves the objective of improving bilateral relations with Washington to the extent that it becomes a "partner" for global denuclearization, *Songun* may prove to be beneficial to the long-term interest of the DPRK.

Notes

1. For an in-depth and detailed account of the political climate in those years, refer to Robert A. Scalapino and Chong-Sik Lee, *Communism in Korea* (Berkeley: University California Press, 1972); Bruce Cumings makes a direct assessment of the ideologically and politically divided factions competing for power in the formative stage of regime formation in the peninsula. See Bruce Cumings, *The Origins of the Korean War: The Roaring of the Cataract 1947–1950* (Princeton: Princeton University Press, 1990).
2. Refer to Dolf Sternberger, "Legitimacy," in David Shill, ed., *International Encyclopedia of Social Sciences Volume 9* (New York: Macmillan and The Free Press, 1968), 244; Also, Richard Merelman, "Learning and Legitimacy," *American Political Science Review* LX, 3 (September 1966): 548.
3. Han S. Park related the different bases to different stages of political development, thus, when a system is faced with the challenge of political integration, ideology looms large, and when it is faced with prosperity or economic growth as the primary challenge, performance works more forcefully as the basis of legitimacy. See his *Human Needs and Political Development* (Cambridge: Schenckman Books, 1984).
4. Initially, in 1948, the Soviet Union and the East European states recognized the DPRK, China recognized it in 1949 immediately after the establishment of the PRC government, followed by Vietnam in 1950. Only a handful of African nonaligned states established diplomatic ties with North Korea until the mid-1970s, when the European Nordic states followed course.
5. Over 250,000 South Koreans, some 54,000 U.S. troops, and 132,000 Chinese soldiers were killed in the conflict. The accurate number of North Korean casualties has not been officially documented, but the war left devastating effects in terms of human and structural destruction.
6. This fear led North Korea to construct the Pyongyang Subway System underground, with an average depth of 100 meters, which can be used as a bomb shelter for the entire citizenry of the capital city. It is known that every community has also built deep bomb shelters to avoid the same consequence if there should be another conflict.
7. In 1968, a specially selected, thirty-one-man North Korean commando team infiltrated across the demilitarized zone (DMZ) to conduct a raid on the Blue House, the South Korean equivalent to the U.S. White House, to assassinate President Park Chung-Hee by cutting off his head.

8. The "*dependencia* school," which emerged in the 1950s, is a school of economic theory that explains the lack of development in Latin America. The theory attributes the backward nature of the economy in the Third World to the structural exploitation of the peripheral economy by the entire economy of the West.

9. The theory that foreign hostile elements must be forcefully and militarily destroyed was similar to Mao Zedong's Two Stage Theory of Revolution, that the initial stage of expelling foreign sectors must be pursued through militant means but the ensuing phase of the revolution will be approached peacefully by "self criticism."

10. Unfortunately, I have no credible way of showing the volume of arms sales.

11. One might see the current emergence of Kim Jong Il's son, Kim Jong Un, in this cultural context. On this particular theme, see my own article, "Succession in North Korea," *Global Asia* 4, 2 (Summer, 2009): 13–16, http://www.globalasia.org/Current_Issues/V4N2_2009/Han_S_Park.html.

12. These features of Songun have been introduced initially in "Military-First Politics (*Songun*): Understanding Kim Jong Il's North Korea," *KEI Academic Paper Series* 2, 7 (September 2007): 118–130.

13. This term, *Suryong*, refers to "the Supreme Leader and Father of the State," a name reserved originally only for Kim Il Sung but being used of late for Kim Jong Il as well.

14. North Korean scientists and experts on renewable energy and sustainable development have participated in conferences and seminars in Norway and Denmark, the first of which was a ten-person delegation to the two Nordic countries in November 2005.

15. In November 2009, North Korea invited the Fuller Center for Housing from the United States for a groundbreaking ceremony as a peacemaking project from the grass roots, with the plan of building a large number of homes. The blueprint for the initial group of homes was designed by North Korean architects, and it is entirely powered by passive energy sources.

16. This refers to the fact that rather pricey blue jeans manufactured in the DPRK have made their way to Sweden in late 2009, and scores of other Western companies have established contacts with Pyongyang as of early 2010.

PART 2

Challenges from the Changing International Environment

CHAPTER FIVE

"China Rising" and Its Implications for North Korea's China Policy

DAVID C. KANG

Since the introduction of market reforms in 1978, China has rapidly emerged as a major regional and even global power, averaging over 9 percent economic growth over the next thirty years. Although China's economy in 1980 was less than 10 percent the size of the United States' economy, by 2006 it had grown to almost half that of the United States and surpassed that of Japan when measured by consumption. Foreign businesses have flocked to invest in China, while Chinese exports have begun to flood world markets. China is modernizing its military, has joined numerous regional and international institutions, and is increasingly visible in international politics.

The world has reacted in two ways to China's rise. On one hand, policy-makers, business executives, and the popular press have marveled at China's successes and scrambled to participate in the tremendous economic opportunities that have arisen in the past few decades. Indeed, seven consecutive U.S. presidents have encouraged China's integration into the global system, from Richard Nixon's belief that "dealing with Red China...means pulling China back into the world community," to President George W. Bush welcoming "the emergence of a China that is peaceful and prosperous, and that supports international institutions."[1]

On the other hand, there is increasing concern that the arrival of a new superpower may challenge the United States politically and perhaps even lead to military conflict, and the Pentagon's 2008 assessment of China's military power concludes that "much uncertainty surrounds China's future course, in particular in the area of its expanding military power and how that power might be used."[2] Whether China can rise peacefully, or whether it can even continue its rise, is thus one of the major policy and scholarly issues of our time.

Nowhere will China's emergence have a greater or more immediate impact than on the Korean peninsula. Sharing a long land border with China and with literally centuries of deep interactions between the two, both South Korea and North Korea must deal with China on a daily basis. North Korea in particular remains closely tied to China, both in its dependence on Chinese economic aid and in its political and diplomatic reliance on China. And thus, China's relations with the Korean peninsula provide a good case study for exploring larger questions about China's intentions, actions, and impact on international relations.

Chinese policies toward North Korea are of continuing relevance given the tensions on the peninsula. In the spring of 2009, North Korea's second nuclear test, its long-range missile tests, and provocative rhetoric once again threatened stability in Northeast Asia. Once again, North Korea has engaged in bluster designed to project strength and resolve in the face of international disapproval. And once again the underlying issues remain the same: how to reign in North Korea's nuclear programs and entice North Korea to open its markets and borders to greater foreign interactions.

This chapter will explore Chinese-North Korean relations by discussing three main questions. First, do Chinese actions toward North Korea give us any evidence of their status quo or revisionist impulses? Second, does China have any irredentist intentions toward the peninsula? That is, is China likely to use instability in North Korea, or historical disputes over the ancient Koguryo kingdom, as a pretext for reneging on the 1962 treaty? Finally, what are current Chinese attitudes and policies toward North Korea? In the wake of the 2009 provocative actions by North Korea, has China finally begun to consider abandoning its longtime ally, or even imposing economic sanctions on the North Korean regime?

These questions are of more than intellectual interest, because the Korean peninsula remains a troubled and potentially unstable area. While old rivalries have either disappeared or at least evolved in the past twenty years, inter-state relations on the Korean peninsula remain essentially unchanged. The most salient and enduring security issue on the peninsula remains how to deal with North Korea and its nuclear programs. The past fifteen years have seen almost as much failure as progress, and the issue itself remains basically the same: North Korea continues to pursue a nuclear weapons program, but it offers to disarm if the outside powers—in particular the United States—can credibly reduce the North's fear for its survival. The outside powers themselves have moved between engagement and coercion in dealing with the North, leading to policies that both occasionally contradict each other and lack consistency.

I argue that identities and interests are central to explaining both the sources of stability and potential instability in East Asia, and that relative capabilities and economic relations, while important, do not provide a clear picture of the fundamental dynamics in the region.[3] What states want is more important than how powerful they are, and it is the question of state intentions, and how they view their own position in the world and their relationship to their neighbors, that will ultimately determine whether Northeast Asia continues to move toward stability or slides into instability. In this respect, Chinese intentions toward the Korean peninsula are in the process of being formed, and nothing is as yet fixed. Although many of China's actions have shown it to be increasingly willing to engage in multilateral negotiations, and China clearly desires stability on its borders, the question remains whether China can be seen as a "responsible stakeholder" if Chinese interests conflict with U.S. interests. China continues to prioritize stability over denuclearization on the Korean peninsula.

Approaches to Explaining Chinese Intentions and Behavior

Neither realism nor liberalism provides a comprehensive explanation for the relative salience and importance of these issues. With its focus on relative power, realists would argue that China's rising power and its potential regional and perhaps even global hegemony should be the primary concern among states, that it would create fear on the part of its neighbors, and that this would lead to clear expectations for state behavior. For example, John Mearsheimer confidently argues that "China cannot rise peacefully...Most of China's neighbors, including India, Japan, Singapore, South Korea, Russia, and Vietnam, will likely join with the United States to contain China's power."[4] The implications are clear, as Richard Betts asks, "Should we want China to get rich or not? For realists, the answer should be no, since a rich China would overturn any balance of power."[5] Yet China is not foremost on policy-makers' minds; other issues such as North Korea and territorial disputes are more salient to policy-makers. Furthermore, South Korea appears to be accommodating, rather than fearing, China's rise. Realism not only has difficulty explaining this situation but also does little to explain the enduring importance of issues such as historical disputes.

Scholars who emphasize material power—both military and economic—have long predicted that states would fear China and balance against it. Offensive realism, with its emphasis on balance of power politics and the maximization of power, has had the most consistently pessimistic expectations for East Asia.[6] The offensive realist logic is fairly straightforward: because states can never be sure about the intentions or even the capabilities of other states, they must constantly fear and guard their own interests, which usually requires military power. As states become more powerful, they inevitably wish to control more of their own fate and to guard their interests, thus leading them to become increasingly interventionist. Furthermore, international relations theorists have traditionally associated the rise and fall of great powers with war and instability.[7] Robert Gilpin reflects conventional wisdom when he writes that "as its relative power increases, a rising state attempts to change the rules governing the system."[8]

Yet, in contrast to offensive realists, other realists are more sanguine about the potential threat that China may pose. These "defensive realists" tend to argue that both nuclear weapons and geography mitigate against an inevitable showdown between China and the United States.[9] Both these factors make territorial conquest much more difficult now, in contrast to the nineteenth century when imperial expansion was an input to power. Nuclear weapons in particular are seen to stabilize deterrence among great powers, in what has become known as the "nuclear peace."[10] Geography also places an ocean between the United States and China, and because China is a continental power while the United States a maritime power, this may mitigate the influence of the security dilemma.[11]

Liberals, with their focus on economic interdependence and the constraining effect of international institutions and the potential pacifying effect of democratic states, tend to see China's rapid and deep economic integration with the rest of the world as a positive aspect to its rise.[12] These scholars see deep and multiple economic relations between two states as creating ties that increase the benefits of stable relations between the two sides, and decrease the benefits of going to war. Thus, as China continues to grow, and because that growth relies heavily on deep interactions with world markets and investment, China and other states have much to gain from stable relations and much to lose from conflict.[13]

Two other strands of liberalism hold that global and domestic institutions can mitigate conflict and promote cooperation. The more that China becomes involved with international institutions, the more it both adjusts its own grand strategy to accommodate the needs of other countries and also sends signals about its intentions and willingness to work with the broader international community.[14] Furthermore, many scholars argue that democracies are less prone to fight each other than authoritarian regimes, and thus if China does become a democracy, they would expect it to be less destabilizing than if it remains an authoritarian regime run by the Communist Party.[15]

Yet, liberal arguments are not entirely optimistic, and some of those who argue that China's increased economic interdependence with the world will constrain its behavior are skeptical that this by itself can solve the security fears of East Asian states.[16] Furthermore, although China may one day become a democracy, it certainly remains a repressive authoritarian regime today, and the prospects for its democratization appear far in the future at best.

As for the liberals, their emphasis on the pacifying effect of domestic and international institutions and increasing levels of economic interactions has neither dampened concerns about Japan's intentions nor resolved historical disputes, despite over half a century of Japan's economic integration with its neighbors.[17] Although interdependence is part of the explanation for East Asian stability, by themselves economic interests do not explain the variation in threat perceptions in East Asia. In fact, increased economic relations between China, South Korea, and Japan have not had a noticeable impact on their political relations.[18] As John Ikenberry writes, "Economically, most East Asian countries increasingly expect their future economic relations to be tied to China...Can the region remain stable when its economic and security logics increasingly diverge?"[19] Furthermore, Korea and Japan are both advanced industrial democracies with deep economic ties to each other and to the United States, but this has not helped the two sides resolve their long-running disputes about history and territory.

The foregoing arguments, whether optimistic or pessimistic, tend to emphasize material and structural factors, such as military power, economic interdependence, or domestic and international institutions. Yet, an alternative theoretical approach sees ideas as independent of

118   David C. Kang

power, and as Robert Powell writes, "Although some structural theories seem to suggest that one can explain at least the outline of state behavior without reference to states' goals or preferences...in order to specify a game theoretic model, the actor's preferences and benefits must be defined."[20] Material capabilities do not necessarily lead directly to intentions, and while stronger states can do more than weaker states, their intentions may vary quite widely. Thus, what China wants may be more important for stability than how big it becomes, and states are constantly engaged in the process of interpreting and updating Chinese goals, values, and intentions.[21] Here, too, ideational theories provide both optimistic and pessimistic hypotheses.

One common way in which international relations theories incorporate identity and intentions into theories of threat in the context of a rising power lies in the distinction between status quo states and revisionist states. Definitions of status quo and revisionist powers vary, but they tend to center on the satisfaction of a state regarding the current international order.[22] That is, the main driver of instability is the difference between a state's desired situation and the status quo: the greater the difference between the two, the greater the likelihood that a state will use force to redress the difference. A powerful, revisionist China seething with resentment would prompt different responses from East Asian states than would a powerful, status quo China that desires peace and stability.

In sum, the theoretical literature contains a number of competing hypotheses, both positive and negative, about China's rise. The most spare and power-based offensive realists are most pessimistic, while defensive realists are somewhat more optimistic, as are those who emphasize economic interdependence and the constraining influence of international institutions. Those who focus on ideas believe China's rise depends on how Chinese goals and identity evolve, and they think that what China wants may be more important than how big it becomes.

Is China a Status Quo Power?

Although other foreign policy issues have a higher priority in the region, an emerging question is how regional relations with China will evolve. Rising powers pose opportunities as well as threats, and the Chinese economic opportunity and military threat toward its regional neighbors are both potentially huge. Yet, East Asian states see substantially more economic opportunity than military threat associated with China's rise. Furthermore, East Asian states prefer China to be strong rather than weak, because a strong China stabilizes the region, while a weak China invites chaos as other states attempt to control it. No state is moving toward outright containment of China, and indeed all states in the region are increasing their economic, political, and cultural ties with it.[23] China is in the middle of a long ascent, and thus any conclusions at this point about the ultimate course of China's rise are partial at best. Yet China's rise is not a new phenomenon—it has been growing rapidly for three decades—and it is possible to draw some initial conclusions.

Perhaps the most energetic movement has been in Northeast Asia, where China has involved itself in environmental, energy, trade, and other multilateral and bilateral institutions. Our concern, of course, is the Korean peninsula, and in particular Chinese relations with North Korea. Using the criteria of "responsible stakeholder,"—that China involve itself in multilateral diplomacy and eschew unilateral moves, that China not compete with the United States but rather work with it cooperatively, and that China provide leadership and influence to stabilize, and not destabilize, potential crisis situations—while one may complain that China's interests are not identical to those of the United States, it is difficult to argue that China has not worked increasingly within larger global norms and expectations regarding both the goals and how to manage the North Korean problem. As for the ties between the Republic of Korea (ROK) and the People's Republic of China (PRC), South Korean Prime Minister Han Seung Soo recently described the rapid growth of bilateral ties with China as "unprecedented," adding that "We can see profound changes take place in almost all the fields of bilateral cooperation since then, especially in trade and economy, culture, education and youth exchange."[24]

In fact, in 2003 it was China that first proposed multilateral dialogue by offering to host negotiations between North Korea and the United States; this eventually became the "Six-party Talks," involving South Korea and North Korea, China, the United States, Russia, and Japan. Mike Chinoy points out the increasing frustration Chinese diplomats had with *both* United States and North Korean intransigence, quoting a Chinese official:

We like to do things behind the scenes in Washington and Pyongyang by encouraging them to have more dialogue and exchanges. But by early 2003 the situation was very dangerous...Bush said "All options are on the table." China did not see this statement as an idle threat. Also, we hated to see North Koreans withdraw from the Non-Proliferation Treaty and restart the reactor. Only when China realized the dangers of confrontation, even military confrontation, did China change its low-key manner.[25]

China has hosted each of these talks in Beijing. Indeed, China expended considerable diplomatic capital to keep these talks continuing. While China was hardly alone in its diplomatic efforts, the evidence suggests that China's role as facilitator and locus for the talks has been considerable. Indeed, that China and the United States have been able to meet productively over an extremely tense issue with widely differing goals, interests, and perceptions is at least one positive outcome of the depressingly perplexing problem of North Korea.

But an important question, which will only be answered in the future, is whether China can be considered a responsible player in international politics even when its interests diverge from those of the United States. Is merely working within the accepted conventions, norms, and institutions enough to make China a status quo power? Or does the substance of Chinese foreign policies need to be consistent with those of the major established states?

In sum, this perspective on the North Korean problem and its affect on both regional and U.S.-PRC relations offers a few hopeful signs amid the bad news. The North Korean problem has caused China to play a central mediating role in the region; it has caused the United States and China to cooperate closely even while their interests diverge; and it has caused all the countries in the region to sit down at the same table numerous times to discuss and negotiate their differences. Although the North Korea problem remains as intractable as ever, one positive consequence may be greater cooperation and stability among the actors in the region, and in particular between the United States and China.

Could China Make Irridentist Claims to North Korea?

Another concern that often occurs is whether China makes irridentist claims on parts of North Korea, based on the ancient Koguryo kingdom. Or, could China simply formally or informally "conquer" North Korea and set up a puppet regime of some type?

Formal delineation of borders is important because clear boundaries between states are a good indicator of states' status quo interests toward each other. In this way, borders as the "political divides [are] the result of state building," and they are a useful indicator of a state's acceptance of the status quo.[26] Yet, borders are not solely functionally rationalist institutions designed to communicate preferences—they also inherently assume the existence of two parties that legitimately recognize each other's existence and right to exist. Demarcation of a boundary is a costly signal that a state intends to have stable relations with a neighbor, and Wendt and Friedheim note, "Recognizing the sovereignty of subordinate states imposes certain restraints on dominant states,"[27] while Beth Simmons notes that "when they are mutually accepted, [borders] drastically reduce external challenges to a government's legitimate authority...and clarify and stabilize transnational actors' property rights."[28]

Although there are numerous issues that could be categorized as "historical," I concentrate on only two here, the contrasts of which serve as examples that reveal both underlying causes and yet some notable differences. These two cases are Japan's continued claims to islands such as Dokdo/Takeshima in the East Sea, and China's potential claims to the ancient kingdom of Koguryo. While these two territorial disputes superficially appear similar, they are fundamentally different, and the prospects for their resolution or continued existence are thus also different. The starkest difference between the two disputes is that China signed a formal treaty delineating their border with North Korea in 1962, while Japan and South Korea have never formalized their border. This has major implications for the possibility of resolution and conflict. While South Korea's President Lee pledged not to confront Tokyo over historical issues, these issues remain dormant and always a potential problem for Korea-Japan relations. Indeed, Lee has been the third consecutive South Korean president to have a "false start" with Japan: both Kim Dae Jung and Roh Moo Hyun pledged to look to the future, only to be limited by the past.

In contrast, the China-Korea dispute over Koguryo appears superficially similar, yet in reality it is not nearly as salient an issue. The most important difference between the two issues is that China and North Korea formally delineated their border in 1962, with China ceding 60 percent of the disputed territory. In contrast to South Korea's territorial dispute with Japan over the Tokdo/Takeshima islands that was never formally resolved, the dispute over Koguryo is restricted to claims about history, and at no time has the Chinese government made any attempt to abrogate the 1962 treaty or to renegotiate the actual border.[29] In 2004, the two countries clashed verbally over the nature of the ancient kingdom of Koguryo (37 BC–AD 668), with both sides claiming that Koguryo was a historical antecedent to their modern nation.[30]

This dispute does not, however, appear likely to have any substantive effect on relations between the two countries, in part because the dispute is not a function of official Chinese government policy but rather is limited to unofficial claims made by Chinese academics.[31] Furthermore, China has not pressed any claims since that time. By the tenth century, Korea and China had established the Yalu river as their border, and by the fifteenth century, Korea's long northern border— along both the Yalu and Tumen rivers—was essentially secure and peaceful, and these two rivers have formed the border between China and Korea ever since.[32] Perhaps most significantly, the debate over Koguryo—which has died down considerably since 2004—is about history, identity, and national narratives, not power.

None of us know the future, of course, but there is reason to doubt that the Chinese government harbors a secret plan to renege on the 1962 treaty and move the border farther south. Why is a treaty—a mere piece of paper—so significant for stability? China has been extremely concerned about its own territorial integrity following the "unequal treaties" era of the late nineteenth century. China also faces sizable ethnic populations in Tibet and Xinjiang, both of which only came under Chinese rule relatively recently, during the Qing dynasty of the eighteenth century. David Shambaugh notes that "China has managed to peacefully resolve all of its land border disputes except one (with India), having concluded treaties that delimit 20,222 kilometers of its boundaries."[33]

Even the Indian border dispute has seen recent progress. China and India have made significant progress in stabilizing this relationship. In April 2005, China and India signed an agreement focused on resolving the fifty-three-year-old border dispute. On April 11, 2005, Chinese Premier Wen Jiabao and Indian Prime Minister Manmohan Singh released a joint statement pledging to establish an "India-China strategic and cooperative partnership for peace and prosperity."[34] China officially recognized the Himalayan territory of Sikkim as part of India, and reached agreement with India about how to resolve the rest of their boundary dispute, offering at one time readiness to accept only 29 percent of the disputed land.[35] The comprehensive agreement also covered areas including civil aviation, finance, education, and tourism. Evan Medeiros and Taylor Fravel conclude that as a result of China's efforts,

"China's long land border, the site of many of the country's major wars, has never been more secure."[36]

Why is this relevant to Korea? The worldwide protests against Chinese control of Tibet in 2008 serve as a reminder that Chinese concerns are with the stability of its borders. Significant about the 2008 protests was that no major government joined the protests, even symbolically. This is because the Westphalian set of international rules is very clear, and quite conservative: states only renege on treaties that demarcate borders under the most extreme of conditions. That no government got involved serves as a notice about the unwillingness of other governments to broach the subject with China. Given China's concerns about "one China" and the claims made for its territorial integrity, the worst thing China could do is to begin unilaterally renegotiating treaties that define its borders. If the Korea-China border is up for reconsideration, then *all other borders* are also up for reconsideration. Thus, it appears unlikely that China would voluntarily open an issue that currently works in its favor and which currently keeps under control troubles much larger than North Korea. The world would otherwise be immediately convinced that China *is* a major threat, and adjust their policies accordingly.

There are also practical, immediate reasons why China has little interest in extending political control across its historical limit. To actually occupy and control Korean territory would be a prohibitively difficult task: to incorporate even more Korean ethnic minorities into China would cause untold problems, no Chinese mayor of a northern city wants more unemployed low-skill workers who can't speak Chinese, and of course China would have no interest in being financially and politically responsible for cleaning up the mess that is North Korea.

The nightmarish scenario, for both Chinese and other states, is a situation in which instability in North Korea causes China to send troops either to the border or even into North Korea in an attempt to stabilize the situation. Such moves would doubtless be seen by South Koreans and the United States as a preemptive move by China to expand its influence and perhaps even incorporate territory into the PRC. Gregory Moore notes that, "China would prefer not to have to intervene, it does not fancy the notion of North Korea as a northeast Asian version of the pre-2001 Taliban-ruled Afghanistan ... [yet] it is not certain how a unified Korea would treat China."[37] A United States Institute of Peace study release in January 2009 cited Palestinian Liberation Army (PLA) researchers as noting that China's "strong preference is to receive formal authorization and to coordinate closely with the UN," but the PLA does have contingency plans in place to perform humanitarian, peace-keeping, and environmental issues in the North, should the world not respond in a timely manner.[38]

Thus, the implications of what a renegotiation of the North Korean border would mean for the rest of China's borders, its impact on perceptions of Chinese intentions, and practical difficulties in extending political control lead to the cautiously optimistic conclusion that China—while intending to have major influence over Korea—is unlikely to actually attempt to exert political control and move the border.

Chinese Policy toward North Korea in 2009

The most relevant question regarding relations between China and the Democratic People's Republic of Korea (DPRK) is the extent and level of influence and the Chinese goals regarding the peninsula today. The early moves from 2009 indicate a North Korean regime in chaos, increasingly belligerent, and totally focused on internal palace dynamics. Kim Jong Il's poor health over the past year has surely intensified the internal maneuvering over his successor, and North Korean elites are almost surely engaged in "palace politics" as they attempt to position themselves for power and to protect their interests in the future. That Kim Jong Il has not yet anointed a successor implies that none of his possible successors has built enough factional support to become the clear choice. As a result, the internal factions and potential future leaders have every incentive to show their loyalty to the Kim family and to prove their nationalist credentials.

The logical results of this leadership instability is both a decreased long-term planning and strategic vision, as well as an incentive for nationalistic and assertive acts, as various factions attempt to prove their loyalty to the Kim family and the North Korean regime. If North Korea can resolve the succession issue quickly, the regime might survive well into the future. On the other hand, we could be seeing the beginning of the internal collapse of the Kim dynasty, and governments around the region might do well to begin reviewing their contingency plans regarding how to deal with the chaos that such a collapse would surely cause.

China's policy is important because the only country that could affect North Korea in a direct manner is China. Indeed, the Chinese appear to be fairly angered by North Korea's provocative moves of this past spring, and the nuclear test in particular has been a real insult to Chinese diplomatic efforts. There has also been intense debate within China about the best way to deal with North Korea and even whether North Korea remains strategically important to China. The range of political opinion following North Korea's second nuclear test in 2009 varied widely, but an emerging consensus held that China was the key player in negotiations, and that China was potentially more willing to reconsider its relationship with the DPRK.

The sad fact is that the range of policy options available to both China and other countries is quite thin. Few countries would consider military action to cause the regime to collapse, given that Seoul is vulnerable to North Korean conventional weapons and that war in the region or regime collapse could potentially unleash uncontrolled use of nuclear weapons and potentially draw all the surrounding countries into conflict with each other. At the same time, the United States, South Korea, and Japan are unwilling to normalize relations with North Korea and offer considerable economic or diplomatic incentives in the hopes of luring Pyongyang into more moderate behavior. As a result, both Chinese and U.S. governments are faced with the choices of rhetorical pressure, quiet diplomacy, and mild sanctions.

Chinese political influence is quite limited. As Adam Segal noted, "The idea that the Chinese would turn their backs on the North Koreans is clearly wrong."[39] As to nudging North Korea into economic reforms and opening up, the only country that could affect North Korea's economy in a major way is China. North Korea's latest moves, and the nuclear test in particular, appear to have angered the Chinese and have been a real insult to Chinese diplomatic efforts.

After the first North Korean nuclear test in 2006, China called the test "flagrant and brazen," and voted with other United Nations (UN) Security Council members for resolution 1718, which imposed a series of sanctions on North Korea.[40] However, the Chinese also reduced the severity of those sanctions, including opposing the use of military action to enforce the sanctions. Marcus Noland estimates that Chinese exports, including export of luxury goods, have actually increased since the imposition of sanctions. Noland estimates that China's export of luxury goods increased 140 percent between 2007 and 2008.[41] Thus, the prospects of China putting any significant pressure on North Korea are dim.

Furthermore, China is North Korea's main trading partner, and despite the economic sanctions imposed by UN resolution 1718 and

1874, trade between the two countries continues to increase. Total trade in 2008 was 41.3 percent greater than it was in 2007, and amounted to between half and two-thirds of North Korea's total foreign trade.⁴² In fact, Chinese trade now accounts for between 60 percent and 80 percent of North Korea's entire foreign trade.⁴³

Thus, China retains considerable economic leverage over North Korea. However, it is unlikely that China would use such economic pressure, or that such pressure would work. China has continued to build economic relations with North Korea over the past few years, and, to a considerable degree, Chinese economic policies toward North Korea have been designed to prevent instability, through expanded economic assistance. That is, China faces the same problem that other countries do—how to pressure and persuade North Korea to take a more moderate stance without pushing it so hard that it collapses. In this way, North Korea's dependence on Chinese aid limits China's ability to pressure North Korea—North Korea is so vulnerable that China needs to be quite careful in its policies toward it.

And China, like South Korea, must concern itself with the potential consequences of a North Korean collapse, which could include hundreds of thousands of North Korean refugees, a large and well-armed North Korean military that may not voluntarily disarm, nuclear weapons unaccounted for and uncontrolled by any central authority, and the subsequent social, economic, and cultural costs of dealing with an implosion.

Although the spring of 2009 saw a number of policy analyses that either predicted or encouraged China to impose sanctions on North Korea (or to actually enforce the 2006 UN sanctions), it appears unlikely that there will be a major shift in Chinese economic support for the North Korean regime.⁴⁴

The reasons are simple—the United States continues to view North Korea primarily in military terms, and is worried about North Korean strength, in particular its nuclear weapons program. The United States is concerned about the potential sale of nuclear material or missiles to terrorist groups, such as al-Qaeda, that would in turn use such weapons against the United States. To that end, the United States has generally attempted to isolate North Korea, and is pursuing a complex mix of negotiation and coercion in its attempt to convince North Korea to halt its nuclear programs.

In contrast, China has come to view the North Korea problem primarily in economic and political terms, and is now more concerned about North Korean weakness: the possibility of its collapse or chaos.

Chinese analysts tend to believe that North Korea can be deterred, and they are worried about the economic and political consequences of a collapsed regime. To put the matter in perspective, should North Korea collapse, the number of refugees could potentially exceed the entire global refugee population.[45] Even assuming a best-case scenario in which collapse did not turn violent, the regional economic and political effects would be severe.

However, China did evince growing frustration with North Korea over the past few months, and China also agreed to the UN sanctions of June 9, 2009. China's UN ambassador, Zhang Yesui, said, "We strongly urge the DPRK to honor its commitment to denuclearization, stop any moves that may further worsen the situation and return to the six party talks... [but] under no circumstances should there be use or threat of the use of force."[46] Yet China has also signaled fairly clearly that it was unlikely to be in favor of too precipitous a move toward punishment of North Korea. An official analysis published in the *Beijing Zhongguo Jingji Shibao* on June 11, 2009, argued that:

> If nothing unexpected happens in the third DPRK nuclear crisis triggered by the second DPRK nuclear test, there will again be a return to the negotiating table, as in the past... The DPRK is using nuclear weapons as a means to demand that the United States give it a security and development guarantee... the question of how China can preserve its national interests and at the same time truly take responsibility for regional security expresses a power's demeanor and responsibility.[47]

The real question for China is to what extent its own priorities regarding North Korea have shifted. As Greg Moore has noted, "Chinese policy is *both* to bring North Korea to heel and to prop up North Korea's struggling economy, and this behavior... is based on a careful calculation of China's national interests."[48] If China decides that a nuclear-armed North Korea is harmful for its own security than the aftermath of a North Korean collapse, it could begin to shift policy and put more pressure on the regime. Alternatively, if China continues to fear instability arising more directly from a weakened North Korea, its policies—rhetoric aside—will remain roughly the same as they have been over the past decade. At this point, it is unclear how Chinese officials and policy-makers view the current situation, and it is unclear how their policies will evolve in the coming months.

Conclusion

This exploration of China's relations with North Korea yields a number of important implications for our theories of international relations. The extent and limits of balance of power theory, especially when applied to the rise and fall of great powers, has long been a central preoccupation for students of international relations. Yet, privileging the distribution of power as the key determinant of stability and state behavior is a mistake. What states aspire for is more important to determining whether or not states are threatening than how big they are. Security-seeking status quo states provoke different responses from other states than do revisionist, expansionist powers, and states design their policies based on what they believe these interests and identities are. China is in the middle of a long transition, and at this point the future place of China in the world is still unclear. Indeed, at this point, prediction is mere speculation. How Chinese identity and power will develop is not known, and speculation is not a very satisfying scholarly exercise.

Chinese—and other states'—goals, intentions, power, and identities, and how these evolve will be central to determining whether states adjust to and accept China, or whether they increasingly compete with and fear China. Indeed, Chinese goals and identities are still in the process of being determined. How the Communist Party evolves, and whether it will still exist thirty years from now, is also unclear. These are the key questions to ask, and how their answers develop will determine whether the future of East Asia is increasingly stable or increasingly unstable. As Richard Samuels wrote last year, "the challenge for China is how to become socialized into a world order with rules and norms valuing democracy and human rights...For the rest of us...the challenge is to socialize ourselves to an emerging new order that makes room...for Chinese power—even in terms of moral authority."[49]

As to China-North Korean relations, the prospects for the time being are that China will continue to attempt to achieve all its goals, however incompatible. That is, China may exert influence over North Korea, but it remains limited, partial, and tenuous. China will attempt to nudge North Korea toward economic reforms and pressure North Korea to give up its nuclear weapons and missile programs, while not putting so much pressure on the regime that it collapses or chooses to lash out in anger. At the same time, China will continue to support multilateral talks on Northeast Asia and work with the United Nations, the United States, and other countries in the region. However, Chinese interests are not the same as U.S. interests, and while the two share the goal of avoiding further instability in Northeast Asia, the United States tends to prioritize nuclear weapons and missile programs, while China tends to prioritize regime stability as more important. Whether China can continue to balance these competing priorities and interests in the face of an inflexible and opaque North Korean regime remains to be seen.

Notes

1. R.M. Nixon, "Asia after Viet Nam," *Foreign Affairs* 46 (1967–1968): 123; "U.S. President George W. Bush and Chinese President Hu Jintao," *Washington Post*, April 20, 2006, http://www.washingtonpost.com/wp-dyn/content/article/2006/04/20/AR2006042000694.html.
2. "Annual report to Congress: Military Power of the People's Republic of China," *U.S. Defense Department*, 2008, http://www.globalsecurity.org/military/library/report/2008/2008-prc-military-power.htm.
3. Richard Ned Lebow, *A Cultural Theory of International Relations* (Cambridge: Cambridge University Press, 2008); J.D. Fearon, "Signaling Foreign Policy Interests: Tying Hands Versus Sinking Costs," *Journal of Conflict Resolution* 41 (1997): 68–90.
4. Z. Brzezinski and J. Mearsheimer, "Clash of the Titans," *Foreign Policy* 146 (2005): 47.
5. Betts, R.K. "Wealth, Power, and Instability: East Asia and the United States after the Cold War," *International Security* 18 (1993–1994): 55.
6. A. Friedberg, "Ripe for Rivalry," *International Security* 18 (1993–1994): 5–33; K.A. Waltz, "The Emerging Structure of International Politics," *International Security* 18 (1993): 44–79; D. Roy, "Hegemon on the Horizon? China's Threat to East Asian Security," *International Security* 19 (1994): 149–168; C. Layne, "The Unipolar Illusion: Why New Great Powers Will Rise?" *International Security* 17 (1993): 5–51.
7. P. Kennedy, *The Rise and Fall of Great Powers: Economic Change and Military Conflict From 1500 to 2000* (New York: Random House, 1987); S. Chan, *China, the U.S., and the Power-Transition Theory: A Critique* (London: Routledge, 2008); J. Kugler, "The Asian Ascent: Opportunity for Peace or Precondition for War?" *International Studies Perspectives* 7 (1998): 36–42.
8. R. Gilpin, *War and Change in World Politics* (Cambridge: Cambridge University Press, 1981), 187.
9. A. Goldstein, *Rising to the Challenge* (Stanford, CA: Stanford University Press, 2005).
10. K.A. Waltz, "Nuclear Myths and Political Realities," *American Political Science Review* 84 (1990): 731–45.
11. R. Ross, "The Geography of the Peace: East Asia in the Twenty-First Century," *International Security* 23 (1999): 81–118.
12. J. Grieco, "China and America in the World Polity," in C.W. Pumphrey, ed., *The Rise of China in Asia: Security Implications* (Carlisle: Strategic Studies Institute, 2002); P. Papayounou and S. Kastner, "Sleeping with the Potential Enemy: Assessing the U.S. Policy of Engagement with China," *Security Studies* 9 (1999): 164–95; M. Wan, "Economic Interdependence and Economic Cooperation: Mitigating Conflict and Transforming Security Order in Asia," in M. Alagappa, ed., *Asian Security Order* (Stanford, CA: Stanford University Press, 2003).
13. Brzezinski and Mearsheimer (2005).
14. R. Keohane, "International Institutions: Can Interdependence Work?" *Foreign Policy* 110 (1998): 82–96.

15. B. Gilley, *China's Democratic Future: How It Will Happen and Where It Will Lead* (New York: Columbia University Press, 2004).

16. John Ikenberry, "American hegemony and East Asian Order," *Australian Journal of International Affairs* 58, 3 (September 2004): 353–367.

17. Alexis Dudden, *Troubled Apologies Among Japan, Korea, and the United States* (New York: Columbia University Press, 2008).

18. Miles Kahler and Scott Kastner, "Strategic Uses of Economic Interdependence: Engagement Policies on the Korean Peninsula and Across the Taiwan Strait," *Journal of Peace Research* 43, 5 (2006): 523–541.

19. Ikenberry, "American Hegemony and East Asian Order," 354.

20. R. Powell, "Bargaining Theory and International Conflict," *American Review of Political Science* 5 (2002): 17.

21. J. Legro, "What China Will Want: The Future Intentions of a Rising Power," *Perspectives on Politics* 5 (2007): 515–34.

22. A.I. Johnston, *Social States: China in International Institutions, 1980–2000* (Princeton, NJ: Princeton UP, 2008); A.F.K. Organski and J. Kugler, *The War Ledger* (Chicago: University Of Chicago Press, 1981); R. Schweller, "Bandwagoning for Profit: Bringing the Revisionist State Back In," *International Security* 19 (1994): 72–108.

23. David C. Kang, *China Rising: Peace, Power, and Order in East Asia* (New York: Columbia University Press, 2007).

24. "Rapid growth of ROK-China relations 'unprecedented,' says ROK PM," *Xinhua*, June 12, 2009, http://news.xinhuanet.com/english/2009–06/13/content_11533612.htm.

25. Quoted in Mike Chinoy, *Meltdown: The Inside Story of the North Korean Nuclear Crisis* (New York: St. Martin's Press, 2008), 165.

26. Michiel Baud and Willem Van Schendel, "Toward a Comparative History of Borderlands," *Journal of World History* 8 (1997): 214.

27. Alexander Wendt and Daniel Friedheim, "Hierarchy under Anarchy: Informal Empires and the East German State," *International Organization* 49, 4 (1995): 704.

28. Beth A. Simmons, "Rules over Real Estate: Trade, Territorial Conflict, and International Borders as Institutions," *Journal of Conflict Resolution* 49, 6 (1995): 827.

29. Taylor Fravel, "Regime Insecurity and International Cooperation: Explaining China's Compromises in Territorial Disputes," *International Security* 30 (2005): 46–83.

30. Peter Gries, "The Koguryo Controversy: National Identity, and Sino-Korean Relations Today," *East Asia* 22 (2005): 3–17.

31. David Scofield, "China Puts Korean Spat on the Map," *Asia Times*, August 19, 2004.

32. Gari Ledyard, "Cartography in Korea," in J. B. Harley and David Woodward, eds., *Cartography in the Traditional East and Southeast Asian Societies* (Chicago: Chicago University Press, 2005), 290.

33. David Shambaugh, "China Engages Asia: Reshaping the Regional Order," *International Security* 29, 3 (2004–2005): 66.

34. "China and India Sign Border Accord," CNN, April 11, 2005, www.cnn.com

35. Fravel (2005): 56.

36. E. Medeiros and M.T. Fravel, "China's New Diplomacy," *Foreign Affairs* 82 (2003): 26.

37. Gregory J. Moore, "How North Korea threatens China's Interests: Understanding Chinese Duplicity on the North Korean Nuclear Issue," *International Relations of the Asia-Pacific* 8, 19 (2008): 1–29.

38. Bonnie Glaser, Scott Snyder, and John S. Park, "Keeping an Eye on an Unruly Neighbor: Chinese Views of Economic Reform and Stability in North Korea," *United States Institute of Peace Working Paper*, January 3, 2009, 19.

39. Jayshree Bajoria, "The China-North Korea Relationship," *Backgrounder*, Council on Foreign Relations, July 21, 2009, http://www.cfr.org/publication/11097/.

40. David E. Sanger, William J. Broad, and Thom Shanker, "North Korea Says It Tested a Nuclear Device Underground," *New York Times*, October 9, 2006, http://query.nytimes. com/gst/fullpage.html?res=9E0CE0DC1330F93AA35753C1A9609C8B63&sec=&spo n=&&scp=1&sq=%22North%20Korea%20Says%20It%20Tested%20a%20Nuclear%20 Device%20Underground%22&st=cse.

41. Russia defined "luxury goods" loosely—as watches costing over US$2,000 and coats over US$9,000. Marcus Noland, "The (Non)-Impact of UN Sanctions on North Korea," *Asia Policy* 7 (January 2009): 61–88.

42. Mary Beth Nikitin, Mark E. Manyin, Emma Chanlett-Avery, and Dick K. Nanto, "North Korea's Second Nuclear Test: Implications of UN Resolution 1874," *Congressional Research Service* R-40684, Washington, DC, July 1, 2009, 10–11.

43. Jayshree Bajoria, "The China-North Korea Relationship," *Backgrounder*, Council on Foreign Relations, July 21, 2009, http://www.cfr.org/publication/11097/.

44. See, for example, Scott Snyder, "Reaching Out to Touch North Korea: The Sanctions Debate and China," *Global Security*, May 28, 2009, http://sitrep.globalsecurity.org/ articles/090528355-reaching-out-to-touch-north-ko.htm; Jay Solomon, Ian Johnson, and Gordon Fairclough, "China's Anger at North Korea Test Signals Shift," *Wall Street Journal*, May 29, 2009, http://online.wsj.com/article/SB124353389041863413.html.

45. "World Refugee Survey 2004," *U.S. Committee for Refugees and Immigrants*, http://www. refugees.org/data/wrs/04/pdf/key_statistics.pdf.

46. "China urges North Korea to scrap nuclear weapons," *Reuters*, June 12, 2009, http://www. reuters.com/article/newsMaps/idUSTRE55B49O20090612.

47. Quoted in Bonnie Glaser, *Beijing Zhongguo Jingji Shibao* [China Economic Times], Online in Chinese, OSC Translation, June 11, 2009.

48. Moore, "How North Korea Threatens China's Interests."

49. Richard J. Samuels, *Securing Japan: Tokyo's Grand Strategy and the Future of East Asia* (Ithaca, NY: Cornell University Press, 2007), 208.

CHAPTER SIX

Multilateralism and Pyongyang's Foreign Policy Strategy

GILBERT ROZMAN

Management of North Korea has proven difficult for all countries that have tried. China and the Soviet Union struggled with this challenge, competing for Pyongyang's favor even as they grasped for the slightest leverage.[1] South Korea made at least three earnest attempts: in the early 1970s in the shadow of Sino-U.S. reconciliation; in the early 1990s after the end of the cold war; and from 1998, guided by the Sunshine Policy.[2] When it sought reciprocity under Lee Myung Bak in 2008, relations deteriorated abruptly. Since 1993 the United States has groped for a strategy to achieve denuclearization, above all. It signed the bilateral Agreed Framework in 1994, supported the Sunshine Policy putting South Korea in the forefront in 2000, and launched the Six-party Talks that, after rocky periods, produced the Joint Agreement in 2007. Yet, through the spring of 2010, despite overtures from the Obama administration, North Korean rhetoric was bellicose and its behavior aggressive. Without prospects for bilateral U.S.-North Korean talks in the short run, particularly after the sinking of the South Korean naval vessel, the Cheonan, the chances were high for a multilayered or nested approach combining "strong carrots and strong sticks." The prospects for such an approach rest heavily on the responses of the "other four" (China, South Korea, Japan, and Russia) and can be evaluated against the backdrop of the three previous U.S. attempts at multilateralism. Pyongyang's strategy can be assessed, in the coming period as in recent years, in the context of how well the others work together.

The first layer consists of a strong defensive posture based on triangular relations among the United States, South Korea, and Japan.[3] Although the U.S.-Japan alliance will mark its fiftieth anniversary in 2010 and the U.S.-South Korean alliance has stood firm since the Korean War, triangularity has proven elusive and still requires bolstering even after the past two decades of concern about North Korean nuclear weapons development. The second layer that warrants attention is the bilateral forum of Sino-U.S. dialogue.[4] In the context of the overall relationship between the two most important great powers, a balance must be reached between enticements to the North when it is cooperative and sanctions against it if it stubbornly fails to respond to sincere compromises. This dialogue lies at the core of deliberations over sanctions among the permanent members of the United Nations (UN) Security Council. The third layer of the Six-party Talks has become fixed as Northeast Asia's regional security framework and the appropriate venue for offering incentives to the North.[5] Finally, the fourth layer of U.S.-North Korean bilateral talks operates, if conditions permit, against the background of these other layers. It is nested firmly within a multilateral framework.

The Obama approach to Pyongyang comes on the heels of three previous U.S.-led attempts to utilize multilateralism in order to provide security and ensure stability in post-cold war Northeast Asia. In 1993–1994, in the first North Korean nuclear crisis, Bill Clinton groped unsuccessfully for an effective combination of the first two layers while, after the intervention of Jimmy Carter that led to the Agreed Framework, becoming amenable to a formal multilateral structure in the form of four-party talks consisting of the two Koreas, the United States, and China.[6] This set in motion policy changes in each state, especially Kim Young Sam's call for "humanitarian engagement." Yet, in the midst of a devastating famine, progress had practically ground to a halt in 1997. A second try at multilateralism under Bill Clinton became known as the "Perry Process," when former Secretary of Defense William Perry reinforced Kim Dae Jung's launching of his Sunshine Policy by drawing the states of Northeast Asia together in 1998–1999 in more intensive diplomatic exchanges, offering many more rewards to North Korea. Although this process survived until the fall of 2002, it was only limping along following Kim Dae Jung's failed meeting with George W. Bush in March 2001. Finally, on the ruins of the tense U.S.-North Korean standoff, a third path toward multilateralism was launched in 2003. It operated at a rather low key until Bush's second term began in 2005 and Chris Hill was given the green light to back China's formal chairing of the Six-party Talks, with vigorous U.S. shuttle diplomacy.[7] It, too, failed from the fall of 2008, when Pyongyang refused to proceed, and then, in a mist of uncertainty about Kim Jong Il's health and his succession, became increasingly defiant. Drawing lessons from these three rounds of multilateralism in dealing with North Korea, we find that diplomacy becomes increasingly intense, the number of countries in the process keeps expanding, and the multilayered nature of managing the North grows more complex. This experience has proven that China is indispensable to any resolution of the problem, South Korea and the United States will each suffer if they cannot coordinate closely, Japan may appear at times to be aloof but remains vital to a lasting solution, and Russia can be a spoiler and must be accepted as a relevant player.[8] Even if, at times, U.S. receptivity to the full implications of multilateralism was tenuous, particularly in 2001–2006, its shift in 2007 at the time of the Joint Agreement appears to lay a foundation for a lasting approach to building on the experiences of these three rounds. No longer is it likely to be a barrier to a multilateral framework as long as all of the layers are present in a balanced manner.

Of course, critical to the resolution of North Korea's challenge to regional and global order is the strategy chosen by the North's leadership. Rather than speculate about their choice, the approach here is to clarify the setting in which it is likely to be made and then consider their response. With U.S.-North Korean talks nested in a multilayered framework, the North's options can be specified, including the costs and benefits of different choices. A desperate regime playing a bad hand, however, may be drawn to an unusual calculus.

The Alliance Triangle

The need to forge a three-way alliance gained urgency in 1989–1992 as the cold war ended, the Soviet Union collapsed, and Seoul succeeded in its *nordpolitik* of establishing diplomatic relations with Moscow and Beijing. Ironically, during the cold war, despite encouragement by Washington, neither Tokyo nor Seoul saw any compelling reason for forging the third leg of the alliance triangle to complement and make more meaningful Washington's strong ties to both capitals. The impetus to do more arose from complaints aired to U.S. officials that the other side was behaving in an untrustworthy fashion. South Koreans were aghast at a high-level Japanese delegation to Pyongyang led by

Kanemaru Shin that sought, without consultation, full-scale reconciliation with North Korea on terms deemed inimical to the South's plans
for reconciliation and, eventually, reunification. In turn, the Japanese
were dissatisfied with the intemperate drive of Roh Tae Woo to achieve
normalization with the Soviet Union and China without regard to
Japan's interests, while also changing direction toward North Korea in
a manner that could leave Japan isolated. In these circumstances, during the final year of his presidency, George H.W. Bush made efforts
to tighten the triangle. Tokyo promised to keep Seoul informed of its
intentions, and both sides reassured Washington, but with the onset of
nuclear crisis, Washington needed to provide them with reassurances
that it would not resort to force or make far-reaching concessions.[9]

Although during the first nuclear crisis Bill Clinton looked for ways
to draw both allies closer, neither Tokyo nor Seoul was satisfied with
the U.S. handling of North Korea, fearing for a while that a unilateral
strike could put their countries in jeopardy and fretting about the deal
that was finally reached, which left them paying for the construction
of two light-water nuclear reactors. Triangularity did not become a
priority until after North Korea fired a missile over Japan in August
1998 and the visit of Kim Dae Jung to Tokyo in October in a bid to
upgrade relations across a wide spectrum. When Clinton launched the
Perry Process to respond to the North's provocation, close consultations among the three states resulted in an unprecedented commitment to security cooperation.[10] In 1999, they established the Trilateral
Coordination and Oversight Group (TCOG), as Perry prepared one
plan for engagement, testing Kim's new Sunshine Policy and a backup
plan for containment of the North. Yet, when George W. Bush took
office, it was perceived that the promise of a triangular alliance and
ties in 1992 had not been realized. Richard Armitage, who had been
involved in this effort eight years earlier at the Defense Department,
was now expected at the State Department to orchestrate the diplomatic synchronization necessary for TCOG to thrive. Early optimism
of achieving success soon stumbled owing to the worsening U.S.-
South Korean distrust and also the repeated revival of the history issue
between Japan and South Korea.[11]

The worst nightmare for South Koreans is for them to be bypassed
again, with their fate left to foreign powers pursuing their own national
interests. Unlike Japan's ambivalence over the United States alternating
bashing and passing it, South Koreans do not make a special issue of
being bashed by the United States and save their alarm for being passed
over, as in 1993–1994 and 2001–2006, in the U.S. handling of North

Korea's nuclear weapons program. "Shuttle diplomacy" with Japan in 2004–2005 failed to alleviate this situation.[12] Increased coordination with China, with aspirations to be taken seriously as a kind of regional "balancer," made little headway. Lee Myung Bak departed from Roh's arms-length treatment of the United States after Bush's diplomacy shifted toward multilateralism, and when he visited Washington in June 2009, he continued to stick closely to the U.S. approach after Obama took a hard line to the North's nuclear tests and missile tests while readying the ground for a multilayered strategic approach.

South Korea's status goals have shifted over time. They included confirmation of its rise as an ally, an economic actor, an advanced industrial society, a political actor, and recognition as a force in the international relations of East Asia. Each president had reason to resent some lack of recognition. The balance gradually shifted from seeking confirmation to showing Korean autonomy, albeit progressives were keener on doing the latter. Koreans share the desire for autonomy in international relations, a higher status in relation to key states, and unification of the peninsula. Yet, conservatives are prone to put these in the context of preservation of the existing social order at home and coordination with a dependable ally as part of international society that can be trusted. In contrast, progressives impatiently set aside some restraints in search of some breakthrough process with the North, with far-reaching identity consequences from the outset. Unlike China or Japan, South Korea is not a great power and has no memory of making any challenge for leadership. Recently, there has been a repeat of these frustrations: The United States in 2001–2003 was blamed for stifling Kim Dae Jung's diplomatic endeavors; Japan is accused of repeatedly insulting Korean feelings in textbook revisions or territorial claims; and China with its historical assertions about the Koguryo state and treatment of South Korea during the Olympics has reminded people of the arrogance of sinocentrism. After repeated reminders of marginalization, the reality has fallen far short of expectations, as economic crises a decade apart compounded fears of national vulnerability squeezed between "arrogant" China and "desperate" Japan.

In comparison to the illusory nature of U.S. expectations for an "alliance triangle" in 2001–2003 and the unraveling of rudimentary forms of this arrangement in 2005,[13] the situation became more promising in 2008–2009. Although Japan in 2007–2008 had grave misgivings about the U.S. position toward the North being too soft, it was firmly behind U.S. demands for verification in Stage 2 and full abandonment on an accelerated timeline in Stage 3. After Lee Myung Bak took office in

2008, he was ready to act in concert too, requiring denuclearization as a precondition for advancing the bilateral agenda approved by Roh Moo Hyun, and reciprocity if blandishments to the North are to be forthcoming. When the United States presented a proposal or draft to North Korea, it now represented the common agenda of the three states. In 2009, Obama found that Lee and Prime Minister Aso Taro agreed on antipathy toward the North's provocative moves and were receptive to a coordinated strategy. Yet, the possibility remained that South Korean-Japanese relations would again be derailed by Japanese revisionist moves, arousing the South Korean public once again and complicating anew the long-illusive pursuit of alliance triangularity.

Just as Kim Dae Jung's eagerness to boost relations with Japan aroused optimism among Japanese from 1998, a decade later Lee Myung Bak's even greater enthusiasm led to another wave of hope. Yet, the response was not how to avoid the same mistakes that had soured Koreans' attitude toward Japan after Kim's supposedly breakthrough summit, but how to pressure the South to do what it had refused repeatedly: forget history regardless of how Japan chooses to reinterpret it; recognize how important Japan is for South Korea in economic cooperation, especially during a financial crisis as in 2009, and in its defense when the North threatens it; be pragmatic in calming emotions over the territorial dispute; and awaken to the danger from China's rise, overcoming gullibility. Insistent that Seoul and Tokyo need closer cooperation, Nishihara Masashi, president of the Research Institute for Peace and Security, placed the entire burden on Seoul.[14] Blaming Bush for ignoring East Asia and being soft on North Korea despite the hopelessness of the Six-party Talks, he stressed that Obama would have to stop neglecting bilateral ties with Japan and avoid succumbing to China's efforts to strengthen U.S. ties at Japan's expense in order to set the right tone for regional security. Similar to other Japanese officials and conservative academics, he left no doubt that Japanese leaders have no reason to temper historical revisionism and territorial demands out of concern for South Korean feelings.

Prospects for the alliance triangle are the best they have been, but they remain far from promising due to many reasons: Japan's political paralysis in which obsession over the abductions issue with North Korea distracts attention from coordinated diplomacy; Japan's hesitation to improve interoperability of military forces with the United States in the shadow of an ongoing struggle over revising Article 9 of its Constitution; South Korean polarization as progressives keep Lee Myung Bak on the defensive and capitalize on explosive emotions, such as after Roh committed suicide in late May 2009; the inevitability of Japan raising the history issue again in an inflammatory manner, which is bound to antagonize South Koreans, as seen in the media coverage of General Tamogami Toshio's explosive essay in November 2008;[15] and the U.S. difficulty of finding a reassuring strategy for the frontline countries, the populace of which, after stark memories of past warfare and lengthy exposure to postwar appeasement thinking, is not prepared to bear the costs of what could be a devastating hot war or even a protracted cold war with possible repeated threatening spikes of danger.

Pyongyang has sought to divide this triangle, removing U.S. bases from South Korea. It concentrated on Seoul as the weak link and reacted angrily to Lee, who insists on bolstering ties with both Washington and Tokyo. Although the public's ambivalence may interfere with Lee's intentions, Pyongyang's strategy has backfired in recent years. Its hardball tactics in 2008–2009 have made it easier for Lee to gain support for his policies. While in the late spring of 2009, after Roh's suicide, there were sympathy demonstrations amid charges that prosecutors had hounded him at the behest of Lee in a manner that cast doubt on the country's democratic foundations, North Korea continued to remain deeply unpopular. When South Korea determined that a North Korean torpedo had sunk its naval vessel in April 2010, anger mounted. Yet, Lee would have to proceed cautiously, given the staunch progressive opposition to his leadership and the grave danger of war sensed by large numbers of South Koreans.

Sino-U.S. Bilateralism

The core of multilateralism in dealing with North Korea is Sino-U.S. relations. In the fall of 2006 they were tested, and their relations appeared to strengthen. On the one hand, Beijing voted in favor of Security Council sanctions and toughened its posture toward the North. On the other, Washington intensified bilateral talks that led to the Joint Agreement at the Six-party Talks that conformed to Chinese thinking over several years. There seemed to be an understanding that the former would keep compromising and giving Pyongyang ample opportunity to show it was ready to denuclearize and the latter would withhold rewards and join in pressuring Pyongyang if it stalled or reverted to belligerent behavior. Yet, this implicit deal assumed the existence of mutual trust, which at least on the Chinese side was lacking. China over the next two years alternated between feeling bypassed in the two-way talks, apprehending that an agreement may be reached at its expense, and feeling suspicious that the United States' dropping of bank sanctions against North Korea meant that words did not match deeds and that values were only a smokescreen for U.S. moves to cut a separate deal to strengthen its presence on the peninsula; China also began fretting anew that North Korea would provide an excuse to increase U.S. pressure for regime change. No matter how much Chris Hill and others assured China of U.S. intentions, suspicions were intense, at least prior to the North's May 2009 nuclear test.[16] At the same time, many doubted China's intentions. Instead of fulfilling its part of the apparent bargain, China accelerated trade with North Korea even as the North was uncooperative in talks and became stridently insistent on retaining and further developing its nuclear assets. When China hesitated to condemn North Korea after the sinking of the Cheonan despite the clear findings of an international investigation, criticisms of its irresponsibility mounted.

China's role as host and coordinator of the talks put it in a critical position as to the nature of the emerging multilateralism. It drew praise from U.S. officials for its even-handedness and hard work to achieve a successful outcome. At times it has successfully urged the United States to moderate its demands or accept language chosen by North Korea. In September 2005, its active intervention resulted in a last-minute compromise allowing for the construction of light-water reactors, as the North desired. In 2008, China found it sufficient that the North's declaration covered the production of nuclear material and facilities without, as the United States had expected, including the military programs. At this point in the process, direct talks between Washington and Pyongyang had intensified, and Beijing's role was secondary, but Washington compromised in order to put the focus on verification. Beijing also tried to strengthen the multilateral nature of the process by getting Japan to give its full approval and join in supplying heavy fuel oil on a schedule coordinated with the disabling of the Yongbyon reactor. Appealing to Washington to pressure Japan, it misjudged the leverage Washington had and failed in its objective. As the North Korean leadership in late 2008 and 2009 took a harder line, Beijing was tested again in how far it would go in supporting sanctions through the Security Council and the direction of its own recently accelerated trade with the North. Given signs that Moscow was reluctant to apply pressure, the focus shifted to testing Beijing. There was no doubt about its criticism of the North's nuclear test and concern for regional instability, but the degree to which it would apply pressure on the North was uncertain.[17] This was also a test for Obama in how persuasive he could be in drawing China into a five versus one multilateral group. According to Wu Xinbo, China approached multilateralism with suspicion in the 1990s, fearing that it would be used to contain China or to internationalize disputes in ways that would reduce China's leverage. Only if the U.S. role was missing or marginal did China consider participation, apart from the instance of entering the Asia-Pacific Economic Cooperation (APEC) in 1991, as its agenda of trade liberalization matched China's needs. The Six-party Talks were different, but Wu's controversial conclusion is that China has won so much appreciation that it is ready to embrace more multilateralism of a similar type. He notes serious concerns in China that Washington will try to wrest leadership of various multilateral groups in its own hands and block community building. Yet, he describes a process of pluralization of security arrangements in the 2000s, whereby U.S. fears of exclusion are alleviated even as Chinese hopes for an Asian-centered East Asian Community are gradually realized.[18] In the case of Northeast Asia, however, such pluralization had not occurred by 2009. The issue for Washington was not exclusive Asian regionalism led by China, while the challenge for Beijing was not forging a new community in Asia. Americans feared that North Korean nuclear weapons and threats would set off a global chain reaction of Weapons of Mass Destruction (WMD) proliferation and a regional arms race in which all would be insecure. In contrast, China seemed more concerned that North Korean regime collapse or capitulation to pressure would strengthen the U.S. alliance system and undercut aspirations for China's rise at the center of Asia's reorganization and as the dominant player on the Korean peninsula.[19]

One angle for interpreting the struggle under way is to focus on the Sino-Japanese relationship, with the United States in the background. Korea is situated between the two states and, arguably, stands as the foremost test of their relative influence in Asia.[20] If Russia and Southeast Asia are other tests,[21] Korea's role has a longer history and gained newfound importance, with South Korea's "economic miracle" and the peninsula's post-cold war situation at the nexus of four great powers. In 2003–2006, U.S. officials strove to improve Sino-Japanese relations, worrying that the downturn focused on Koizumi's visits to the Yasukuni Shrine was complicating regional cooperation. In late 2006 to 2009, Sino-Japanese summits stabilized relations, but that did not overcome the sense of divergent values and clashing interests, not the least of which was the Korean peninsula. When a new push occurred in 2009 for three-way U.S.-Sino-Japanese talks, concerns were aired that this would merely serve as a transition from preferential treatment of U.S.-Japanese ties to the ascendancy of Sino-U.S. ties as Japan grew increasingly marginalized.

After North Korea fired a missile, U.S. officials, in an effort to bridge the gap at the Security Council between Japan's strong resolution invoking sanctions and China's cautious warning not to overreact, explored a compromise with Japan on a statement by the chair. Japan doubted the resolve of the Obama administration, which was seen as split between hard- and soft-liners, while they heaped more scorn on Chinese officials, who were urging self-restraint.[22] A different view, represented by former diplomat Tanaka Hitoshi, welcomed Sino-U.S. coordination and stressed the importance of unity in the face of North Korea's divisive tactics and of strong U.S.-Japanese relations.[23] In this perspective, Sino-U.S. cooperation is in Japan's interest. The fact that it dominated the UN search for a response did not escape Japanese notice.[24] More than a month after the nuclear test, a similar scene would occur, as Japan waited suspiciously for China, after consulting Russia, to decide on how strong a UN response it would let slip past its veto, while watching the Sino-U.S. dialogue at the center of deliberations. In contrast to voices that repeated the old mantra that the North was seeking regime security, which depends only on U.S. assurances, the main split in Japan's debate centered on whether Sino-U.S. talks contribute positively to a multilayered approach favorable to Japan or should be viewed with suspicion as bypassing Japan and likely to betray its vital national interests. Yet, by mid-April a media reversal had taken place in Japan. With North Korea furious over the compromise resolution and insistent it would not return to the Six-party Talks, far right *Sankei shimbun* depicted the struggle that followed as an isolated North versus international society, including China.[25] In contrast, the progressive *Asahi shimbun* saw the Security Council outcome as a joint Sino-U.S. decision from which an isolated Japan had no choice but to accede.[26] A new bilateralism prevailed, different even from 2006.

The Obama administration carefully assembled a team prepared to engage China intensely on many fronts. It was characterized by professionalism, planning, and patience. North Korea provided one of the most important tests of the new relationship sought with China. With the occurrence of the nuclear test, this team found more determination in China's leaders to impose restraints on the North's belligerent moves. While unsure about how much enforcement there would be of the June 12 Security Council resolution 1874, which approved inspection of traffic from the North involving possible arms exports, in conjunction with the Proliferation Security Initiative (PSI), and tightly restricting various North Korean financial dealings, Obama was intent on following this agreement by continuing to work closely with China as the core diplomatic partner that can contain North Korea's security threat. This effort did not bear fruit over the next year, but it was renewed in the spring of 2010 when South Korea sought to win consensus in condemning North Korea for sinking the Cheonan.

The Six-party Talks

Five states are convinced that their geopolitical interests depend heavily on what happens in North Korea. South Korea is especially anxious about being bypassed, as in 1993–1994 during the first nuclear crisis and in 2001–2003 after the optimism of the Sunshine Policy. Russia was alarmed about being marginalized during the first crisis and moved quickly to seize the opportunity of the Sunshine Policy to insert itself into the picture. In the case of Japan, it has had the most recurrent alarm about irrelevance: in 1993–1994 in the midst of trade tensions with the United States; in 1999–2000 when it was slow to become part of the Sunshine Policy; and in 2007–2008 when it dissented in the Six-party Talks. For China there has been no shortage of rejection by North Korea, which has been intent on two-way talks with the United States, but in 2007–2008 China began to fear that Bush was bypassing it too, as Chris Hill met separately with the North Koreans. A U.S. nightmare is that the real aim of China is to gain dominance over North Korea, stealthily expanding economic ties to leverage its position while playing a double game of cooperating in the Six-party Talks. The second nuclear crisis brought these conflicting strategies and anxieties to the surface.[27]

The other four states were caught in 2002–2003 between two stubborn adversaries: North Korea, whose most hard-line elements were loathe to negotiations as they prepared to take their state down the path of nuclear weapons pariah, and the United States, where the neoconservatives at their peak were determined to use pressure rather than Clinton-like negotiations to force the North to capitulate on its nuclear plans and, some suspected, on regime change. After both sides sobered up somewhat—the United States in June 2004 abandoning the insistence on the North, as a starting point before rewards could be discussed, committing to "complete, verifiable, irreversible, denuclearization"

(CVID) in the Six-party Talks; and North Korea accepting a formula of action-for-action along with the principle of denuclearization—the other states became involved in intensified consultations on how to achieve simultaneous concessions and rewards through multistate progress in negotiations. For the United States, the goal was to achieve early verification, with the fewest possible stages. In the Joint Agreement of February 2007, U.S. attention concentrated on complete information and initial verification in Stage 2 and abandonment of the nuclear program and weapons in Stage 3. In contrast, North Korea sought to make Stage 2 as reversible as possible with only limited information disclosure, while dragging out the talks through many additional stages in which it would be generously rewarded without loss of its nuclear arsenal. The test of multilateralism was whether the other states would commit to a process that kept the pressure on the North to denuclearize or, if U.S. demands proved unreasonable, whether the other states would pursue compromise that would make it easier for the North to proceed as per its plan.[28]

The Joint Agreement of the Six-party Talks produced a plan for five working groups, including one for establishing a peace and security mechanism. China's refusal to proceed on the basis of five states, excluding North Korea when it was uncooperative, left the pursuit of this mechanism in limbo. As host to this group, Russia was pleased to gain a central role in the search for regionalism, but it too insisted on North Korea's presence. The result of the June 2009 Security Council resolution, approved by the three great powers involved in the Six-party Talks with veto power in the Security Council and by Japan, as well as the object of consultations and acceptance by South Korea, gives a boost to five states working together. As North Korean defiance continues and the Six-party Talks fail to convene, the rump group of five can be expected to continue consultations. It serves as a holding group, but to the degree the North is belligerent, the remaining five states will have increased reason to keep consulting each other. In the process, informal multilateral gatherings may become institutionalized as the five-party holding operation for the Six-party Talks in the absence of North Korea. Fearing marginalization, South Koreans eyed this option, and the Japanese as well as the Russians shared the need to be actively involved.

Realizing that Moscow was frustrated by its exclusion from talks related to the Korean peninsula after its decision to normalize relations with Seoul in 1991, Pyongyang patiently turned aside its entreaties for resuming cooperation until the end of the 1990s when the Sunshine

Policy brought multilateralism to the fore. Only when Vladimir Putin personally wooed Kim Jong Il did Moscow envision a central role in the next stage of talks; but in January 2003, as various states groped for a way to launch them, Russia's bid for leadership was rejected. Kim rightly calculated that it did not have enough clout with the other countries or enough rewards as enticements to play more than a secondary role. In the first round of the Six-party Talks, where Pyongyang had sought Moscow's presence to provide some balance, Moscow sided too closely with Washington for Pyongyang to be satisfied. Yet, as talks progressed, increasingly adversarial relations with Washington pushed Moscow to first take a passive position and then express stronger responses deemed closer to Pyongyang.[29] Even so, it remained opposed to nuclear weapons, as seen in its June 2009 support for the Security Council resolution.

While annoying some of the other participants in the Six-party Talks, Russia was trying to position itself for a successful outcome in its favor, when reconstruction of the North's economy and its regional integration could bring massive contracts for energy and transportation infrastructure linked to the Russian Far East. No less important, it was also positioning itself for the talk's failure, when increasing tension in the region would put a premium on any country that could serve as a bridge to the North. Playing a weak hand in regional maneuvering, Moscow took more extreme outcomes more seriously. Pyongyang found it useful to cultivate more positive ties with Russia than with any other state in the Six-party Talks, also preparing for the possibility of an extreme outcome. Although, in June 2009, Russia approved the Security Council resolution, its hesitation left further support unclear.

Abstract debate pondered if the multilateral outcome of the Six-party Talks would be six countries managing, after repeated setbacks, to work together in a comprehensive regional framework, or five states together fending off North Korean machinations and divisive tactics. Hard evidence revealed, however, that strains among the five states left the prospects for effective multilateralism in doubt in the face of the North's defiance. In the five years of Roh Moo Hyun's presidency, U.S.-South Korean and Japanese-South Korean relations were strained by differences over how to deal with the North, damaging not only coordination in the Six-party Talks but also three-way alliance building.[30] Then, after Lee Myung Bak took office, Sino-South Korean differences over how to treat the North rose to the surface and affected relations. Russia was the most peripheral member of this group, but this did not spare it from problems of coordination. In the first session of the Six-party Talks it drew rebukes from North Korea for siding too closely with the United States. Subsequently, it kept a low profile as it stuck closely to the Chinese stance. Starting in 2006, Sino-Russian coordination also became more difficult. Despite a shared sense of impending destabilization if the North could not be controlled, narrow national agendas prevailed.

With U.S. support for multilateralism unquestioned, uncertainty prevailed about China's strategic thinking. Over the past decade it had shifted from "multi-polarity" as its favorite mantra to seeming approval of multilateralism. Along with its organizational role in the Shanghai Cooperation Organization (SCO) and its energetic backing of the Association of Southeast Asian Nations "plus three" (ASEAN + 3; the "three" referring to Korea, Japan, and China), China's hosting of the Six-party Talks had fostered the impression that it has become a strong backer of regionalism. Yet, its ambivalence remains obvious, which is linked to its narrow notions of sovereignty, persistent concern about U.S. alliances, and advocacy of values that clash with those of the Chinese Communist Party.[31] The future of the rump group of five in the Six-party Talks depends largely on China's seriousness about multilateralism.

U.S.-North Korean Bilateralism

North Korea seeks direct talks with the United States for recognition as a nuclear state, removing pressure on it for regime change or on human rights, and accepting it into international organizations that will assist its economic revival and growth. The United States rejects such talks as a betrayal of universal values and of its alliances with South Korea and Japan, as well as a green light for further proliferation of nuclear weapons. If the two states managed in 2006–2008 to conduct bilateral discussions in the context of the Six-party Talks, the agenda remained much narrower than what the North sought. In any new round of bilateral talks it is unlikely that Obama would proceed without the rubric of the Six-party Talks and an agenda that again stresses denuclearization as well as control over the testing of missiles. The North Korean leadership, in transition due to Kim Jong Il's ill health and his inexperienced third son's uncertain succession, appears resistant to such an agenda, but when Bill Clinton was lured to Pyongyang in order to bring back two journalists sentenced to hard labor after being arrested at the border, Kim made clear his desire for bilateral talks. Yet, without evidence that he was serious about denuclearization, Obama would approach the two-way talks cautiously and insist on the need for Six-party Talks. Obama has made it clear that no repeat of the Agreed Framework and the Joint Agreement will occur on his watch. He will not trust a North Korean promise to end its nuclear programs and will not "pay for the same horse" a third time. The stakes would be higher in new talks, as Obama insisted on the North committing to more far-reaching and faster actions to remove their threat capacity. In turn, the North would be expected to demand more immediate and substantial rewards for its concessions. Also, aware of how distrust of U.S. policies and rhetoric under George W. Bush reduced U.S. effectiveness in securing cooperation from other states,[32] Obama will stress a broad framework. Should there be a new bilateral round, attention to consensus-building is expected. The round might begin with the specific aim of crisis prevention in a hostile atmosphere, but the previous notion of "word-for-word" and "action-for-action" through a gradual buildup of bilateral trust would not apply in a situation where only decisive actions in one fell swoop could possibly overcome the distrust North Korea has aroused.

Pyongyang apparently intends to up its threat capacity and behavior to the point that Washington will be obliged to negotiate with it directly on favorable terms. This may produce a dangerous situation, but it is unlikely to achieve Pyongyang's objectives. The case is compelling for the United States sticking to a multilayered approach in which bilateral talks are just one layer within the framework established by the other layers. In Washington there is no constituency for prioritizing bilateralism. In turn, Pyongyang is unlikely to accept the status quo for long. It is proceeding unilaterally with arms sales and weapons tests, and in the face of sanctions, it is inclined to more provocative behavior. Yet, as financial sanctions squeeze an already impoverished Pyongyang, a comprehensive package being discussed by Seoul and Washington may eventually attract attention. In the spring of 2010 a torpedo attack proved that the North's choice was belligerence.

At some point, Pyongyang is likely to rediscover the benefits of enlisting the other four states, each of which, through different strategic objectives or threat assessments, has reason to seek a compromise agreement. Beijing is most inclined to orchestrate a soft landing. Moscow is most eager to use Pyongyang as its ticket to influence in the region. Seoul is most divided on how to respond and could turn supportive due to nationalist sentiment and war alarm. Even Tokyo remains interested in a breakthrough as well as nervous about war, in ways that could be used to Pyongyang's advantage. Multilateralism may not now seem appealing to North Korean leaders, who are aiming for stakes that are likely unachievable. When their ambitions are tempered, the benefits of maneuvering among this range of states, as done with some success in 2003–2008, may again look more promising than other alternatives. This return to a degree of multilateralism may await a military showdown and more clarity over the succession process, but the situation may unfold without long delay, given the severity of the challenge to the global system.

Conclusion

North Korea has a multilateral option through the Six-party Talks that would give it a favorable atmosphere for negotiations to facilitate domestic reform and international acceptance. As seen in the pressure exerted on the Bush administration during the course of talks in 2003–2006, this format does not support efforts at regime change. It is conducive to compromise, and rewards to the North, for each step it takes in the direction of regional stability. Yet, the North's ambitions outrun what any other state finds acceptable, making multilateralism unappealing to it as long as its leaders believe that these ambitions can be realized. The foremost challenge following the June 2009 Security Council resolution to impose sanctions is to convince the North's leadership that its ambitions cannot be realized. They must experience new financial pain, recognize the firm resolve of the United States and others to enforce the sanctions and respond to military provocations, and understand that they face a united front when they resort to the extreme behavior observed in 2009 and in the spring of 2010.

After the North's leadership overcomes the current uncertainty over succession and agrees on a new strategy beyond isolated defiance, it is likely to resume the search for a regional balance of power. Before 2013, South Korea under Lee Myung Bak will be a doubtful partner for the North. Japan's appeal as a partner is greater at the conclusion of successful negotiations than it was at an earlier stage. That leaves China and Russia as potential sources of balance for U.S. power. In the 1990s Russia was the less desired partner, as seen in the way North Korea reacted to its 1990–1991 normalization of relations with the United States. Yet, since Putin visited Pyongyang in July 2000, Russia has usually escaped the venomous rhetoric that has been leveled against China. Not only was Moscow eager in 2001–2003 to play the role of intermediary in ties between Pyongyang and the outside world, it was most hesitant to blame Pyongyang from 2005 onward for troubles in the Six-party Talks or with the United States. Russia is still groping for a regional strategy in Northeast Asia.[33] Although it is not ready to provide large-scale assistance to North Korea, and does not have the presence in this region that it has in Europe, it could be a tempting partner for a besieged North Korea in search of renewed multilateralism. Russia is likely to patiently prepare for this outcome.

Ultimately, North Korean frustration with the United States will lead it primarily to China. It is well aware that Sino-U.S. rivalry and Chinese strategic thinking about the Korean peninsula provide it with the opportunities to resist U.S. pressure. While Russia's utility may be appealing in breaking a logjam, any long-term strategy cannot bypass reconciliation with China, to the degree of resuming summit diplomacy and encouraging China to take an active part in negotiations involving the United States, if not others. With the alliance triangle and Six-party Talks in the background, U.S.-North Korean and Sino-U.S. talks may well reflect what will happen in Sino-North Korean talks, as the shadowy pairing in this triangle is what is likely to matter most in determining how the nuclear crisis is resolved. Kim Jong-il's trip to China in May 2010 appeared to be inconclusive in the shadow of accusations against his aggression toward South Korea and signs of expanding economic dependency on China.

If Pyongyang seeks to cut a deal with the Obama administration, it might bypass the Six-party Talks. Yet, given Washington's demands and the lack of leverage on it, this seems improbable. Seoul, Tokyo, and even Moscow are unlikely to provide such leverage. Instead, Pyongyang can expect the best outcome from recommitting to multilateralism in which Beijing and Washington are the prime targets, while Moscow plays a supportive role, Seoul becomes involved at an early stage, and Tokyo eventually becomes a factor too. The prospects for multilateralism have slipped, but they are far from dead. U.S. moves to sustain what has been achieved through the Six-party Talks will be tested first by the degree of consensus reached in the alliance triangle and, above all, by the degree of understanding achieved in diplomacy with China. While sustained, skillful wooing of China matters, the most important factor will be how far Chinese strategic thinking will shift away from the suspicious reasoning of past decades and toward regional cooperation.[34]

Notes

1. Sergei N. Goncharov, John W. Lewis, and Xue Litai, *Uncertain Partners: Stalin, Mao, and the Korean War* (Stanford: Stanford University Press, 1993); Don Oberdorfer, *The Two Koreas: A Contemporary History* (New York: Basic Books, 1997).
2. Gilbert Rozman, In-Taek Hyun, and Shin-wha Lee, eds., *South Korean Strategic Thought toward Asia* (New York: Palgrave, 2008).
3. Victor D. Cha, *Alignment Despite Antagonism: The US-Korea-Japan Security Triangle* (Stanford: Stanford University Press, 1999).
4. Gilbert Rozman, "The North Korean Nuclear Crisis and U.S. Strategy in Northeast Asia," *Asian Survey* 47, 4 (July–August 2007): 601–621; Gilbert Rozman, "Strategic Thought on the Korean Peninsula," in *Chinese Strategic Thought toward Asia* (New York: Palgrave, forthcoming), ch. 8.
5. Gilbert Rozman, "Turning the Six-Party Talks into a Multilateral Security Framework for Northeast Asia," in "KEI 2008 Towards Sustainable Economic & Security Relations in East Asia: U.S. and ROK Policy Options," *Joint U.S.–Korea Academic Studies* 18 (2008): 149–166.
6. Joel S. Wit, Daniel B. Poneman, and Robert L. Gallucci, *Going Critical: The First North Korean Nuclear Crisis* (Washington, DC: Brookings Institution Press, 2004); Charles L. Pritchard, *Failed Diplomacy: The Tragic Story of How North Korea Got the Bomb* (Washington, DC: Brookings Institution Press, 2007).
7. Yoichi Funabashi, *The Peninsula Question: A Chronicle of the Second Korean Nuclear Crisis* (Washington, DC: Brookings Institution Press, 2007).
8. Gilbert Rozman, *Strategic Thinking about the Korean Nuclear Crisis: Four Parties Caught between North Korea and the United States* (New York: Palgrave, 2007).
9. Gilbert Rozman, "Japan's North Korean Initiative and U.S.-Japanese Relations," *Orbis* 47, 3 (Summer 2003): 527–539; Gilbert Rozman, "South Korean-Japanese Relations as a Factor in Stunted Regionalism," *IRI Review* 11, 1 (Spring 2006): 99–124; Gilbert Rozman, Togo Kazuhiko, and Joseph P. Ferguson, eds., *Japanese Strategic Thought toward Asia* (New York: Palgrave, 2006).
10. Gilbert Rozman, "Regionalism in Northeast Asia: Korea's Return to Center Stage," in Charles K. Armstrong, Gilbert Rozman, Samuel S. Kim, and Stephen Kotkin, eds., *Korea at the Center*, (Armonk, NY: M.E. Sharpe, 2006), 151–66.
11. Gilbert Rozman, "Japan and South Korea: Should the U.S. Be Worried about Their New Spat in 2001?" *Pacific Review* 15, 1 (2002): 1–28; Tsuyoshi Hasegawa and Kazuhiko Togo, eds., *East Asia's Haunted Present: Historical Memories and the Resurgence of Nationalism* (Westport, CN: Praeger, 2008).
12. Tae-Hyo Kim and Brad Glosserman, eds., *The Future of U.S.-Korea-Japan Relations: Balancing Values and Interests* (Washington, DC: The CSIS Press, 2006).
13. Gilbert Rozman and Shin-wha Lee, "Unravelling the Japan-South Korea 'Virtual Alliance': Populism and Historical Revisionism in the Face of Conflicting Regional Strategies," *Asian Survey* 46, 5 (September–October 2006): 661–684.
14. *The Korea Herald*, January 21, 2009, 4.
15. *Sankei shimbun*, November 11, 2008, 27; *Yomiuri shimbun*, November 11, 2008, 17, and November 12, 2008, 3; *Asahi shimbun*, November 12, 2008, 15.
16. Shi Yinhong, "China and the North Korean Nuclear Issue: Competing Interests and Persistent Policy Dilemmas," *The Korean Journal of Defense Analysis* 21, 1 (March, 2009): 34–36.
17. *China Daily*, June 1, 2009, 4.
18. Wu Xinbo, "Chinese Perspectives on Building an East Asian Community in the Twenty-first Century," in Michael J. Green and Bates Gill, eds., *Asia's New Multilateralism:*

Cooperation, Competition, and the Search for Community (New York: Columbia University Press, 2009), 55–77.

19. Zhang Jinfang, "Chaohe wenti zhanuan huahan [The Uncertain Direction of the North Korean Nuclear Issue]," Shijie xingshi yanjiu [International Political Studies], 51 (December 24, 2003): 23–26.

20. Gilbert Rozman, "Sino-Japanese Competition over the Korean Peninsula: The Nuclear Crisis as a Turning Point," in Jonathan D. Pollack, ed., Korea: The East Asian Pivot (Newport, RI: Naval War College Press, 2006), 287–306.

21. Gilbert Rozman, "Sino-Japanese Relations in the Russian Shadow," in Lam Peng Er, ed., Japan's Relations with China: Facing a Rising Power (London: Routledge, 2006), 213–233; Gilbert Rozman, "New Challenges in the Regional Integration of China and Japan in 2005," in Satow Toyoshi and Li Enmin, eds., The Possibility of an East Asian Community: Rethinking the Sino-Japanese Relationship (Tokyo: Ochanomizu shobo, 2006), 389–410.

22. Yomiuri shimbun, April 9, 2009, 6; Yomiuri shimbun, April 9, 2009, evening, 1.

23. Yomiuri shimbun, April 6, 2009, 6.

24. Nihon keizai shimbun, April 14, 2009, 9.

25. Sankei shimbun, April 15, 2009, 1.

26. Asahi shimbun, April 14, 2009, 5.

27. Gilbert Rozman, "The Geopolitics of the North Korean Nuclear Crisis," in Richard J. Ellings and Aaron L. Friedberg, eds., Strategic Asia 2003–04: Fragility and Crisis (Seattle: The National Bureau of Asian Research, 2003), 245–261.

28. Gilbert Rozman, Strategic Thinking about the Korean Nuclear Crisis.

29. Gilbert Rozman, "Strategic Thinking about the Russian Far East: A Resurgent Russia Eyes Its Future in Northeast Asia," Problems of Post-Communism 55, 1 (January–February, 2008): 36–48.

30. Thomas Hubbard, "Thomas Hubbard (2001–2004)," in Ambassadors' Memoir: U.S.-Korea Relations through the Eyes of the Ambassadors (Washington, DC: KEI, 2009).

31. Gilbert Rozman, Northeast Asia's Stunted Regionalism: Bilateral Distrust in the Shadow of Globalization (Cambridge: Cambridge University Press, 2004); Gilbert Rozman, "Post Cold War Evolution of Chinese Thinking on Regional Institutions in Northeast Asia" (Denver: unpublished manuscript presented at Denver University, May 2009).

32. Jonathan D. Pollack, ed., Asia Eyes America: Regional Perspectives on U.S. Asia-Pacific Strategy in the Twenty-first Century (Newport, RI: Naval War College Press, 2007).

33. Gilbert Rozman, "Russia in Northeast Asia: In Search of a Strategy," in Robert Legvold, ed., Twenty-first Century Russian Foreign Policy and the Shadow of the Past (New York: Columbia University Press, 2007), 343–392.

34. Gilbert Rozman, "Strategic Thought on Regionalism," in Chinese Strategic Thought toward Asia, ch. 10.

CHAPTER SEVEN

Changes in Seoul's North Korean Policy and Implications for Pyongyang's Inter-Korean Diplomacy

SCOTT SNYDER

After a decade of liberal leadership in South Korea that was accompanied by apparent progress in inter-Korean relations, the political winds shifted in 2008 with the election of Grand National Party (GNP) candidate Lee Myung Bak. It was inevitable that this power transition would bring with it new challenges for inter-Korean relations. Lee's campaign based on "pragmatism" gave the impression that his administration would generally seek to continue engagement with North Korea along the lines of his predecessors while introducing greater conditionality into South Korea's relations with the North. This policy came to be known during the 2008 South Korean presidential campaign as Lee's Denuclearization, Opening, 3000 (DNO 3000) policy. This policy promised to make efforts to raise North Korea's per capita income to US$3000 if the North abandoned its nuclear weapons and pursued economic opening to the outside world. Although the North refrained from criticizing Lee himself during the campaign period, the likelihood of difficulty in the relationship following his election was not a surprise given the North's strident criticisms of the GNP. Further complicating the issue, a second inter-Korean summit between Roh Moo Hyun and Kim Jong Il was held and a new inter-Korean agreement was signed in October of 2008, only a little over two months prior to South Korea's presidential election. Given Roh's lame-duck status, the timing of the summit appeared to be intended to lock in and make irreversible the gains that had been made in inter-Korean relations before a new government came to power. Lee Myung Bak's inauguration was inevitably accompanied by a reevaluation of inter-Korean relations on both sides of the Demilitarized Zone (DMZ).

This chapter will examine the precipitous decline and apparent recalibration in the inter-Korean relationship that has accompanied the power transition from Roh Moo Hyun to Lee Myung Bak. It will also consider the role and influence of South Korean domestic politics on inter-Korean relations, the Lee Myung Bak administration's initial policy approaches toward North Korea, North Korea's test of the Lee Myung Bak administration and the setbacks accompanying the Keumgang tourism project, the impact of Kim Jong Il's health situation on the inter-Korean relationship, and the deterioration of relations surrounding the Kaesong Industrial Complex as aspects or stages in the deterioration of the inter-Korean relationship. The chapter will conclude with an assessment of North Korea's aggressive escalatory acts in the spring of 2009, the challenge posed by these actions for both the Obama and Lee Myung Bak administrations, and the implications for Pyongyang's inter-Korean diplomacy.

Divisions in South Korean Domestic Politics

South Korea's power transition posed a new challenge to continued inter-Korean relations for several reasons. First, the inter-Korean summits since 2000 had been accompanied by a deepening ideological division in South Korea's domestic politics between progressives and conservatives (widely referred to from 2001 in South Korea as *namnam kaldeung*). This division was exacerbated by the manner in which the first summit became a partisan issue in South Korean domestic politics in the context of South Korea's 2000 National Assembly elections. The failure of the Kim Dae Jung administration to include opposition GNP representatives as part of a bipartisan delegation to the summit (or the failure of GNP delegates to join the trip) sowed the seeds for likely difficulties down the road, especially in a context in which power once again would come to the GNP. North Korea's consistent demonization of the GNP and efforts to exclude GNP representatives from inter-Korean events fed those divisions and created difficult political terrain in the context of a transition in power back to a GNP-led government.

A related problem was that, despite two inter-Korean summits, progress in inter-Korean relations had remained primarily in the hands of progressives, with GNP representatives largely excluded from the process. One result is that top GNP leaders felt little "ownership" of improved inter-Korean relations as a policy priority. The single exception has been Park Geun Hye, Lee Myung Bak's chief rival within the party. Thus, the transition in power in South Korea also meant that it would be necessary for North Korea to build a new relationship with counterparts who had until Lee Myung Bak's inauguration been strangers to inter-Korean dialogue.

Second, the North's handling of the transition attempted to define the South Korean political field in its favor. The October 2007 inter-Korean summit had at least two critical aims: (1) to influence the South Korean political field in favor of progressives by showing a sense of progress and momentum in the inter-Korean relationship, (2) to "lock in" economic gains with a progressive government as a defensive measure in the event of a South Korean power transition.

Although North Korea had made its antipathy to the GNP well known, the Democratic People's Republic of Korea (DPRK) media was careful not to criticize Lee Myung Bak directly during the election campaign. This restraint was notable, although the decision to hold an inter-Korean summit with Roh Moo Hyun so close to the end of his term gave the impression that North Korea was trying to influence the South Korean election. In particular, the second summit promoted vague but expansive promises of continued economic cooperation, giving the impression that South Korea's new administration would be obligated to continue generous economic assistance to the North.

The DPRK's careful restraint in criticizing Lee Myung Bak during the political campaign left the door open to continuity in the inter-Korean relationship. Through these measures, DPRK authorities appear to have felt that they would be able to manipulate the South Korean domestic political environment sufficiently to ensure that the North would still be able to gain the desired economic and political benefits. They may have been surprised when this did not turn out to be the case. A rumor surfaced in the spring of 2009 that Choe Sung Chol, the party official responsible for the second inter-Korean summit and representative of the Asia-Pacific Peace Committee, may have been executed for misinterpreting South Korean politics. This rumor further suggests that North Korea's grand political strategy toward the South in 2007 had failed.

The Lee Myung Bak Administration's
North Korea Policy

During the transition period following Lee Myung Bak's election in early 2008, the North put out feelers for an invitation to Lee's inauguration, a symbolic gesture that might have signaled continuity in the inter-Korean relationship and would have provided an early opportunity for dialogue. There was also talk of South Korea sending a special envoy to the North during this period, but no such effort materialized. Lee Myung Bak himself referred to progressive administrations as the "lost decade" and referred to the Basic Agreement as the primary foundation for inter-Korean relations during the transition period prior to his inauguration, indirectly calling into question the validity of the two summit declarations as a basis for proceeding in the relationship. In addition, the North Koreans observed the fallout from the recommendation of the presidential transition committee to abolish the Ministry of Unification and the efforts to marginalize the ministry as a factor in policymaking under the new administration.

But the most important change that resulted from the leadership transition is that Lee Myung Bak no longer treats inter-Korean relations as a priority or gives it privileged status to override other issues or be treated as exceptional, as was the case with his predecessors Kim Dae Jung and Roh Moo Hyun. Lee Myung Bak's relative disinterest in and low prioritization of improved inter-Korean relations under his administration had several important effects. First, the Lee Myung Bak administration's low prioritization of the importance of North Korea led to frustration and irritation with South Korea on the North Korean side, especially since this meant that it was more difficult for the North to receive economic benefits from South Korea. As a result, initial North Korean gestures designed to test Lee's willingness to continue the relationship on the same terms as in the past were not reciprocated.

Second, the diminishing of North Korea as a policy priority for the South meant that, in light of the lack of interest and attention on the part of the president himself, others in his administration filled the vacuum and defined his policy more harshly than he himself might have intended. For instance, the North interpreted some initial public statements by senior defense and unification ministry officials under Lee Myung Bak negatively (explored in greater detail below), but these statements reportedly did not necessarily represent considered policy positions of the Lee Myung Bak administration. Lee Myung Bak's relative disinterest in inter-Korean relations appears to have spawned a contest for control of policy toward the North between "pragmatists" and "neo-conservatives" within the administration. During an initial period of adjustment under career foreign ministry bureaucrat Kim Ha Joong, who had served as Kim Dae Jung's national security advisor, the Ministry of Unification was progressively weakened and subordinated to the foreign ministry in the foreign policy formation process.

Third, when troubles arose in the inter-Korean relationship, difficulties were harder to overcome since the Blue House was less likely to weigh in to safeguard the relationship against negative consequences of specific actions, as had been the case under progressive administrations. For instance, the Blue House had little room to act in response to the shooting of a South Korean tourist at Mount Keumgang, so there was no way to resume the project as there could not be a joint investigation of the incident. Moreover, relationships had not yet been built between North Korean authorities and the new leadership in the Lee Myung Bak administration that could be used to conciliate following such an incident, which provided a big shock to South Korean public expectations for North Korea. This made inter-Korean communication more difficult and contributed to the downward spiral in inter-Korean relations.

Fourth, the North sought a relationship in which the accomplishments of prior administrations, especially at the inter-Korean summits held with Kim Dae Jung and Roh Moo Hyun, would be affirmed, but Lee Myung Bak was reluctant to offer an a priori blanket validation of the results of those summits as a basis for continuing the relationship. The North continued to assert the relevance of the inter-Korean summit declarations as the foundation for inter-Korean relations and accused the Lee administration of trying to destroy cooperation that had been established under the prior South Korean progressive administrations. In response, Lee Myung Bak cautiously asserted a willingness to pursue inter-Korean dialogue to discuss the respective interpretations of the inter-Korean summit declarations.

Fifth, many analysts interpreted the deterioration in inter-Korean relations as evidence that North Korea had decided to pursue a *tongmi bongnam* policy (to be explored in greater detail below), through which the North focused on negotiations with the United States while marginalizing South Korea. On balance, these conditions were sufficient to bring about a serious downturn in inter-Korean relations in the first phase of the Lee Myung Bak administration.

Sixth, the Lee Myung Bak administration attempted to respond to a growing South Korean public desire/demand to introduce conditionality or some form of limited reciprocity into the relationship. Lee Myung Bak's DNO 3000 proposal marked the starting point for his effort to introduce conditional reciprocity into the inter-Korean relationship. The proposal contrasted with the focus on engagement and unconditional economic assistance that formed the foundations of Kim Dae Jung's Sunshine Policy and Roh Moo Hyun's Peace and Prosperity Policy toward North Korea. The proposal itself was designed to have elements that could attract support from both Korean conservatives and progressives, but several factors discussed below made the proposal difficult to implement in the early stages of the Lee administration.

North Korean Testing of New South Korean Leadership

Lee Myung Bak's DNO 3000 campaign proposal was in practice an initial failure, in part due to North Korea's efforts to test the Lee Myung Bak administration and to show who has the upper hand in the relationship. But the new policy also veered off track as a result of indiscipline and misunderstanding of the Lee Myung Bak policy on inter-Korean relations by newly established senior officials in his administration.

Early statements by the new administration provided the immediate pretext for North Korea to go public with its criticisms of Lee Myung Bak and the new administration. The first was a statement by unification minister Kim Ha Joong in his first policy briefing to the president on March 26, in which he said that "the speed and scope of as well as ways to push for any development in inter-Korea relations will be decided according to progress in the North Korean nuclear issue."[1] That statement was followed by a North Korean announcement that South Korean officials would no longer be allowed to stay at the Kaesong Industrial Complex.

The second was a statement by the Chairman of the Joint Chiefs of Staff Kim Tae Young at a March parliamentary hearing in which he stated that there were contingency plans for responding to a possible nuclear weapons strike by North Korea, telling lawmakers, "we would identify possible locations of nuclear weapons and make a precise attack in advance."[2] These statements provided a pretext and possibly confirmation for North Korea's decision to take a publicly adversarial role toward the Lee administration's policy, choosing to interpret it as confrontational and contrary to the spirit of the past inter-Korean agreements. In effect, North Korea was rejecting Lee Myung Bak's bid for conditional engagement, perhaps betting that the South Korean public would eventually put pressure on the Lee Myung Bak administration to soften its policy toward North Korea or that the South would find renewed tensions with the North costly enough to recalibrate its policies and continue to offer a down payment in return for peaceful coexistence.

The Lee administration's handling of humanitarian aid to North Korea in its initial phase further contributed to the deterioration in relations. North Korea analyzed the Lee administration's handling of the issue as a means by which to further test the intentions of South Korea's new government. Although the DNO 3000 policy did not link provision of humanitarian aid to progress in denuclearization, the new administration hesitated to fully separate humanitarian aid provision in its handling of the issue. The situation was complicated by apparent shortages in North Korea and reports that a renewed famine might possibly be developing. South Korean nongovernmental organization (NGO) advocates of continued food assistance to the North raised their voices, but they struggled to gain attention of the South Korean public given the inordinate focus on the controversy in May and June of 2008 over health concerns surrounding the reopening of the Korean market to U.S. beef.

Meanwhile, South Korean officials struggled to show in their first actions toward North Korea that their approach would be different from that of progressive administrations. Ultimately, the Republic of Korea (ROK) government made available 50,000 tons of corn to North Korea that had been approved in the waning days of the Roh administration on the condition that North Korea issue a request for assistance to South Korea. In addition, a debate ensued over whether to provide 300,000 tons of fertilizer and 500,000 tons of grain that had become a regular part of South Korea's foreign assistance budget to the North. Both of these possible contributions from South Korea were also subject to the requirement that North Korea request assistance, but the requirement that the North ask for assistance was precisely the type of precondition the North could never accept, given its implications for the nature and balance of the inter-Korean relationship. North Korea's response put the South Korean government into a situation where it would symbolically be seen as backing down on its own principles of conditionality if it gave food to North Korea without obtaining at least a request for assistance in return, but would be perceived as uncaring and inhumane if it chose not to respond to an emerging humanitarian crisis in North Korea.

The DPRK further tested the mettle of the Lee Myung Bak administration in its handling of the July 11, 2008, shooting of a South Korean female tourist who had crossed outside the boundary of the Mount Keumgang tourism zone and was killed by a North Korean soldier. The incident occurred on the same day that Lee Myung Bak gave an address to the National Assembly in which he attempted to set the parameters for renewed inter-Korean dialogue, pledging a willingness to discuss the meaning of the two inter-Korean summit agreements as a subject of inter-Korean dialogue. Notably, Lee decided to go ahead with his effort to strike a conciliatory tone and offer to renew dialogue despite learning of the incident only hours prior to the speech. The incident led to the closing of Mount Keumgang to South Korean tourists pending a resolution of the incident, with Hyundai Asan caught in the middle. The incident also set off a debate over how to respond and what the conditions should be for resuming the tourist project. North Korea returned the body and offered its own version of events leading to the shooting, but declined to allow a joint investigation with South Korean authorities.

A potential opportunity to reverse this situation appeared to present itself when North Korea proposed a military dialogue with South Korean counterparts at the DMZ in October of 2008. But it turned out that the purpose of the dialogue was not to reopen discussion about Mount Keumgang but rather to pose a new test for the Lee Myung Bak administration over whether the ROK government would be willing to take action to prevent citizen groups from launching balloons containing propaganda fliers. North Korea argued that these efforts by citizen groups were in contravention of the agreement from the first inter-Korean summit in June of 2000 that both sides would stop utilizing propaganda against each other along the DMZ. North Korea raised the stakes by threatening to close down the border with South Korea, including stopping the overland crossings necessary to run the Kaesong Industrial Zone. Many South Koreans thought that the North might be making an empty threat, given that Kaesong had developed into a significant moneymaker for the North Koreans, who received millions of dollars in payments each month for North Korean labor contributions and South Korean private sector access to the site.

The cycle of deterioration in inter-Korean relations has stimulated a variety of public responses in South Korea. In response to the shooting of a South Korean housewife at Mount Keumgang, negative public opinion reached its peak in the summer and fall of 2008. Although public opinion prompted Seoul to suspend civic group visits to the North, South Korea began allowing liberal civic groups to resume their trips to the North two months after the shooting incident, a decision that prompted some analysts to suggest that "Seoul has no leverage in resolving the nuclear crisis due to worsening ties with North Korea."[3] During the first anniversary of the October 2007 inter-Korean summit, some expressed concern that the Lee administration appeared to be abandoning summit commitments in the face of public opinion that remained largely negative.[4]

The negative cycle in inter-Korean relations initially appeared to put pressure on the Lee Myung Bak administration to seek ways of reaching out to North Korea and keeping dialogue alive without sacrificing its core principles. The ROK Government allocated funding to resume grain and fertilizer shipments to North Korea in the budget for shipments to occur in the spring of 2009. Another face-saving possibility in the absence of a request from the North was to consider supplying the assistance via the United Nations World Food Programme (UN WFP), which had already requested funding from South Korea to support its overall aid effort to the North. But with North Korea's suspension of food assistance and expulsion of all food aid workers in the spring of 2009, even the possibility of indirect food assistance via the UN WFP became impossible.

Kim Jong Il's Health Crisis and Its Impact on Inter-Korean Relations

Amidst a precipitous downturn in inter-Korean relations, periodic rumors of Kim Jong Il's poor health drew special attention in the context of his absence from celebrations marking the sixtieth anniversary of the founding of the DPRK on September 9 and similar celebrations of the founding of the Korean Workers' Party on October 10. Although there have been previous rounds of speculation regarding problems with Kim Jong Il's health, these rumors took on renewed significance as American and South Korean intelligence agencies confirmed suspicions that Kim Jong Il had suffered a stroke in early or mid-August. Rumors of recovery in September and October were followed by rumors of a relapse in November, despite desperate North Korean media efforts to quell international speculation by releasing just the right types of pictures that would satisfy external curiosity. This effort on the part of the regime's top propagandists is even more notable for the fact that external media reports now appear to have the capacity to influence internal opinion within North Korea, or at least that the North Korean officials worry about such influence sufficiently to try to rebut reports about the Dear Leader's health directly with counter-reports from the Korea Central News Agency.

But the significance of the impact of reports about Kim Jong Il's health cuts both ways. Every indication that North Korean officials are worried about the vulnerability of the regime to external influence, or are positioning themselves as best they can to manage some form of political succession in case of Kim Jong Il's demise, carries with it reverberations for South Korean policy that in turn may further stoke difficulties in inter-Korean relations. When one considers North Korea's potential vulnerability, the decision by DPRK authorities to protest leaflets by South Korean NGOs that attempt to spread the word inside North Korea about Kim Jong Il's health situation or North Korean attempts to curtail the number of South Korean workers at the Kaesong Industrial Zone are primarily defensive actions related to the uncertainty of North Korea's domestic situation rather than an attempt to test or challenge a new South Korean administration. Nonetheless, the response of the Lee administration might play a potentially critical role in both shaping prospects for inter-Korean relations during the next phase and possibly in shaping the future of North Korea as well.

For this reason, rumors related to Kim Jong Il's health appear to have had the effect in South Korea of intensifying the domestic policy debate over the Lee Myung Bak administration's policies toward North Korea. While progressive groups and North Korea-focused NGOs continue to argue for humanitarian engagement of the North, both to prevent a humanitarian catastrophe and to prevent further deterioration in inter-Korean relations, the debate over Kim Jong Il's health appeared to split South Korean conservatives into two groups: one group sought to step up pressure on North Korea in anticipation that Kim Jong Il's passing will also mean an opportunity for the passing of the North Korean system and that preparations for Korean reunification should be South Korea's highest strategic objective; the second group was primarily concerned with managing to maintain some form of inter-Korean relationship as a defensive measure unless and until reunification is finally clearly in sight. The second group advocated a more pragmatic approach to humanitarian aid and gave priority to stabilization of North Korea's situation, while the first group worried that such an approach would sell short the potential opportunity to finally achieve Korean unification. Differences between conservatives reverberated over the potential role of China and the United States in a North Korean contingency and are relevant to U.S.-ROK coordination efforts under the Obama administration.

Kaesong Industrial Complex: Pressure Point or Breaking Point for Inter-Korean Relations?

Operations at the Kaesong Industrial Complex became a flashpoint for rising inter-Korean tensions from November 2008. An unusual tour of Kaesong by North Korean military authorities at that time suggested the possibility of a shift in DPRK policies regarding the complex. North Korea has increasingly squeezed Kaesong since early 2008, kicking out ROK government officials in March, cutting the number of South Korean workers authorized to visit the complex, and threatening retaliation through Kaesong in response to South Korean leaflet campaigns. Pyongyang's suspension of DMZ crossings into the industrial zone hurt factory production. Hyundai Asan, which runs the Kaesong and Mount Keumgang tourism projects in North Korea, was hit particularly hard.

Further complicating the situation was the North's detention of a South Korean worker in March 2009, an issue that was categorized by ROK Unification Minister Hyun In Taek as a "fundamental issue" to the future of Kaesong.[5] Although Pyongyang proposed the first Kaesong-related talks in April, squabbling over the agenda took most of the day. Finally, a twenty-two-minute meeting took place, in which the North Korean delegation refused to discuss the detainee issue, while demanding wage increases and contract revisions. Pyongyang has subsequently declared all contracts void and vowed to revise them on their own terms, and has also unilaterally proposed a new financial structure for South Korea-based companies operating in the zone, in which North Korea is demanding land-use fees from next year and a fourfold wage hike for North Korean workers, from US$75/day to US$220/day. These rates undermine Kaesong's competitiveness on labor costs and are increasingly threatening the viability of South Korean operations in Kaesong, with several companies moving to curtail their operations or shut them down completely.

Although the Ministry of Unification refuses to consider shutting down the industrial park, the Lee government appears to be left with little leverage over the North. South Korean analysts question whether Seoul should continue to implement inter-Korean cooperation projects given the uncertainty of the North's reform and opening, arguing that the detainee issue and the entire Kaesong project are being held hostage to political and military interests.[6] Grand National Party lawmaker Chung Mong Joon, son of Hyundai Group founder Chung Ju Yung who proposed the project in the late 1990s, has called for withdrawing all South Koreans from Kaesong, suggesting that "there is no point" in continuing the venture. However, a public survey by Hyundai Research Institute showed that 75 percent of respondents still believed Kaesong should continue operations, while 21 percent supported closure.[7]

Kaesong currently employs more than 40,000 North Korean workers compared to over 10,000 in 2006, with an output that reached US$250 million in 2008 compared to US$100 million in 2007. While the ROK government and businesses have invested US$26.86 million to develop the complex, aboutUS$26 million went to the DPRK government in the form of wages in 2008.[8] South Korean small and medium size enterprises have already felt the impact of political tensions, as buyers have canceled orders owing to the crisis that has lasted more than six months.[9] The Kaesong Industrial Council, which represents 106 South Korean firms in Kaesong, has blamed the actions of both North Korean authorities and the conservative Lee government, claiming that business has fallen "victim to policy conflicts between the former and current governments" of South Korea.[10] Experts also point to North Korea's internal issues to explain Pyongyang's recent hostility toward the South, as the regime remains concerned about growing South Korean cultural penetration into the North through Kaesong.

A New U.S. Administration and Inter-Korean Relations

A final challenge is how the Lee Myung Bak administration would align its policies toward North Korea with those of the newly established Obama administration. In 2008, many South Korean analysts thought that North Korea was pursuing a *tongmi bongnam* policy, which attempts to utilize progress in U.S.-DPRK relations as a way of marginalizing and indirectly pressuring the South to ease its policies toward the North. In this approach, it was expected that North Korea would exploit the gap between inter-Korean relations and U.S. policies toward North Korea, heightening the likelihood of potential conflict in the U.S.-ROK alliance. According to this strategy, if sufficient progress can be made in the U.S.-DPRK relationship to the exclusion of progress with South Korea, the Lee Myung Bak administration may be forced by South Korean public pressure, or by the United States, or both, to take a more accommodating stance toward the North without North Korea having to take steps in return to benefit the South. However, as events have unfolded in the early part of 2009, it appeared that North Korea was pursuing a *tongmi bongnam* policy, in which Pyongyang's leadership is alienating all external parties while focusing primarily on its own internal considerations.

As part of the strengthening of U.S.-ROK relations, the Lee Myung Bak administration has prioritized North Korea's denuclearization and appears to have abdicated any particular independent role for South Korea in relation to the North Korean nuclear issue, viewing the nuclear issue as one to be resolved between the United States and North Korea, with little apparent involvement by South Korea. In essence, the Lee administration appeared to have determined that the best way to deal with the North Korean nuclear issue is for South Korea to subordinate its policies and efforts regarding North Korea's nuclear weapons development to the policy of the United States. Likewise, the Obama administration has taken the lesson from the waning days of the Bush administration that the core principle upon which policy should be based is close coordination with allies in Seoul and Tokyo. As long as North Korea continues to engage in escalatory provocations, the task of alliance coordination should be easy to achieve. However, in the context of North Korea's diplomatic reengagement, it is easy to imagine that there may be differences in opinion over the performance thresholds North Korea should meet in order to justify dialogue and on the specifics of how to negotiate effectively with North Korea.

Another factor likely to stimulate conflict between the United States and South Korea is the continuing domestic division within South Korea over policy toward the North. These divisions carry over to and influence Korean judgments of American policy as well. Progressive critics of the Lee Myung Bak administration have indicated their own frustration with Lee's approach and believe that the new administration has squandered a decade of progress in inter-Korean relations by focusing on the nuclear issue and circumscribing South Korea's independent capacity to manage or influence the situation *vis-à-vis* North Korea.

But more significant has been the widespread doubt over whether the United States itself would persist in espousing and implementing a policy that insists on North Korea's denuclearization or whether in fact the United States might decide to recognize North Korea as a de facto nuclear weapons state.

These fears have been most pronounced among South Korean conservatives, who have maintained quiet skepticism over the Bush administration's change in tactics in pursuing dialogue following North Korea's October 2006 nuclear test. They perceive that North Korean tactics have worked and that the 2006 test led to renewed dialogue with the United States while moving North Korea one step closer to, at the very least, being able to effectively utilize nuclear blackmail to perpetuate the existence of the regime. The Obama administration's attempts to change the past pattern of North Korean crisis escalation, negotiations, and lack of implementation will be particularly disappointing to progressives. These progressives had high hopes that the Obama administration's early willingness to engage in direct diplomacy with North Korea would lead in a Sunshine Policy-like direction that would ultimately support enhanced inter-Korean reconciliation. Whenever there is even the faintest sign of progress in the U.S.-DPRK relationship, these progressives utilize those developments as a pretext for criticizing Lee's approach to inter-Korean relations. Whether or not the unfolding policy of the Obama administration toward North Korea favors denuclearization through negotiations, applies multilateral pressure through UN sanctions, or anticipates the need to strengthen contingency planning in anticipation of North Korea's regime change—and whether the United States, South Korea, and other parties might respond to North Korean instability in a coordinated or an uncoordinated fashion to pursue the relative priorities of Korean reunification versus stabilization of the peninsula—are likely to be central issues that require coordination between the Lee Myung Bak administration and the newly formed Obama administration.

Pyongyang's August 2009 "Charm Offensive" and Stabilization of Inter-Korean Relations

Interestingly, the Kaesong Industrial Complex proved to be on the leading edge of an apparent reversal of North Korea's hard-line approach in August of 2009, following former president William Clinton's early August surprise visit to Pyongyang. The main factors leading to this stabilization are all attributable to a shift in North Korea's policies and reveal connections among all the factors listed above. By Kim Jong Il's own choice, the tensions that had been heightened from the end of 2008 and early 2009 began to relax, showing a complex interconnection between North Korea's approaches to the United States and South Korea with Kim Jong Il's apparent recovery of his health and the relaxation of tensions in North Korea's relations with its neighbors. The way these events have unfolded may also be interpreted to signal North Korea's attempt to prioritize the various elements in its own policies according to its own calculation.

First, Kim Jong Il effectively utilized his negotiation with the United States as the main vehicle for attaining prestige benefits associated with former president William Clinton's rescue mission to retrieve the two American journalists from their captivity in North Korea. As a result of this dramatic mission, fashioned by the Obama administration as a private effort tightly focused on the rescue of the journalists and not as an opening to a broader U.S.-DPRK engagement, the two journalists were released, removing a core obstacle to the possible improvement of U.S.-DPRK relations in the future. In that context, Kim Jong Il was able to signal that his health had returned to normal and that he was in control, by meeting directly with a former American president. Such a visit undoubtedly would also provide a boost to Kim's standing internally and to prospects for a stable succession of power to his third son, Kim Jong Eun.

Second, Kim also took steps to stabilize the inter-Korean relationship by meeting with Hyundai Chairperson Hyun Jung Eun and by releasing the South Korean employee who had been held for months at the Kaesong Industrial Complex. Through this meeting, Kim tried to put pressure on the South Korean government to reengage with the North economically by enabling Hyun to make "pre-emptive" announcements regarding the possible reopening of the Mount Keumgang tourism project and the resumption of normal operations at the Kaesong Industrial Complex.

A third element that led to the stabilization of inter-Korean relations was North Korea's decision to send a high-level condolence delegation to the South less than a week later, on the occasion of the passing of Kim Dae Jung. This decision posed several challenges for the Lee Myung Bak administration, particularly because the delegation originally came at the invitation of the Kim Dae Jung Peace Foundation and appeared designed to shun direct contact with the Lee Myung Bak administration. However, upon its arrival, the delegation, led by a close Kim Jong Il confidant and senior party official Kim Ki Nam and including North Korea's chief negotiator with South Korea, Kim Yang Gon, clearly indicated its desire to speak first with Unification Minister Hyun In Taek and to seek a meeting directly with President Lee. This contact appears to have been significant as a basis for jump-starting inter-Korean dialogue, although how this dialogue is likely to develop remains uncertain as of this writing.

An early interpretation of these developments by the Lee administration attempts to vindicate its early approach on the basis of the idea that the dynamics of the inter-Korean relationship have changed fundamentally: instead of South Korean administrations chasing Kim Jong Il, North Korea is now the *demandeur* in the relationship, having recognized that a stable inter-Korean relationship may be essential to its own survival and for going forward. As a related point, it is interesting to note that, according to North Korea's calculus in managing the relaxation of tensions in the summer of 2009, the improvement in U.S.-DPRK relations and the stabilization of the inter-Korean relations are linked according to North Korea's unfolding calculus, and that the North was sure to send the signal that a warming of the U.S.-DPRK relationship, in the form of the Clinton visit, should precede the stabilization of inter-Korean relations. It remains to be seen whether this interpretation is correct or if the current stabilization in the inter-Korean relationship proves to be temporary or lasting.

Lee Myung Bak Administration Policy:
Implications for Pyongyang's Inter-Korean Policy

The end of South Korean policies that put inter-Korean reconciliation above all else, in favor of an approach that insists on limited reciprocity, has proven to be a shock and a test for North Korea's leaders. The change in South Korean policy under the Lee Myung Bak administration comes at a particularly challenging moment, as Kim Jong Il is seeking both to ensure his legacy and perpetuate regime survival by choosing an heir and a successor. The North Korean response has been guarded and defensive, with the apparent intent of closing off North Korea to the perceived negative and/or hostile intentions of the Lee Myung Bak policy. However, from an external perspective, the North appears to have either overreacted or taken preemptive actions against perceived negative intent of Lee Myung Bak's policies to the North, which were disproportionate to the reality of the policy. Although Lee's initial policies may have been intended to introduce conditional reciprocity on the part of the North, the overall character of Lee's policy efforts appears to have been shaped more by neglect than by hostile intent.

Initially, North Korea's response to South Korea's change in policy is intended to deepen the *nam-nam kaldeung* as a means by which to force the Lee administration to return to the basic parameters of a policy, in which the North Koreans will continue to receive economic and security benefits without having to give much in return. Following Kim Jong Il's health crisis, however, North Korea's policy response appeared to be primarily defensive and intended to protect North Korea from the negative effects of contact with South Korea, as North Korea's leadership focuses on the conditions necessary to carry out a smooth political succession. In either event, North Korea has reason to regard both the Lee administration's policies and the extent of South Korean cultural and economic penetration into North Korea as two different forms of threat. From this perspective, it is natural to expect that North Korea's leaders would feel a need to take defensive countermeasures to limit North Korea's exposure to South Korean influence.

North Korea's handling of the Kaesong Industrial Zone is a case in point. Many outside analysts anticipated that the North had become addicted to the cash flows accompanying the zone, to the extent that it would be foolish for the North to do anything to threaten the project. However, North Korea's leadership appears to have prioritized its own stability, and is guarded about the potentially transformative economic effects that the Kaesong project can have on the mind-set of the North Korean people. On one hand, North Korea's leadership has taken steps that have a direct effect on the financial viability of the zone in an attempt to crack down on South Korean social influences by reducing the number of South Koreans who can be at the zone and by holding a South Korean Hyundai Asan employee incommunicado for months, allegedly for influencing a North Korean employee at the zone to defect. These steps appeared to put the entire project at risk and could cost North Korea tens of millions of dollars in annual returns. But, to the extent that the project undermines or threatens the viability of the North Korean regime, the leadership must cut off the negative effects of the Kaesong project and go cold turkey. On the other hand, the North Koreans appear to perceive that such influences can still be managed, but only for the right price. Under "non-threatening" conditions, the North Koreans were willing to settle for a lower price, but with a change in policy under the Lee administration the North Koreans may feel justified to ask a higher price of entry for less friendly

counterparts. So they have unilaterally imposed higher fees on South
Korean firms and have demanded a fourfold increase in payments for
North Korean workers. This suggests that North Korea's addiction to
money has only grown stronger, and that, ultimately, it will be impossible for North Korea to cut off the project entirely.

The South Korean change in approach may not have been completely
unwelcome to North Korean leaders, since these changes have provided
a pretext for North Korea to make defensive adjustments designed to
contain some of the negative side-effects of increased interactions with
South Korea. Moreover, a South Korean regime that is perceived as more
threatening to the North may be useful to North Korean leaders as a
means by which to heighten a sense of external threat so as to strengthen
internal political controls while the North lays in place the foundations for a leadership succession process. Nonetheless, a South Korean
leadership that is watching its pocketbook and scrutinizing its return
on investment does make "fundraising" more difficult for a leadership
that increasingly must rely on its ability to extract resources from external actors as the basis for assuring its own legitimacy, rather than rely-
ing solely on ideology as the primary source of legitimacy. As relations
between the two Koreas appeared to stabilize in the summer of 2009, the
primary explanation has been that North Korea may have realized that
it was overreaching and that a sacrifice of the essential economic flows
from South to North, which had developed under a decade of progressive administrations, would be impossible to replace. In this sense, the
conservative critique of inter-Korean engagement under Kim Dae Jung
and Roh Moo Hyun as having been too generous to the North may in
actuality be a core contributing factor to any success the Lee Myung
Bak administration may have in "taming" North Korea, or in achieving
a stabilization in the inter-Korean relationship. With the negative turn
in North Korea's relations with the international community following
its nuclear and missile tests, the contradiction inherent in North Korea's
twin objectives of being both "strong" and "prosperous" is deepening.
For these reasons, North Korea's task of managing inter-Korean relations
while continuing to secure regime legitimacy is likely to become a more
difficult challenge for North Korea's leaders to manage.

Notes

1. "Minister Vows to Raise Nuclear Issue in Inter-Korean Dialogue," *Yonhap*, March 26,
   2008.
2. Kim Min-Seok and Jung Ha-Won, "North's Nukes on Attack Radar: New Military Chief
   Says Plans Exist for Possible 'Pre-emptive Strike,'" *JoongAng Ilbo*, March 27, 2008.

3. Shim Sun-Ah, "S. Korean Group Resume Visits to N. Korea Following Tourist's Death," *Yonhap*, September 23, 2008.

4. "Anniversary of Inter-Korean Summit Marred by Suspicion, Doubt," *Yonhap*, October 4, 2008.

5. "South Korean Minister Urges North to Respond to Proposal for Talks on Kaesong," *Yonhap*, May 21, 2009.

6. Lee Doo-won, "Should We Continue Cooperation with N. Korea?" *Chosun Ilbo*, May 21, 2009, http://english.chosun.com/site/data/html_dir/2009/05/18/2009051800836.html.

7. "Amid Calls for Pullout, Kaesong Park Tests S. Korean Diplomacy," *Yonhap*, May 20, 2009.

8. "Key Dates in Joint Kaesong Complex," *Yonhap*, May 16, 2009; "Amid Calls for Pullout, Kaesong Park Tests S. Korean Diplomacy," *Yonhap*, May 20, 2009.

9. "S. Korean Firms in Kaesong Face Bankruptcy: Businessmen," *AFP*, May 20, 2009.

10. "Amid Calls for Pullout, Kaesong Park Tests S. Korean Diplomacy," *Yonhap*, May 20, 2009.

CHAPTER EIGHT

Domestic Determinants of U.S. Policy toward North Korea and Ramifications for Pyongyang[1]

L. GORDON FLAKE

A well known political science axiom holds that "Only Nixon could go to China." For those unfamiliar with domestic politics in the United States during that era, the notion was that in the furor that followed the "loss" of China to the communists, a relatively progressive Democrat such as President Kennedy or President Johnson would risk appearing weak were they to attempt to initiate relations with the People's Republic of China. For the conservative and vocally anticommunist Richard Nixon, however, the political risk of his historic 1972 visit to Beijing was considerably lower. Put simply, despite the never achieved ideal of politics stopping at the nation's borders, domestic political considerations do indeed have a significant influence on foreign policy considerations.

A version of this axiom, updated for the Bush Administration, might have been phrased "Only Bush can ignore North Korea." After having declared his "loathing" for Kim Jong Il, terming North Korea a member of the "Axis of Evil," and executing a preemptive war against one member of that axis, President Bush could hardly be pilloried as soft on North Korea, and his Administration felt remarkably little political pressure, particularly from the more conservative congressional Republicans who had frequently challenged the Clinton Administration's approach to North Korea.

In the opening months of the Obama Administration there was little opportunity to focus on creative strategies or policy approaches to North Korea. The early timing and pace of North Korean provocations, such as its April 2009 long-range missile test and its June 2009 test of a nuclear weapon, has meant that the U.S. interaction with North Korea to date has been largely reactive. What some analysts assumed would be a relatively smooth transition from the more active engagement and negotiations with Pyongyang that characterized the last few years of the Bush Administration's second term has instead been characterized by a coordinated regional and international effort to exert pressure on North Korea in response to its actions and a marked hardening of the tone of official U.S. statements regarding North Korea.

More recently, North Korea has adopted what might be interpreted as a more conciliatory approach: allowing the release of U.S. journalists, reengaging with South Korea on some level, and expressing a highly conditioned willingness to return to the Six-party Talks. At this writing, there does appear to be the possibility that the United States might send an envoy to Pyongyang in an effort to further coax Pyongyang back to the Six-party Talks; however, expectations are low and the United States continues to focus on coordinating its approach with its allies and other partners in the Six-party Talks and on implementing and enforcing UN Security Council sanctions.

It is still very early period in the U.S. administration, which is currently dealing with events of both historic scope and severity posing both domestic and international challenges, and North Korea has yet to grab the attention of the American public to the same degree as have domestic concerns, Iraq, Afghanistan, Pakistan, and now Iran. There are a number of developing issues that will likely make domestic considerations in the United States a significant factor in forging a policy toward North Korea, which warrant closer examination.

Early Indications of a U.S. "North Korea" Policy

Just nine months into a new administration, particularly one facing many simultaneous crises, it is premature to attempt any definitive description of what might be called a "North Korea" policy of the Obama Administration. It is useful to note that Assistant Secretary of State for East Asia and the Pacific Kurt Campbell was not formally sworn in until mid-September 2009 and there has been no public announcement of a "policy review" let alone a release of its conclusions. Perhaps more importantly, North Korea's actions over the past few months have been of sufficient clarity and severity as to merit little debate on what is widely seen as a "necessary" response.

During the campaign, the transition, and in the early days of the administration, President Obama and his foreign policy team have articulated two fundamental principles related to dealing with North Korea: (1) a firm belief in the efficacy, importance, and necessity of diplomacy; and (2) a strong commitment to close coordination, consultation, and cooperation with the United States' allies and other partners in the region. While such principles may seem unremarkable and even basic common sense, they are both, in part, reactions to the perceived excesses or mistakes of the Bush Administration's approach(es) to North Korea.

While North Korea has allowed scant opportunity for negotiations in the past six months, the Obama Administration has consistently called for a return to negotiations and expressed a willingness to meet with North Korea bilaterally. This is in sharp contrast to the early months of the Bush Administration, when the Cheney mantra of "We don't negotiate with evil, we defeat it" appeared to hold sway in practice if not always in rhetoric. Likewise, the intense focus on prior coordination with U.S. allies in South Korea and Japan is in part a reaction to the last few years of the Bush Administration, when the process of keeping the talks moving forward often meant that the United States would engage in intense bilateral negations with North Korea, secure Chinese support for whatever agreement emerged, and then brief its allies. Understandably, this approach led to considerable consternation in Japan, and even in Seoul following the election of President Lee Myung Bak.

It is useful to recall that there was very real anxiety in both Seoul and Tokyo after the election of President Obama. President Obama's willingness to meet with Kim Jong Il as expressed during the campaign trail led to unrealistic yet very real concerns in both Japan and Korea that the United States under an Obama Administration might seek an early summit with Kim Jong Il and a broad bilateral agreement that would not fully address the domestic concerns of U.S. allies. Instead, there has been a remarkable degree of trilateral coordination at all levels between Washington, Tokyo, and Seoul over the past months, forging a unified position that has been key in negotiations with China and Russia regarding actions taken in the United Nations Security Council (UNSC) to respond to North Korea. That there has been a striking absence of complaints from South Korea and Japan represents an important early success of the Obama Administration's approach.

It is the combination of the two principles discussed above that has facilitated recent and early Obama Administration successes in forging a coordinated regional and international response to North Korea. Given the unmistakable clarity with which during the first nine months of 2009 Pyongyang dismissed any possibility of returning to the Six-party Talks or even to the negotiating table as long as the subject of their nuclear status was on the agenda, some observers declared the demise of the Six-party Talks. Yet, even prior to recent tentative indications of some flexibility on the part of Pyongyang, the Obama Administration and the other four parties continued to express their support for the Six-party Talks and call upon North Korea to return to the process. This is partly due to the fact that it was in the September 19, 2005 Joint Statement of the talks that North Korea committed to abandon "all nuclear weapons and existing nuclear programs."[2] For the United States and its other allies and partners to abandon a commitment to the talks would be to fail to hold North Korea to that commitment. Those who call for the abandonment of diplomacy altogether, however, misunderstand the political dynamics in the region. It is only with a plausible commitment to diplomacy that the United States can hope to convince China, Russia, or even its allies Korea and Japan, to actively participate in a process to ratchet up pressure on Pyongyang. At the same time, it increasingly appears that, absent a serious and coordinated effort to convince North Korea of the costs of abandoning its international commitments, there is little prospect that North Korea will ever even consider abandoning its nuclear ambitions.

Given the heavy priority and practice of close and careful regional coordination, it is clear that the Obama Administration has more of a "Northeast Asia policy" than a "North Korea policy." In other words, the focus of the policy is not on North Korea itself, but rather on ensuring that the United States' real strategic interest—the peace, stability, and prosperity of Northeast Asia—is not threatened. From a Dunkin Donuts view of the world, North Korea is the hole in the Northeast Asian donut. Our primary interests have long been centered in blocking the risks inherent in North Korean proliferation and in ensuring that no matter what direction North Korea takes or whatever happens there—be it collapse, conflict, or unexpected compromise—it does not jeopardize U.S. alliance relationships in the region and that North Korea does not become a source of conflict between the United States and its other partners—China and Russia—in the region. In the past the North Korean "donut hole" has been somewhat of a black hole sucking up all the diplomatic matter in its vicinity and becoming an end in and of itself. While tedious, and certainly less appealing for the individual diplomats involved, the process of regional consultation and coordination is far more directly connected to the United States' fundamental interests in the region. As such, at least for the time being, the process is the policy.

Déjà Vu All Over Again: The North Korean Crisis Cycle

The word "again" seems to be used with alarming frequency in regard to North Korea. One common narrative in recent months has been the fear that Pyongyang is once again provoking a crisis, and will once again return to negotiations in order to alleviate pressure from the international response to its actions, but will ultimately once again break its agreement and reinitiate the cycle. Given the track record of negotiations with North Korea for the past twenty years, this is a scenario that cannot be ruled out. However, there are several factors that would seem to indicate that things might be different this time around, and all of them involve domestic determinants in Pyongyang, in Washington, and in Seoul, respectively.

Domestic Factors within North Korea

Even before Kim Jong Il's stroke last fall there was considerable evidence of a North Korean retreat from what may come to be seen as the apex of openness in 2007. While the reasons may be debated, even with recent easing in rhetoric, within North Korea there appears to have been a clear trend toward less openness, less freedom, and more direct government control over the past year and a half. The closing of the Diamond Mountain resort and Kaesong city tours, new restrictions on NGOs, the rejection of international food aid, attempted crackdowns on markets and cell phones, and greater visa and tourist restrictions, when viewed together paint a picture of a regime that is aware of a pending power transition and which is seeking greater stability, certainty, and control.

In this context the stroke suffered by Kim Jong Il early last fall and the apparently precipitous decline in his health since then has seemed to further galvanize the North Korean regime, at least as is apparent from North Korea's interaction with the outside world. One possible explanation for this is that in a society as closed as North Korea and with such highly stove-piped internal information flows, Kim Jong Il's stroke has meant that every individual, every party member, and every institution is likely keenly aware of a possible power transition but unable to talk about it. The resulting anxiety and uncertainty create an environment in which individuals and institutions have no incentive to be moderate. In fact, it is logical that most feel a necessity to prove their strength and loyalty to the regime and to Kim Jong Il. In such an environment it is difficult to imagine individuals or institutions advocating sensitivity to international concern about missiles, nuclear tests, or detained journalists. Until recently, there have been few serious signs of a North Korean willingness or perhaps even capacity to back off from its recent statements and return to the negotiating table. Further evidence for this view is seen in a series of conciliatory statements, if not real compromises, that appear to have coincided with Kim Jong Il's apparent recuperation. Absent a direct role by Kim Jong Il, it is hard to imagine the release of the two journalists who had been detained, tried, and convicted by the regime, or of the relative easing in North-South communications. Yet, until there is some degree of clarity reestablished regarding a power transition in Pyongyang—something that seems unlikely in the short term—North Korea may be in effect unengageable. If true, this question of North Korean capacity has serious policy implications that at a minimum do not bode well for a return to business as usual.

While Kim Jong Il reportedly expressed the DPRK's willingness "to attend multilateral talks, including the six-party talks, depending on the progress in its talks with the United States" during his early October 2009 meeting with Chinese Premier Wen Jiabao,[3] the reaction in Washington to this statement and its inherent preconditions has been understandably cool. The United States may ultimately decide to send an envoy to Pyongyang; however, Obama Administration officials have gone out of their way to make it clear that the objective of any such contacts would be intended to convey the U.S. commitment to the Six-party Talks and would not be "for the purpose of having bilateral negotiations."[4] Moreover, North Korea has continued to test missiles and gives every indication of its intent to continue with not only future missile tests but also future nuclear tests.

Domestic Factors within the United States

When North Korea tested a nuclear weapon in October of 2006 it was widely seen as the failure of the Bush Administration policy. This was true internationally as well as domestically and arguably within the

Bush Administration itself. As such, the pressure in the late fall of 2006 fell just as much on the United States as it did on North Korea, and ultimately resulted in a markedly different U.S. approach to negotiating with North Korea. In sharp contrast to this, few have blamed, domestically or internationally, the North Korean nuclear test in May 2009 on the nascent Obama Administration. The Obama Administration campaigned on a promise of continuing the Six-party Talks process, to which the other parties in the region remain committed, and continued to articulate a willingness to engage North Korea diplomatically. If anything, there is an increased view that in the final years of the Bush Administration the United States had bent over backward in its attempts to maintain some semblance of progress in the talks, a view certainly shared in Tokyo and in some segments in Seoul.

This pressure inversion is evident in differing degrees in all of North Korea's neighbors, in public opinion and in practice, as China and Russia have been pulled step-by-step into constructing a growing body of international law and precedence in response to North Korean actions. This process of coordinating an international response—while slow and unsatisfactory to some—has real significance in that any future North Korean provocations or violations will demand a response that can only build upon the existing body of precedence.

Finally, on the domestic front there is remarkably little pressure on the Obama Administration to engage North Korea. On May 25, the day after North Korea announced its most recent nuclear test, a *Washington Post* editorial entitled "No Crisis for North Korea" called on the Obama Administration not to "lavish attention on North Korea and offer it economic and political favors,"[5] and the opposite page carried an Op-Ed from conservative scholars Dan Blumenthal and Robert Kagan[6] that made essentially the same argument. Thus the domestic and diplomatic climate following North Korea's nuclear test in 2009 could not have been more different than the climate in 2006. If anything, current domestic factors in the United States are likely to urge greater pressure on North Korea.

Domestic Factors in South Korea

While the question of how to deal with North Korea is still a divisive issue in Seoul, perhaps the most important change between 2006 and 2009 has been in South Korea's dealings with the North. Under former president Roh Moo Hyun, South Korea greatly downplayed North Korea's 2006 nuclear test and actively sought to limit international pressure on North Korea. While the primary intent of the Roh government was certainly to protect the inter-Korean relationship and to avoid a rise in tension on the peninsula, South Korea's position had a disproportionately large impact on the ability of the United States to forge a consensus position in the region. Most significantly, South Korea's position allowed China to fall back upon its mantra of noninterference in other countries' internal affairs and to justifiably argue that if the United States' ally in South Korea was not willing to fully implement the requirements of the UN Security Council's resolutions, then certainly China could be expected to do no more.

As was clearly evidenced during the June 2009 Summit in Washington between President Obama and President Lee Myung Bak, any such divergence in the U.S. and South Korean approaches is long past. In fact, it is arguable that, both after the April 2009 long-range missile test and the May 2009 nuclear test, it was the unprecedented degree of unanimity in the U.S.-ROK-Japan position that was largely responsible for convincing China and Russia to agree to a remarkably strident Presidential Statement in the UNSC in April and to sign, in June, the most significant sanctions resolution to date (UNSCR 1847).

Domestic Factors Influencing U.S. Policy Toward North Korea

The initial policy of the Bush Administration toward North Korea has at times been characterized as ABC—anything but Clinton—and, on the part of at least some members of the administration, marked a visceral reaction to the 1994 Geneva Agreed Framework and a negotiating process that President Bush referred as "rewarding bad behavior." While the Obama Administration's approach is also inevitably a reaction to the policy of the Bush era, as discussed above, it can in no way be described as a knee-jerk ABB—anything but Bush—policy. To begin with, the Obama Administration has continued to voice its support for the Six-party Talks. More significantly, rather than a pendulum swing back to Clinton era rhetoric or policies, the Obama Administration has staked out a harder line on North Korea than the Bush Administration.

This position has been in large part necessitated by North Korean actions, and has been facilitated by the Obama Administration's approach to diplomacy and coordination. It is arguable that, without ever holding a single negotiating session, the Obama Administration is closer to realizing the original goal of the Six-party Talks—the mobilization of maximum multilateral pressure and policy coordination—than the Bush Administration ever was.

Still, to fully understand how in just a few short months President Obama has been transformed from someone feared to be the great appeaser, who would sit down to tea with Kim Jong Il, to the head of a government that the North Korean Foreign Ministry described as "...nothing different from the preceding administration which frantically worked to stifle by force other countries which incurred its displeasure,"[7] one also needs to understand the role of domestic factors in the United States

On June 15, 2009, a *Fox News* Poll reported that 69 percent of respondents felt that President Obama "has not been tough enough" on North Korea.[8] Lest this be dismissed based on the source of the poll data, it is notable that among those polled and who voted for President Obama in the 2008 elections, 59 percent felt that the President had not been tough enough. One can only assume that, if anything, those numbers would have grown in the ensuing weeks as news regarding North Korea focused on the saga of the two journalists being held in North Korea, the threat of a long-range missile test linked—however unrealistically—with a direct threat to Hawaii, regular updates of a North Korean ship suspected of trafficking arms being tracked by the U.S. Navy that ultimately turned back from Burma, and a North Korean threat to "...wipe out the aggressors on the globe once and for all and achieve the cause of national reunification without fail."[9]

Over much of the past fifteen years, North Korea has been a source of derision and some amusement in the United States. Kim Jong Il is arguably the most well known Korean to Americans, largely due to his hairdo and the strange and wacky reporting that tends to come out of what many regard as the last communist Disneyland. Recently, however, that image has taken a more serious turn, and one that has brought the North Korean threat home to the American public. A quick survey of news articles since President Obama took office in January is sufficient to understand how North Korea is currently framed by the U.S. media and perceived by the American public. In addition to the intense focus on the long-range missile test and the nuclear test, North Korea's declaration that the Armistice was null and void reminded Americans that the Korean War was still unfinished business and not merely something from the history books. The lack of ambiguity surrounding North Korea's second nuclear test gave new and more ominous meaning to North Korea's hyperbolic rhetoric, and references to North Korea's offensive nuclear capability and over-the-top reprisals are no longer easily dismissed

There has also been an emerging human dimension to how the public in the United States views North Korea. A diverse and vibrant group of human rights organizations have continued to raise the profile of the situation inside North Korea, as well as the plight of refugees. One issue which had the potential to gain significant public traction was the case of the two female journalists who were detained, tried, convicted, and then sentenced to hard labor in North Korea. Had this issue not been resolved by the timely intervention and travel to Pyongyang by former president Bill Clinton, it could well have developed into a very emotional, complex, and difficult diplomatic and humanitarian challenge.

Another international development that has the potential to greatly influence the U.S. perceptions of and approach to North Korea is the crackdown in Iran. The sharp criticism of and pressure on President Obama to speak out more strongly in response to violence in the streets of Tehran demonstrated the necessity of the U.S. government to be sensitive to how issues are framed in the press and impact public perceptions. This is a lesson that cannot be missed when responding to developments in North Korea. It was already evident in the rapid assurances from both the Pentagon and the White House regarding the United States' preparedness to respond to North Korean missiles feared to be likely launched in the direction of Hawaii over the course of the early summer of 2009.

Ultimately, it remains a political reality that Pyongyang has no advocate or constituency in Washington, DC. Of course, the United States has fundamental national strategic interests in the peaceful resolution of the situation in the Korean peninsula. If a clear opportunity for meaningful progress in resolving the North Korean nuclear issue or other tensions were to emerge, any U.S. administration would likely be willing to take advantage of such an opportunity. However, such opportunities are rarely clear and more often hold more risk than promise. At present, the door to meaningful negotiations appears to be closed. Even if North Korea returns to the table, there are only a few who think that a relatively rapid or satisfactory outcome is likely. The best-case scenario would still appear to be an unsatisfactory compromise with a drug smuggling, counterfeiting, human right abusing pariah state—hardly something that would sell well in Peoria.

Ramifications for North Korea

The few remaining critics of the coordinated international effort to increase international pressure on North Korea in response to its nuclear and missile activities argue with some merit that international pressure will actually serve to bolster the regime, and that backing North Korea into a corner will increase the likelihood that North Korea might lash out. In other words, as per the proverb, "The cornered rat bites the cat." Such critics decry the recent spate of strong official statements made by the Obama Administration.

For example, during his June 2009 news conference with President Lee Myung Bak, President Obama noted that "there has been a pattern in the past where North Korea behaves in a belligerent fashion and, if it waits long enough, it is rewarded. I think that is the pattern they have come to expect. The message we are sending them is that we are going to break that pattern." Early comments by Secretary of Defense Robert Gates described North Korea's nuclear program as a "harbinger of a dark future," and yet he too indicated clearly, "I am tired of buying the same horse twice."[10]

It is important to recognize that such statements were nearly always accompanied by statements indicating an ongoing commitment to diplomacy. More important still, such statements were not issued out of the blue, but rather in response to North Korean actions. For example, while some in Seoul criticized the U.S. reaffirmation of its nuclear umbrella and extended deterrence as provocative to North Korea, these reaffirmations only followed North Korea's threat of the offensive use of nuclear weapons and its declared unilateral annulment of the Armistice Treaty. In the context of North Korean actions and statements, the U.S. response has been, if anything, measured. Perhaps this is what has lead to the general sense among the U.S. Public that the Obama Administration has not been "tough enough," at least during the height of North Korea's provocations earlier this year.

Ultimately, and tragically, given the domestic situation in North Korea described earlier, it is North Korea that is backing itself into a corner and which has not provided room for a more flexible approach from the Obama Administration. Clearly, President Obama is neither a Nixon nor a Bush. To date, he has demonstrated neither the inclination to visit Pyongyang nor to ignore North Korea's actions. Instead he has worked to construct a carefully coordinated regional and international response. North Korea is increasingly facing an environment in which its actions cannot be targeted at, and will not be responded by, a singular U.S. leader. Given President Obama's personal mantra "Yes, we can," it is probably not wise to conclude that due to domestic considerations there is something that his Administration "can't" do. It is perhaps time to apply a new axiom to the North Korean crisis, one favored by President Obama's Secretary of State Hillary Clinton "... It takes a village to raise a child." It clearly will take the entire region to address the challenge posed by North Korea in a manner that will protect the mutual interests of all involved.

Notes

1. The author would like to acknowledge the assistance of The Asia Foundation Center for U.S.-Korea Policy Research Associate See-Won Byun.
2. Secretary for Political Affairs: Bureau of East Asian and Pacific Affairs, Regional Topics, "Six-Party Talks, Beijing, China," *U.S. Department of State*, September 19, 2005, [as released by the Ministry of Foreign Affairs of the People's Republic of China], http://www.state. gov/p/eap/regional/c15455.htm.
3. See, "US Envoy Bosworth in Seoul before Talks in North Korea," BBC News Web site, http://news.bbc.co.uk/2/hi/8398570.stm; and "Six-party Talks Face Opportunities of Getting Out of Difficulties: Chinese Vice FM," *Xinhua*, October 7, 2009, published on the PRC Embassy Web site, http://www.china-embassy.org/eng/zmgx/t618737.htm.
4. Comments by U.S. Deputy Secretary of State James Steinberg in an interview with the *Asahi Shimbun*, "Reassuring Japan: N. Korean Nuclear Issue Limited to 6-party Agenda," *The Asahi Shimbun* (English edition) October 3–4, 2009, 26.
5. Dan Blumenthal and Robert Kagan, "What to Do About North Korea," *Washington Post*, May 26, 2009, http://www.washingtonpost.com/wp-dyn/content/article/2009/05/25/AR2009052501391.html.
6. Ibid.
7. "N. Korea Says Obama administration Same as Bush's," *San Francisco Chronicle*, May 4, 2009, http://www.sfgate.com/cgi-bin/article.cgi?f=/n/a/2009/05/04/international/i051049D07.DTL.
8. "FOX News Poll: Americans Say Obama Not Tough Enough on North Korea, Iran," *FOX News*, June 15, 2009, http://www.foxnews.com/story/0,2933,526480,00.html.
9. "U.S. Imperialists, Provoker of Korean War," *Korean Central News Agency*, June 24, 2009, www.kcna.co.jp/item/2009/200906/news24/20090624-14ee.html.
10. "Gates: N. Korea's Nukes Point to a 'Dark Future,'" MSNBC, May 30, 2009, http://www.msnbc.msn.com/id/31007296/.

CHAPTER NINE

Challenges for North Korea's Nuclear Endgame[1]

Victor D. Cha

Negotiating with North Korea is all about contradictions. What can be important one day can become unimportant the next day. A position they hold stubbornly for weeks and months can suddenly disappear. But these contradictions tell us a lot about the core goals that may lie beneath Pyongyang's rhetoric and the provocative actions that culminated in a second nuclear test on May 25, 2009. Understanding these core goals, moreover, offers insights into how spectacularly unsuccessful North Korean leader Kim Jong Il has been as he prepares to step down.

In the paragraphs below, I offer an assessment of what the North Koreans ultimately want with their recent spate of provocative behavior. It is not based solely on formal statements or evidence per se of their stated policy objectives. What is often stated through the mouths of their foreign ministry officials is only a part of the Pyongyang leadership's broader goals. Instead these judgments are also informed by the experiences and "gut instincts" of those who have negotiated with the regime over the past sixteen years.

What do They Really Want?

The latest statements out of North Korea appear to be telegraphing their next set of provocative moves. They have threatened everything from further ballistic missile tests, another nuclear test, withdrawal from the 1953 armistice that ended Korean War hostilities (there is no peace treaty), and cyber warfare. They have demanded that the United Nations "apologize" for its punitive statement against the April missile launch. They have threatened to retaliate with "nuclear war" against any sanctions implemented as a result of United Nations (UN) Resolution 1874 taken by the UN Security Council in response to their May 2009 nuclear test. They refuse to return to Six-party Talks. And in an unprecedented act, the North Koreans sentenced two American journalists, Euna Lee and Laura Ling, to twelve years of hard labor and reform. Had these two women been sent to labor camps in North Korea, they would have been the first civilian American nationals ever to have suffered such a fate.

In the past, this litany of Democratic People's Republic of Korea (DPRK) threatening actions was always understood as a tactic to get the attention of the United States and to draw Washington into bilateral talks.[2] Indeed, this was often the argument that the George W. Bush administration had to contend with whenever the North undertook provocative actions. Even after unprecedented provocations like the October 2002 revelations regarding the North's second uranium-based nuclear program (in violation of the 1994 Agreed Framework) or the October 2006 nuclear test, pundits would "blame" these actions on the Bush administration's reluctance to engage in high-level bilateral negotiations with Pyongyang. Terms like "a bombshell that's actually an olive branch" were how people rationalized what would otherwise be considered exceptionally brash and rogue actions in international relations.[3] The interpretation of North Korean threatening actions was that they constituted cries for help and attention. Pyongyang sought a grand bargain with the United States, the armchair psychologists of North Korean behavior argued. And quite frankly, a very unhelpful dynamic developed in which the causes for North Korean bad behavior were thereafter pinned on U.S. diplomatic inaction rather than on North Korean intentions.

Barack Obama managed to correct this vicious cycle, at least for now. He came into office with none of the allergies that the first Bush administration had to his predecessor's agreements, and signaled early his interest in high-level negotiations with Pyongyang through Special Envoy Ambassador Stephen Bosworth's trips to the region. He made clear to the other members of the Six-party Talks, Japan, China, Russia, and South Korea, his commitment to the multilateral negotiating forum and to moving forward with the September 2005 Joint

Statement, a watershed roadmap agreement that promised energy and economic assistance for a freeze in the North's nuclear programs, and then large scale assistance, diplomatic normalization (with the United States and Japan), a peace treaty ending the Korean war, and the creation of a new Northeast Asian Peace and Security Regime for North Korean denuclearization.[4] The hope was that the new administration's willingness to join Six-party Talks, augmented by higher-level bilateral talks with Pyongyang, would accelerate the denuclearization process, which was not possible even in the forward leaning second term of Bush because of that administration's inherent aversion to meeting the North Koreans at levels higher than the then Assistant Secretary of State Christopher Hill.

The plan seemed like a good one and was widely accepted in the region (with some mild anxiety in Japan), until Pyongyang responded with the April 5 ballistic missile test, its second nuclear test on May 25, and a series of ballistic missile tests on July 4. These latest North Korean provocations can no longer be rationalized as an attempt to engage the United States. Many of the proponents of this view were at a loss to explain the second nuclear test as they no longer could reflexively blame it all on the Bush administration. At the June 11, 2009 hearing on North Korea before the Senate Foreign Relations committee, the normally taciturn and eminently reasonable Richard Lugar (R-Indiana) responded in stern tone to one of the panelists who trotted out the same tired arguments blaming U.S. inaction and lack of negotiations for the North's provocations. The experienced Senator responded: "I will say respectfully, Professor, of course we want negotiations. The whole point we're trying to make is the North Koreans have deliberately walked away from it, have shot missiles across Japan, and have done a nuclear test. Of course [the United States government] want[s] negotiation, but until we really do something as an international community, I don't see much movement in that respect."[5] Lugar is right that negotiations have been proffered to Kim Jong Il, yet the North continues to threaten and refuses to come to the table.

So what do they really want?

They Want Nuclear Weapons... For Keeps

In social science, graduate students learn about a term called "Ockham's razor." Proposed by William of Ockham, a Franciscan living at the turn of the fourteenth century, the principle is "*Pluralitas non est ponenda sine neccesitat*," which translates as "entities should not be multiplied unnecessarily." This has become adopted in social science theorizing to mean that the best theories or explanations are often the simplest ones. Hence, the simplest explanation for North Korean actions is the desire to improve their nuclear weapons and ballistic missiles. Countries do not pursue intercontinental ballistic missiles (ICBMs) or nuclear weapons simply to accumulate negotiating chips. Pyongyang's commitment of massive amounts of very scarce resources to such projects suggests it actually wants to acquire these capabilities and be accepted by the world as a nuclear weapons state. It is unlikely to be willing to trade them away in return for international acceptance and a peace treaty with the United States. Tests of the types conducted on April 5, May 25, and July 4—whether they succeed or fail—are opportunities to demonstrate, learn from, and improve upon their nuclear weapons and short- and long-range delivery capabilities. The April 5 missile test, for example, believed to be a test of the long-range Taepo-dong II ICBM with ranges potentially as far as Hawaii and Alaska, was more successful than the July 4, 2006 ballistic missile test that failed in its ascent stage. The 2009 test successfully deployed its first stage and overflew the Japanese archipelago, deploying the second stage in the Pacific Ocean, though it failed to put a satellite into orbit. The ensuing July 4 test of seven ballistic missiles about 300 miles into the Sea of Japan appeared aimed at improving the accuracy of their short and medium range arsenal. Similarly, the May 25 nuclear test registered seismic magnitude wave activity of 4.7, indicative of a 3–8 kiloton weapon, which is larger than the "fizzle" test of October 2006 of less than one kiloton (0.5–0.8 kilotons), according to scientific analysis in the public domain.[6] Rather than "upping the ante" with the United States or seeking attention, as many of the posttest analyses argue,[7] Pyongyang seeks to build a better nuclear weapon and ballistic missile, and there is no substitute for learning than doing.[8]

North Korean leader Kim Jong Il may want nuclear weapons, but is that all that he wants? After all, you can't eat plutonium. This logic leads many to argue that Pyongyang seeks nuclear weapons only for lack of a better deal out there offering them food, energy, and a new relationship with the international community. The problem with this logic is that Kim has been offered such a deal, twice. The 1994 Agreed Framework negotiated by the Clinton administration initially froze North Korea's plutonium production facilities at Yongbyon in return for U.S.-supplied heavy fuel oil, but the agreement also laid out the vision of a peace regime, normalized relations with the United States, and economic and energy assistance for denuclearization.[9] The 2005 Six-party Joint Statement, as noted above, offered all of these benefits and more in return for the same denuclearization. It is no wonder, then, that members of the Obama administration have stated their disinterest in buying the same horse three times.

They Want an India Deal

I believe that North Korea wants a deal ultimately, but not one that requires full denuclearization on their part. In later rounds of Six-party Talks, North Korean negotiators used to demand that the Bush administration deliver the light water reactors for civilian nuclear energy promised by the 1994 agreement negotiated by Clinton. They asserted in formal sessions that this was the quid pro quo for giving up the small experimental reactor at Yongbyon, ostensibly for nuclear energy, but from which they produced plutonium for nuclear weapons. Yet, in the course of sometimes heated talks, the North Koreans would assert to Ambassador Chris Hill, our lead negotiator, that the United States should simply accept North Korea as a nuclear weapons state, much as they had done for India and Pakistan. When they were told that this was not likely (nor should they want to be treated like Islamabad), their negotiators countered that the Six-party Talks should not be about the one-sided denuclearization of North Korea. This was tantamount to "stripping us naked" without any corresponding actions. Instead, the talks should be about mutual nuclear arms reductions between two established nuclear powers. They would say, "you know, like you used to have with the Soviet Union during the Cold War."

Doves have always maintained that North Korea is willing to trade their nuclear weapons for security. Hawks say that the North equates nuclear weapons with ultimate security. But the record of negotiations implies that Kim's true goal may be a deal with the West, but not the deal believed by the doves. Pyongyang has told countless visiting American scholars and experts in recent months that the U.S. government should simply accept North Korea as a nuclear weapons state.[10] As their candid comments alluded to above demonstrate, moreover, their model may be to turn the Six-party Talks into a bilateral U.S.-DPRK nuclear arms reduction negotiation, in which the North is accorded a status as a nuclear weapons state. The ideal outcome of this negotiation, in the North's view, is a situation similar to the arrangement that the United States negotiated with India. That is, an agreement in which

North Korea is willing to come back under International Atomic Energy Agency safeguards and monitoring, but it is also assured of a civilian nuclear energy element (i.e., Pyongyang's long-held desire for light water reactor technology and a national energy grid capable of supporting these reactors). Most important, they would want to control a portion of their nuclear programs outside of international inspection, which in their eyes could then serve as their nuclear deterrent. This was, of course, the most controversial element of the U.S.-India civil nuclear energy agreement. Pyongyang would certainly want a great deal in return for these "concessions," including energy assistance, economic development assistance, normalized relations with the United States, and a peace treaty ending the Korean War. But on the nuclear side of the equation, they want the rules of the Nonproliferation treaty regime essentially rewritten for them as they were done for India.

The North Koreans have never tabled an India-agreement as a formal negotiating position at the Six-party Talks or in bilateral dialogue with the United States. Despite their relative isolation from the world, perhaps they understand that such a position is a bridge too far. And frankly, they would have been laughed out of the room for proposing this formally, even by the Chinese. But the North Koreans are acutely aware that the ground constantly shifts in a protracted negotiation, and what seemed implausible at one point could become plausible later. After all, they witnessed the Bush administration move from a position of non-dialogue during the first term to allowing Assistant Secretary Hill to do bilateral negotiations in Pyongyang at the end of its second term. The North's incessant rejection of the Six-party Talks as one-sided denuclearization, their continuing references to their de facto nuclear weapons status, and their demand that they be treated like India and Pakistan offer insights into their goals.

But these are not all that North Korea wants. North Korean leader Kim Jong Il's stroke last year and his reported pancreatic cancer has led many experts to see Pyongyang's recent nuclear and missile tests as Kim's way to kill two birds with one stone. The tests establish the North's nuclear status and security from external threats, such that the ailing Kim can hand power over to one of his sons without worries. The tests also serve to secure the Dear Leader's place in Korean history, having bequeathed to the nation the ultimate weapon against all future enemies in fulfillment of *kangsong tae'guk* ("rich nation, strong army"). After all, even dictators need to polish their legacies.

Yet, on closer analysis, Kim's recent provocations don't appear to represent the final jewels in the crown he will hand over to his son.

Indeed, Kim's nuclear tests and ballistic missile barrages may represent desperate attempts to achieve the bare minimum of more ambitious goals, like an India-type deal, rather than the mere demonstration of nuclear capabilities. If an India-type deal—including acceptance as a nuclear state, the promise of civilian nuclear energy, and exclusive control of a portion of its programs outside of international rules—is the Dear Leader's ultimate goal, he has fallen far short of that. What the world sees as Kim's successful second nuclear test (and our failure to stop him) may actually be the last gasps of a dying regime, bankrupt materially and ideologically, trying to secure the first step in a longer-term and distant goal of becoming the next India. Like the poor student who rushes to finish the exam before time runs out, Kim races against the geriatric table to achieve the minimum for his son, rather than the maximum for his legacy.

They Want the "House of Kim"...Forever

Apologists for North Korea often argue that the regime's nuclear programs derive from insecurity. The small, isolated state had few friends during the cold war and even fewer ones after East Germany and the Soviet Union collapsed (Kim Il Sung was good friends with Erich Honecker and vacationed together). After China normalized relations with South Korea in 1992, the relationship between Pyongyang and Beijing, which had been "sealed in blood" through the Korean war, was never the same thereafter. Pyongyang validated the apologists' theories by saying that they desired an end to the hostile policy of the United States, and they pointed to comments like Bush's "axis of evil" and Secretary of State Condoleezza Rice's reference to it as an "outpost of tyranny" as evidence of this hostile policy. While virtually no one in the United States (or the world for that matter) believes that any U.S. president is itching to attack North Korea (not even Bush), it is natural for a small paranoid state to have such concerns, apologists argue.

There is some truth to this claim, and for this reason the United States on countless occasions has stated that it does not have a hostile policy toward North Korea. Table 9.1 lays out all such statements by the United States government, from Barack Obama to George H.W. Bush.

U.S. negotiator Chris Hill was fond of saying that the United States did not have a hostile policy toward North Korea, but that it did have a hostile policy toward its nuclear weapons. The North's response once

Table 9.1 Statements of Non-Hostile Intent by the United States government toward North Korea

Date	Administration	Statement	Context
February 27, 1989	George H.W. Bush	"I will work closely with President Roh to coordinate our efforts to draw the North toward practical, peaceful and productive dialogue, to insure that our policies are complementary and mutually reinforcing."	Presidential Address to ROK National Assembly
January 6, 1992	George H.W. Bush	"If North Korea fulfills its obligation and takes steps to implement the inspection agreements, then President Roh and I are prepared to forgo the Team Spirit exercise for this year."	President Bush, News Conference with ROK President Roh Tae-Woo
June 11, 1993	George H.W. Bush	"The Democratic People's Republic of Korea and the United States have agreed to principles of: - *Assurances against the threat and use of force, including nuclear weapons;* - Peace and security in a nuclear-free Korean Peninsula, including impartial application of fullscope safeguards, *mutual respect for each other's sovereignty, and non-interference in each other's internal affairs*; and - Support for the peaceful reunification of Korea. In this context, the two Governments have agreed to continue dialogue on an equal and unprejudiced basis."	**1993 US-DPRK Joint Statement**
July 10, 1993	William J. Clinton	*"We are seeking to prevent aggression, not to initiate it. And so long as North Korea abides by the U.N. charter and international non-proliferation commitments, it has nothing to fear from America."*	Presidential Address to ROK National Assembly

June 5, 1994	William J. Clinton	*"I approached them in the spirit of peace.... I would like to have a relationship with North Korea.... But we are not trying to provoke North Korea.* We are only asking them to do what they have already promised to do."	President Clinton, CBS Interview
June 22, 1994	William J. Clinton	"We also always kept the door open. We always said—*I always said I did not seek a confrontation; I sought to give North Korea a way to become a part of the international community.* I have sought other means of personally communicating to Kim Il Sung that the desires of the United States and the interests of the United States and the policy of the United States was to pursue a nonnuclear Korean Peninsula and to give North Korea a way of moving with dignity into the international community and away from an isolated path...."	Presidential Press Conference on North Korea
October 21, 1994	William J. Clinton	*"The U.S. will provide formal assurances to the DPRK, against the threat or use of nuclear weapons by the U.S."*	1994 US-DPRK Agreed Framework
April 17, 1996	William J. Clinton	"The four-party talks are simply a way of providing a framework within which the South and the North can ultimately agree on the terms of peace in the same way that the armistice talks provided that framework 43 years ago. And if the United States can play a positive role in that, we want to."	President Clinton, News Conference with ROK President Kim Young-Sam
September 17, 1999	William J. Clinton	"Our policy of seeking to ease tensions, prevent destabilizing developments, and explore the possibilities of a different and better relationship with North Korea, are fully in accord with the positions of our allies. So is our staunch support for the Agreed Framework, which is the linchpin of our effort to end North Korea's nuclear weapons program."	Secretary of State Albright, North Korea Briefing
October 12, 2000	William J. Clinton	*"Hostility between our two nations is not inevitable, nor desired by our citizens, nor in the interests of our countries....* This is why we must seize the opportunity to take the concrete steps required to open a new and more hopeful chapter in our relations."	Secretary of State Albright, Speech at Dinner with North Korean official, Gen. Jo Myong-Rok

Continued

Table 9.1 Continued

Date	Administration	Statement	Context
October 12, 2000	William J. Clinton	"[T]he United States and the Democratic People's Republic of Korea have decided to take steps to fundamentally improve their bilateral relations in the interests of enhancing peace and security in the Asia–Pacific region.... As a crucial first step, *the two sides stated that neither government would have hostile intent toward the other and confirmed the commitment of both governments to make every effort in the future to build a new relationship free from past enmity....* In this regard, the two sides reaffirmed that their relations should be based on the principles of respect for each other's sovereignty and non-interference in each other's internal affairs, and noted the value of regular diplomatic contacts, bilaterally and in broader fora."	**2000 US-DPRK Joint Communiqué**
February 20, 2002	George W. Bush	*"We're a peaceful people. We have no intention of invading North Korea. South Korea has no intention of attacking North Korea. Nor does America.* We're purely defensive, and the reason we have to be defensive is because there is a threatening position of the DMZ, so we long for peace. It's in our nation's interest that we achieve peace on the peninsula."	President Bush, Joint News Conference with ROK President Kim Dae-Jung
May 1, 2002	George W. Bush	"[The] president made it clear that we were willing to talk to them any time, any place, and without any preset agenda."	Secretary of State Powell, Senate Hearing
October 22, 2002	George W. Bush	"The United States hopes for a different future with North Korea. As I made clear during my visit to South Korea in February, *the United States has no intention of invading North Korea.* This remains the case today."	Presidential Remarks in Meeting with NATO Secretary General Lord Robertson
October 27, 2002	George W. Bush	*"We have no intention of invading North Korea or taking hostile action against North Korea."*	Secretary of State Powell, News Conference at APEC in Los Cabos

Date		Quote	Source
February 7, 2003	George W. Bush	*"[We] have no intention of attacking North Korea as a nation.... We're prepared to talk to them."*	Secretary of State Powell, Senate Foreign Relations Committee Testimony
October 20, 2003	George W. Bush	"[What] [the President] himself has said, which is that *there is no intention to invade North Korea*. But the President is very committed to the six-party talks, believes that it is the forum in which we are most likely to get a satisfactory resolution of the nuclear problem on the Korean Peninsula. And so he reiterated the importance of moving those talks forward.... We are not going to go in, all guns blazing, say take it or leave it, this is it."	National Security Advisor C. Rice, Press Briefing
October 27, 2003	George W. Bush	*"The president has made it clear that he has no intention of invading North Korea or attacking North Korea."*	Secretary of State Powell, "Meet the Press"
February 11, 2005	George W. Bush	*"The North Koreans have been told by the president of the United States that the United States has no intention of attacking or invading North Korea."*	Secretary of State C. Rice, News Conference in Luxembourg
July 12, 2005	George W. Bush	"Now that they've decided to return to the talks, *let's just remember that we have stated that this is a sovereign state, that we have no intention to attack it....*"	Secretary of State C. Rice, SBS Interview in Seoul
September 15, 2005	George W. Bush	*"The United States affirmed that it has no nuclear weapons on the Korean Peninsula and has no intention to attack or invade the DPRK with nuclear or conventional weapons...."*	**2005 Six-Party Talks Joint Statement**
October 10, 2006	George W. Bush	*"The United States of America doesn't have any intention to attack North Korea or to invade North Korea.... But the United States somehow, in a provocative way, trying to invade North Korea—it's just not the case."*	Secretary of State C. Rice, CNN Interview with Wolf Blitzer
October 11, 2006	George W. Bush	*"The United States affirmed that we have no nuclear weapons on the Korean Peninsula. We affirmed that we have no intention of attacking North Korea.* The United States remains committed to diplomacy.... But the United States' message to North Korea and Iran and the people in both countries is that we have—we want to solve the issues peacefully."	Presidential News Conference

Continued

Table 9.1 Continued

Date	Administration	Statement	Context
November 18, 2006	George W. Bush	"Our desire is to solve the North Korean issue peacefully. And as I've made clear in a speech as recently as two days ago in Singapore, that we want the North Korean leaders to hear that if it gives up its weapons—nuclear weapons ambitions, that we would be willing to enter into security arrangements with the North Koreans, as well as move forward new economic incentives for the North Korean people."	President Bush, Meeting with ROK President Roh Moo-Hyun
June 26, 2008	George W. Bush	*First, I'm issuing a proclamation that lifts the provisions of the Trading with the Enemy Act with respect to North Korea. And secondly, I am notifying Congress of my intent to rescind North Korea's designation as a state sponsor of terror in 45 days.* The next 45 days will be an important period for North Korea to show its seriousness of its cooperation. We will work through the six-party talks to develop a comprehensive and rigorous verification protocol. And during this period, the United States will carefully observe North Korea's actions—and act accordingly…. Multilateral diplomacy is the best way to peacefully solve the nuclear issue with North Korea. Today's developments show that tough multilateral diplomacy can yield promising results."	Presidential Press Conference on North Korea
July 31, 2008	George W. Bush	"I will do nothing to undermine the six-party structure, the credibility of the six-party structure, and our partners"	President Bush, Roundtable Interview By Foreign Print Media

Date		Quote	Source
February 15, 2009	Barack H. Obama	"Our position is when they move forward in presenting a verifiable and complete dismantling and denuclearization, we have a great openness to working with them.…It's not only on the diplomatic front.…the United States [has] a willingness to help the people of North Korea, not just in narrow ways with food and fuel but with energy assistance."	Secretary of State H. Clinton, En Route to Asia
April 5, 2009	Barack H. Obama	"The United States is fully committed to maintaining security and stability in northeast Asia and we will continue working for the verifiable denuclearization of the Korean Peninsula through the Six-Party Talks. The Six-Party Talks provide the forum for achieving denuclearization, reducing tensions, and for resolving other issues of concern between North Korea, its four neighbors, and the United States."	Presidential Statement on North Korea Launch
April 5, 2009	Barack H. Obama	"The United States and the European Union stand ready to work with others in welcoming into the international community a North Korea that abandons its pursuit of weapons of mass destruction and policy of threats aimed at its neighbors and that protects the rights of its people. Such a North Korea could share in the prosperity and development that the remainder of northeast Asia has achieved in recent years."	**US-European Council Joint Statement**
June 16, 2009	Barack H. Obama	"So I want to be clear that there is another path available to North Korea—a path that leads to peace and economic opportunity for the people of North Korea, including full integration into the community of nations. That destination can only be reached through peaceful negotiations that achieve the full and verifiable denuclearization of the Korean peninsula. That is the opportunity that exists for North Korea, and President Lee and I join with the international community in urging the North Koreans to take it.… *We are more than willing to engage in negotiations to get North Korea on a path of peaceful coexistence* with its neighbors, and we want to encourage their prosperity."	President Obama, Joint Press Availability with ROK President Lee Myung-Bak

it received such assurances was, even at the presidential level, "Words were not enough." The United States must document its nonhostile policy. So, in September 2005, the North Koreans won the negative security assurance that they had long sought—a written statement in full view of China, Russia, Japan, and South Korea, that the "The United States affirmed that it has no nuclear weapons on the Korean Peninsula and has no intention to attack or invade the DPRK with nuclear or conventional weapons" (Joint Statement, Paragraph 1, clause 3). All of the other parties were impressed by this statement, including the Russians and Chinese. The Russians in fact pointed out to the North Koreans the significance of this negative security assurance. Yet, the North dismissed this as a piece of paper with no meaning.

So what do they really want?

The North wants a special type of "regime security assurance" from the United States. This is different from a negative security assurance. The negative security assurance was given to North Korea by the Bush administration in the 2005 Joint Statement, stating that the United States would not attack North Korea with nuclear or conventional weapons. This assurance went further in text than the statement of nonhostile intent provided by the Clinton administration in October 2000, which read "[T]he US and the DPRK sides stated that they are prepared to undertake a new direction in their relations. As a crucial first step, the two sides stated that neither government would have hostile intent toward the other and confirmed the commitment of both governments to make every effort in the future to build a new relationship free from past enmity."[11] Yet, neither of these seems to appease the North because they seek a deeper, more fundamental form of protection for the Kim family and its cronies, which is more problematic for the United States to give. The desire for this very personal type of security assurance stems from the fundamental reform dilemma that the DPRK faces, which I wrote about in *Foreign Affairs* in 2002. It needs to open up to survive, but the process of opening up could lead to cracks in the hermetically sealed country, precipitating the regime's demise.[12] Thus, what Pyongyang wants is an assurance from the United States not against nuclear attack but that it will not allow the House of Kim (that is, Kim Jong Il or his son, Kim Jong Eun) to collapse as Pyongyang (partially) denuclearizes and goes through a modest reform process to absorb the economic assistance and opening to the outside world, which would come with a grand deal.

This type of regime assurance must be an even more prescient concern for the North Korean leadership given Kim Jong Il's deteriorating health condition. The likely leadership transition to Kim Jong Eun, the youngest of his three sons who lacks any experience or revolutionary credentials like that of his grandfather Kim Il Sung, would be an inherently unstable process in the best of times. The fluidity created by this process in combination with the imperative for reform probably makes regime assurance a topline preoccupation.

So if escaping the horns of the reform dilemma has been one of Kim's goals, here too he has failed miserably. He leaves his son with a regime that has neither reformed economically nor gained an ounce of international goodwill to help it out of its current state. Moreover, the sentencing of the two American journalists, Euna Lee and Laura Ling, to twelve years of hard labor in a prison camp (although later released) have put North Korea's human rights abuses squarely in the sights of many Americans who might otherwise care less about a nuclear-toting country on the distant side of the globe ruled by a quirky dictator. Many news reports saw this ordeal as an attempt by Pyongyang to link the fate of the two journalists with the nuclear issue. Governor Bill Richardson (D-New Mexico), a frequent visitor to North Korea, described the two women as "chips" in a "high stakes nuclear poker game."[13] I believe the Lee and Ling case and the nuclear test occurred within the same time frame, but that is about the only link between the two events. In the former case, the two journalists, of their own admission, went into North Korean territory from the Chinese border illegally to report on the trafficking of women who try to escape the country for a better life in China. They were captured by North Korean authorities and detained in Pyongyang. The harsh sentence against the two Americans in this regard was meant as a measure to defend against yet another vulnerability of the regime—the slow but steady trickle of refugees seeking to vote with their feet, to leave the country for China and South Korea—as it goes through its shaky power transition. Yet, even here, Kim and his son are caught in a vicious circle. They are compelled to make an example of these two Americans in order to deter further attempts to document or encourage a growing refugee problem on the Sino-North Korean border. This is important to secure the regime in an inherently unstable leadership transition, but it also removes any shred of empathy in the international system for the North's reform dilemma.

Obama's Conundrum?

Where does this leave the Obama administration? If the goals for North Korea enumerated above are correct, then the negotiations, if they ever resume, will invariably reach a dead end. The United States is unlikely to offer Kim or his son a civil nuclear deal like that of India, and absent any real improvement in human rights, no American president could possibly offer regime assurances to the butchers of Pyongyang. This pessimistic prognosis should not, however, mean abandoning the opportunity to negotiate. If the choice is between dealing with a dictator with a runaway nuclear weapons program or one with a program capped and under international monitoring, the latter surely serves U.S. and Asian interests. The Six-party Talks or any future derivative can still serve the purpose of freezing, disabling, and degrading North Korea's nuclear capabilities, even as the stated goal remains total denuclearization.

By signaling a willingness to negotiate with the North during his campaign and then early in his administration through envoys Steve Bosworth and Sung Kim, Obama has positioned the United States well for a negotiation track and the sanctions track. The emphasis now is on implementing the sanctions in UN Security Council Resolution 1874, passed in the aftermath of the May 2009 nuclear test, and institutionalizing a multilateral counterproliferation regime against North Korean weapons of mass destruction (WMD). Many initially criticized the resolution as lacking teeth because it did not authorize the use of force in its provisions for inspection of suspect North Korean cargo. But after the DPRK ship, the Kang Nam, reversed course because the government of Burma/Myanmar stated publicly its intention to comply with the provisions of 1874 and inspect the cargo, critics began to appreciate the potential for building an effective counterproliferation mechanism. Ironically, the resolution institutionalizes, in a UN context, the proliferation security initiative of the Bush administration, making it both more effective and more inclusive. One of the challenges the administration will face is to keep the Chinese honest in terms of complying with the sanctions in United Nations Security Council Resolution 1874 (UNSCR 1874), even after the North Koreans show interest in returning to the table for negotiations. Removing sanctions against DPRK proliferation should not be a quid pro quo for the resumption of multilateral or bilateral negotiations, tempting as this might be for Beijing to advocate. The other negotiation trap the administration must avoid is the dilemma of "relative reasonableness." What this means is that every agreement in the Six-party Talks process is negotiated with painstaking care in which parties hammer out specific quid pro quos, the synchronization of steps, timelines, with concomitant rewards and penalties. Yet, sooner or later, Pyongyang plays brinksmanship and demands more than it was promised or does less than it should. While everyone accepts that the DPRK is being completely unreasonable, they also realize that a failure of the agreement could mean the failure of the Six-party Talks and the precipitation of another crisis. To avoid this, the parties end up pressing the United States, knowing full well that the DPRK is at fault and has traversed the bounds of fairness and good faith, but at the same time certain that the only chance of progress can be had from American reasonableness rather than DPRK unreasonableness. The result is that any additional American flexibility is widely perceived in the region as evidence of American leadership, but is viewed in Washington as some combination of desperation and weakness.

So that's the playbook for President Obama. The talks, even if they should resume after Special Envoy Stephen Bosworth's bilateral meetings with the North Koreans, will never achieve what either Washington or Pyongyang wants, but they serve as a way to manage the problem, contain the proliferation threat, and run out the clock on the regime. There will definitely be a mess on the back end when the Kim family falls from grace. But planning today for that eventuality with Seoul, Beijing, and Tokyo could help tidy things up. The administration would do well to consider a set of separate dialogues, either bilaterally or multilaterally among the United States, South Korea, and China. The North Korean leader's time in office is severely limited given the new revelations about his rather serious health problems, including pancreatic cancer. While the United States and South Korea have restarted planning on how to respond to a sudden collapse scenario north of the 38th Parallel, they need to also begin a quiet discussion with China. The purpose of such a discussion would be to create some transparency about the relative priorities and likely first-actions by the three parties in response to signs of political instability in the North. Presumably, the United States would be interested in securing WMD weapons and materials, and South Korea would be interested in restoring domestic stability. China would be interested in securing its border against a mass influx of refugees. Coordination in advance will help to minimize misperception and miscalculation in a crisis. South Koreans are suspicious about China's intentions in a North Korean collapse scenario, given Beijing's investment in the North's mineral resources, but such a three-way discussion is important to ensuring China's support in any United Nations Security Council resolutions that might accompany any sudden change in the North.

Notes

1. The views expressed in this chapter are the author's own and should not be construed as representing the position of CSIS or the U.S. government. An earlier version of this chapter, titled "What Do They Really Want?: Obama's North Korea Conundrum" appeared in *The Washington Quarterly* 32, 4 (October 2009): 119–138.

2. Proponents of this argument include Michael Mazarr, "The Long Road to Pyongyang," *Foreign Affairs* 86, 5 (September–October 2007); Leon Sigal, *Disarming Strangers: Nuclear Diplomacy with North Korea* (Princeton, NJ: Princeton University Press, 1998); Selig Harrison, *Korean Endgame* (Princeton, NJ: Princeton University Press, 2003); Joel Wit, "Enhancing U.S. Engagement with North Korea," *Washington Quarterly* 30, 2 (Spring 2007): 53–69; Victor D. Cha and David C. Kang, *Nuclear North Korea* (New York: Columbia University Press, 2003); John Feffer, "Responding to North Korea's Surprises," *Foreign Policy in Focus* 17, 14 (December 2002), http://www.fpif.org/briefs/vol7/v7n14nk.html.

3. Leon Sigal, "A Bombshell That's actually an Olive Branch," *Los Angeles Times*, October 18, 2002.

4. See Secretary Clinton's Remarks in "U.S.-Asia Relations: Indispensable to Our Future," *U.S. Department of State, Bureau of Public Affairs: Office of Electronic Information and Publications*, February 13, 2009, http://www.state.gov/secretary/rm/2009a/02/117333.htm; Secretary Clinton's Remarks in "Putting the Elements of Smart Power Into Practice," *U.S. Department of State, Bureau of Public Affairs: Office of Electronic Information and Publication*, February 19, 2009, http://www.state.gov/secretary/rm/2009a/02/119411.htm.

5. "North Korea: Back at the Brink?" Senate, Foreign Relations Committee hearing, June 11, 2009.

6. For seismic activity, see "Magnitude 4.7—North Korea 2009 May 25," *U.S. Geological Survey*, http://earthquake.usgs.gov/eqcenter/recenteqsww/Quakes/us2009hbaf.php#summary. For assessments of the October 2006 and May 2009 tests, see M.B. Kalinowski and O. Ross: "Data Analysis and Interpretation of the North Korean Nuclear Test Explosion of 9 October 2006." *INESAP Information Bulletin*, 27, 39–43, http://www.inesap.org/bulletin27/art12.htm; Martin Kalinowski, "Second Nuclear Test Conducted by North Korea on 25 May 2009 Fact Sheet," *Carl Friedrich von Weizsäcker Centre for Science and Peace Research (ZNF)*, University of Hamburg, www.armscontrolwonk.com/file_download/177/Kalinowski.pdf.

7. For examples of the "up the ante" argument, see John Glionna, "North Korea's Nuclear Test may be for Kim's Legacy," *Los Angeles Times*, May 26, 2009.

8. It is worth noting that while the North Koreans learn from their tests, the United States learns a great deal more about the state of their programs and their level of development. See Richard Halloran, "How U.S. Exploited N. Korea Missile Tests," *Honolulu Advertiser*, July 12, 2009.

9. Robert L. Gallucci and Kang Sok Ju, "Agreed Framework Between the United States of America and the Democratic People's Republic of Korea, October 21, 1994," The Korean Peninsula Energy Development Organization, http://www.kedo.org/pdfs/AgreedFramework.pdf.

10. See Statement by Evans Revere before the Senate Foreign Relations Committee, June 11, 2009, http://foreign.senate.gov/testimony/2009/RevereTestimony090611p.pdf.

11. "U.S.-DPRK Joint Communique," October 12, 2000, http://www.fas.org/news/dprk/2000/dprk-001012a.htm.

12. Victor Cha, "Korea's Place in the Axis," *Foreign Affairs* (May–June 2002). The first to write on this dilemma was Byong-Joon Ahn, "The Man Who Would be Kim," *Foreign Affairs* 73, 6 (November–December 1994): 94–108.

13. Bill Richardson, interview with John Roberts, *American Morning*, CNN, June 8, 2009, http://transcripts.cnn.com/TRANSCRIPTS/0906/08/ltm.03.html.

CHAPTER TEN

Rapprochement in Postwar History: Implications for North Korea

BRUCE CUMINGS

By the end of 2009, Obama had fulfilled his pledges by reaching out to Iran, Cuba, Burma, and, like his predecessor, Libya; it may well be that this "engagement" train is leaving the station, and leaving North Korea behind. But that cannot be known at this writing, and so I want to focus on several cases of engagement and rapprochement with former enemies, in hopes of shedding light on Obama's policies toward North Korea and Iran—two countries that we specialists keep separate, but that interact daily in the minds of policy-makers—and to critique the long-term American strategy of blockade and isolation toward regimes that Washington does not like.

Remembering the Value of Diplomacy

Diplomacy arose in history to fill the empty space existing between the nation-states of the world, to try and bridge the vacuum and the anarchy long posited by the dominant theory of international affairs, realism. Diplomacy arose from distance, from estrangement, from alienation, and of course from interstate violence.[1] Here was a method for influencing enemies, short of conflict and war. Establishing an embassy was not a gift to the enemy: both antagonists thought that it was in their interest to do so. The clear heyday of diplomacy, when many of its modern traditions were established, was during the "long peace" of the nineteenth century. The extreme ideologies of the twentieth century inhibited the play of diplomacy, but it is worth remembering that the United States maintained an embassy in Berlin from 1933, when Hitler took power, until 1939, and not only kept an embassy in Madrid all during Franco's fascism, but established military bases there during the cold war.

By contrast, since the establishment of the Union of Soviet Socialist Republics (USSR), the United States has denied recognition to all the major left-wing revolutions of the past century. Roosevelt normalized relations with the Soviet Union in 1933 and Carter did the same with China in 1979, yielding a gap of sixteen years for Russia and three decades for China. It is merely prudent to withhold recognition for a newly formed regime, of course, and when that regime is an insurgent power on the world scene a longer period of estrangement is predictable. But it is difficult to see what the United States gained by withholding recognition from either Moscow or Beijing. Both were probably weakened in some ways and strengthened in others by their isolation, but the United States lost any opportunity to influence either of the regimes, short of war or threat of the use of force. What if a U.S. embassy had been in Moscow in the early 1920s, and had been able, with various inducements, to encourage Lenin's New Economic Policy? What if an American embassy had been in China in 1959–1961, as Beijing broke with Moscow? When normalization finally came, the USSR was in the midst of its most destructive period, with the war on the kulaks and the purges, so it can hardly be said that this "gift" came because of good behavior. But that can be said about the rapprochement with China— not the one in 1971–1972, in the midst of the Cultural Revolution, but in 1978–1979, when normal relations coincided with Deng Xiaoping's epochal reforms bringing China into the world economy. In neither case, however, was the totalitarian character of Stalin's Russia or Mao's China an obstacle to normalization.

Isolation from America undoubtedly hurt the USSR and China, but it never came close to achieving its desired result, namely, to push them into (or merely await) the collapse of their systems, and it unquestionably made repression of their own people easier, by invoking foreign threats. Likewise, in the two longest-running cases of nonrecognition today, North Korea (61 years) and Cuba (48 years), the regimes may have been strengthened or weakened, but neither has collapsed or been changed in the positive directions that the policy of nonrecognition presumably anticipated. Cuba, of course, is also a matter of domestic politics, given the exile community in Florida, but North Korea could be recognized tomorrow without any noticeable effect on the next elections. In any case, we again confront decades of isolation that did nothing to change these regimes in a positive direction, seriously limited American influence, and undoubtedly imposed much hardship on the multitudes of innocent people who live in both countries. We have embargoed Iran's economy for thirty years, Cuba's for fifty years, and North Korea's for sixty years: what good has it done? What positive changes have resulted? When the nonrecognition policy and the quarantines are judged in the bright light of their results, decades of history have found them wanting.

American policy in this regard is also, of course, a stark contrast to that of our allies and friends. The British kept an embassy in Beijing through its transition to the People's Republic of China (PRC), France was quite close to the Mao regime (at least in the 1960s), and Italy also had good relations. Cuba now has diplomatic relations with all of America's friends and allies, and, since 2000, North Korea does too, save primarily with Japan. Many reasons might be cited for this American divergence—the shelter of two oceans, the provincialism of most Americans until recently, the isolation between the wars, the solipsistic belief that our truths are self-evident—but the prime one, in my view, is the absence of a serious diplomatic tradition in the United States. A fact that seemed stunning a few years ago, but by now has become a cliché, is nonetheless revealing: the Pentagon's marching bands have more members than the entire Foreign Service. Indeed the Pentagon is far more likely to be involved in nation building, foreign disaster relief, rescuing missing or captive Americans, and so on, than is the State Department. In countries where conflict is ongoing or likely, our ambassadors often seem to sit in the shadow of the local Pentagon commander. (This disparity, of course, has led to much recent conflict between these agencies in the wars in Iraq and Afghanistan.)

Creating Friends After War

I am unaware of another rapprochement between belligerents in modern history that can compare to American policy toward defeated Japan and (with the aid of our allies) defeated Germany. In both cases, industrial countries with their cities flattened by all-out air attacks turned around within five years to be essentially what they are today—democracies, productive engines of the world economy, and that rare thing, nations with a long history of aggression newly instilled with the strongest inclinations toward peace. Japan and West Germany got a very soft peace (particularly when contrasted to the World War I settlement), which still rankles among Japan's neighbors because many lingering questions regarding Japan's conduct during the war remain unsettled. West Germany, by contrast, thoroughly scrubbed out its sordid history in the schools and textbooks, and developed what might be called a "good neighbor" policy toward the rest of Europe. In the main, it is hard to argue that this rapprochement did not work to the great benefit of both the United States and the defeated populations.

It is difficult to distill applicable lessons from these two cases, however. The historical situation is non-replicable, in that the soft peace was in reaction to the harsh terms of Versailles, and it deepened as the cold war made Japan and West Germany into key allies of the United States. Both countries surrendered unconditionally (except for the retention of the emperor in Japan), and both were in no position to resist whatever the Allies wanted to do with them. Both populations were undoubtedly almost as happy to be free of Hitler and Tojo as Americans were, a relief often not characteristic of other situations (for example, the Taiwanese traded Tojo for Chiang Kai-shek, and later came to think that was a bad bargain).

China is a different case of "creating friends after war." American and Chinese soldiers stained Korean soil with rivers of blood in the early fifties, and the United States came close to attacking China with nuclear weapons over Quemoy and Matsu, and perhaps over China's nuclear program. In the meantime, a classic cold war standoff existed from 1949 to 1971, with neither side willing to give an inch. Richard Nixon's rapprochement, signaled while he was a presidential candidate in 1967, was strategic: to contain communism (the USSR) by communism (China). It had absolutely nothing to do with the PRC's internal politics, which were at their very worst. Jimmy Carter's was hegemonic: to bring China out of isolation and into the world economy, and expect that over time the solvent of international exchange across a broad spectrum would retard China's insurgent impulses and slowly erode the nature of the regime. The hindsight of three decades likewise speaks to the brilliance of American strategy in this case. The year 1979 marked one of the grandest victories for American power when China—thoroughly revolutionary, recalcitrant "Red China"—decided to integrate itself into the American-led world system, rather than to continue to resist it. Unlike the 1933 rapprochement with Russia, this one went together with fundamental changes in the PRC's domestic and foreign economic policy that moved it sharply away from a dogmatic socialism. Power is best exemplified by people doing what you want them to do without having to be told: this is the essence of the American victory with regard to China.

Vietnam is another case of successful reconciliation after war—a terrible war. Probably the key reason here is a simple one: they won. This gave Vietnamese leaders tremendous confidence in dealing with the United States, something vivid in the Public Broadcasting System (PBS) thirteen-part documentary on the Vietnam War, where Prime Minister Pham Van Dong triumphantly grins his way through the film. But Vietnam also initiated economic reforms in the late 1980s that convinced many Americans that they wanted to do business. The lessons of China and Vietnam point strongly toward economic reforms turning market forces loose as a necessary prelude to American recognition—at least if we are speaking of socialist economies in transition. But the lessons of all these cases of reconciliation after war point to the virtues of engagement, magnanimity, reward rather than punishment, and looking to the future rather than the past.

Rapprochement After Empire

Intangible factors also play a role in reconciliation. An ocean of ink has been spilled on "the rise of China," but that event happened sixty years ago. The proclamation of the People's Republic in 1949 gave an enormous boost to China's prestige in the world, and especially the Third World, as did its standoff with the United States in Korea. China embodied a force most American leaders never understood, namely, anti-imperial nationalism. This also animated the leaderships of Vietnam, North Korea, Indonesia, and a host of other former colonies around the world. But China wasn't just any country: it was the Middle Kingdom, its civilization spread throughout East, Central, and Southeast Asia for millennia, and that alone always gave it a fascination. Nixon said in 1967 that he couldn't imagine a great nation like China remaining outside the world of international exchange. Vietnam was the unexpected burial ground of the Depression and World War II generation's children, and in the twentieth century no war dug so deeply into the American flesh and soul. A subtle factor in American recognition of the Democratic Republic of Vietnam (DRV) was the presence of powerful politicians, like Senators John Kerry and John McCain, who fought in the war and could not hide their grudging respect for their old adversary—or how deeply the war had penetrated their lives.

Ultimately, though, it was flawed American policy, based on ignorance of the force of anti-imperialism in the colonies, which got us into two wars that we could not win: Korea and Vietnam.

If someone had told Dean Acheson or Henry Stimson in 1945 that their policies would quickly revive Japan and Germany, also war-devastated England and France, and inaugurate a global boom in the 1950s, they would not have been surprised. If a genie had also let them see George Kennan's containment strategy, a limited one of reinforcing the important bulwarks along the Soviet periphery, they would have understood that too. Rebuilding the industrial economies and containing communism were two of the three most important issues of the postwar period. The third was anticolonialism, but if the genie also said that over the next thirty years you will fight two major wars, one in Korea and one in Vietnam, and you will win neither, Acheson and Stimson would have been flabbergasted. And then, if he said conflicts in Korea and Vietnam would also be critical to distending and transforming containment into a world crusade (with National Security Council Report 68), they might have fainted. The mote in their eye was anti-imperial nationalism and, by and large, it remains a mote in the American eye today.

I remember reading a long 1945 Office of Strategic Services (OSS) report in the archives: it said that the United States really had no alternative but to support the reestablishment of British, French, and Dutch rule in Southeast Asia, because the colonies were essential to Europe's postwar rebuilding, and the independence leaders in these colonies would advance the cause of communism. Whatever one thinks of this argument, history demolished it. Anticolonialism was such a powerful force that Burma and India soon got their independence; the Dutch were finished in Indonesia by 1948, the French in Indochina by 1954. Had the United States stood with Ho, Sukarno, Nehru, and others—or simply remained neutral—postwar history would have been rewritten.

Imagine this different outcome: Roosevelt lives a normal life span, is president until 1948, presides over the independence of our only formal colony in the Philippines in 1946, and, because of his disdain for Japanese and French colonialism, reaches out to anticolonial resisters named Kim Il Sung and Ho Chi Minh. He tutors the American people in fireside chats about the March 1, 1919 independence movement in Korea, Kim's decadelong resistance against Japanese imperialism in Manchuria, the nationalist basis of the Viet Minh, Ho Chi Minh being the odds-on father of his country, and the necessity for serious reform of landlordism in Korea and Vietnam. Those readers who are already chuckling need also to grapple with Dean Acheson stating, in early 1947, that it doesn't matter whether Ho is a nationalist or communist, since all agents of Moscow masquerade as nationalists; or Truman and Acheson shipping military aid to the French war in Indochina in May 1949, as part of NSC-48; or Dulles and Eisenhower witnessing the Dienbienphu catastrophe in 1954 and then, together with Kennedy later on, making the stupefyingly bad decision to try to win the anti-colonial war that the French had just contrived to lose.

The point is not to refight policy conflicts from the early cold war, but to suggest that empathy and *verstehen* (a German word with the connotation of understanding across difficult barriers) go a very long way in diplomacy, particularly when you are the most powerful country in the world and can afford to bend in the direction of the enemy: the other, being the weaker and the insecure, who—secretly (Kim) and openly (Ho)—very much wanted your recognition and your support. Anyone who reads through the papers of Stimson or Acheson or, sadly, George Kennan, sees the stain of race clearly: they just could not imagine people of color deploying any serious force in world affairs. Their myopia was a mark of their generation and segregation in the United States, but it badly clouded their perceptions. In different ways it still does, if we consider the demonization of, say, Kim Jong Il that goes on all the time. Ideas have consequences and words make a difference: imagine if the United States were to acknowledge Kim's role in fighting the Japanese, or to "reflect," as the Japanese say, on the carpet bombing of North Korea during the war, or to hold a conference on the Bay of Pigs with high American and Cuban officials, or to open up an inquiry into what, exactly, have been the costs and consequences of exile violence against Cuba.

American leaders have stuck their uninformed noses into the vital politics of many, many countries since 1945, but two remain to be mentioned. I don't know of any capable historian who does not think that the secret overthrow of the Arbenz regime in Guatemala was a disaster, and set in motion a civil war that lasted into the 1980s, killing tens of thousands of people—and Arbenz was no more to the left than most of the leaders in Latin America today. Likewise the Central Intelligence Agency's (CIA) overthrow of the quintessential nationalist (but also a scion of the aristocracy) Mosaddegh in 1953 is the origin of American problems with Iran, and central to the ouster of the Shah in 1979 and the revolution that followed. One of the best accounts of this episode is by a former American official, John Blair, who many years ago in *The Control of Oil* demonstrated how the global oil regime and the Seven Sisters lay at the basis of Mosaddegh's ouster, and fed directly into not just the events of 1979 but the rise of the Organization of the Petroleum Exporting Countries (OPEC) and its oil embargo. But this also came little more than a decade after the British had summarily deposed the Shah's father and put the adolescent Reza Pahlevi (eighteen years old) in his place, and after Mosaddegh had been elected in what was then a parliamentary democracy.

The day after President Obama made his first overture to Tehran, Ahmadinejad asked in a polite way (for him) that the United States apologize for its actions over the past sixty years (starting with the 1953 coup): "Who has asked them to come and interfere in the affairs of nations?"[2] Would this be so hard? Isn't noninterference a core American value, going back to George Washington and John Quincy Adams? I wrote this before President Obama provided an answer, in his signature address to the Muslim world in Cairo: no, it isn't hard. To my knowledge, he issued the only direct apology for the overthrow of Mosaddegh, from any American official, let alone president. He also recalled the anti-imperial origins of the United States.

In other words, simply to acknowledge that overthrowing the democratically elected Mosaddegh was wrong, and that our bipartisan support for the Shah's dictatorship hurt many Iranians, costs little, but the effect goes a long way—or so it seems to me. But then I have never understood why American leaders still pick fights with people like Kim or Ahmadinejad or Castro, leaders whom imperialism brought to power but who lead countries of comparatively little weight in world affairs.[3] And here's the ringer: *they desperately want our recognition*—not to remain in power or build nukes, but to validate their histories and gain the strength to dial down their harsh rhetoric. History has shown that their bellowing gets them nowhere, but we Americans don't seem to know that our own cold war mentalities also invite failure time and again. The leaders of Pyongyang and Tehran always think that they must react with both (rhetorical) barrels whenever Washington appears to slight them;[4] why do we give them so many opportunities? Why get down in the mud? Is this a dignified way for a great power to behave?

Cherishing North Korea and Iran

China has long used a term, *zixiao*, which is usually translated as cherishing friends from afar (or cherishing the lesser), but it really means "not sweating the small stuff" when it comes to relations with allied or tributary states, or enemies who are not really threatening. It is a classic hegemonic device, to show that the power that everyone recognizes as superior nonetheless shows concern and regard for the smaller or lesser party. We don't have good concepts for this in English (although magnanimity comes close), so we use foreign terms like "*noblesse oblige.*" But *zixiao* was a key aspect of the legitimacy of the Chinese world order. Can we not do this? Does being an American leader (Bill Clinton excepted) mean never having to say you're sorry? Are there not highway networks of unplumbed political mileage that could be rolled out just by being *honest* about those places in the postwar world where the United States has not done so well? I am afraid that the divisions and either/or dichotomies of the cold war still linger too strongly in the minds of our leaders for this to happen. Hopefully, Barack Obama will prove me wrong.

Three decades have now passed since the Iranian revolution gained power, and again we confront the question of what, exactly, the United States has gotten from its policy of nonrecognition and isolation. Iran represents perhaps the most difficult type of rapprochement, because it involves historical wounds that result not simply in divisiveness and bitterness, but engender a new regime that is explicitly and ideologically hostile to the United States. In Iran's case, the overthrow of Mosaddegh in 1953, followed by a quarter century of support for the increasingly repressive Shah, was the background to the revolution in 1979, which of course was attended by the seizure of American hostages and effectively ended the Carter presidency. The contemporary rise of militant Islam was like pouring gasoline onto these burning embers, and this region, moreover, has a unique contingency, the state of Israel, a close ally of the United States, and the only nuclear power in the Middle East.

Thus, though there is no clear comparison with Iran, perhaps North Korea is closest to this case, because its leaders believe the United States snatched defeat from the jaws of North Korean victory in 1950, and then plastered the North for three years with an intensive and annihilating air campaign. The post-Korean War regime in the North nursed terrible grievances against the United States that only began to thaw in the 1980s, and those events still inhabit their mass media. Vietnam, by contrast, was an easy rapprochement: once the United States was ready, the Vietnamese were entirely willing, because no matter how or what they suffered, no one could take away from them a cardinal fact—their victory. Japan was the easiest rapprochement because it combined overwhelming defeat, nationwide relief that the militarists were gone, and a very soft peace. China, more than one might have expected, was also easy because Beijing wanted a way out of its difficult strategic cul-de-sac, having the two superpowers as their two biggest antagonists, and saw the United States as a lesser imperialist historically than several others—and especially Japan. But a real set of common interests only emerged when Deng Xiaoping came to power in 1978, as Beijing and Washington both worked to integrate China into the world economy.

For a decade, from 1998 to 2008, South Korea illustrated that rapprochement needs to be preceded by a process of truth and reconciliation, that is, a scrupulous, unblinkered, forensic look at the past, which investigates and acknowledges buried and suppressed aspects of history. And so, mostly unbeknownst to the American people or press, the Korean truth and Reconciliation Commission has dredged up and verified the massacres of tens of thousand of its own citizens by the Syngman Rhee regime, various villages blotted out by American napalm (in the South), and massacres by North Korean and local communists (the latter were mostly the known cases since the Korean War; on the whole, massacre cases have run at a ratio of six killed by the forces of order to one killed by communists).

The purpose of this extended inquiry was not to sow blame or refight cold war battles, but to seek reconciliation between North and South. Though this has been a very slow process, the stark reversal of Seoul's former anticommunist strategy created a sea change in their perceptions of the North—from evil enemy to long-lost cousin, led by a nutty uncle perhaps. The purpose is also to seek an understanding and an orientation that produces *verstehen* of one's former enemy—not sympathy, perhaps not even empathy, but an understanding of the principles that guide one's adversary even if one finds those principles abhorrent or deeply wounding to one's own knowledge of what happened historically with this same enemy. And, of course, full recognition of what one side (the South) did might lead to a better understanding of all the grievances husbanded by the other side. Once the enemy's core principles are understood without blinking, once we view our history with this adversary from all sides, appeals can be made to the adversary that are or appear to be sympathetic to their worldview. But perhaps the greatest gain is self-knowledge, for if you do not know yourself and what others think of you, rightly or wrongly, it is difficult to conduct diplomacy.

The person most responsible for this sea change was Kim Dae Jung, who at his inauguration in early 1998 pledged to "actively pursue reconciliation and cooperation" with the North, seek peaceful coexistence, and declared his support for Pyongyang's attempts to better relations with Washington and Tokyo—in complete contrast with his predecessors who feared any hint of such rapprochement. He soon underlined his pledges by approving large shipments of food aid to the North, lifting limits on business deals between the North and southern firms, and calling for an end to the American economic embargos against the North in June 1998, during a visit to Washington. Kim explicitly rejected "unification by absorption" (which was the de facto policy of his predecessors), and in effect committed Seoul to a prolonged period of peaceful coexistence, with reunification put off for twenty or thirty more years.

Kim Dae Jung also was unflagging in his pressure to get Washington to change its policies toward the North. That finally achieved results when the State Department began a six-month-long review of Korea policy in the fall of 1998, which markedly changed the direction of U.S. policy and culminated in William Perry's mission to Pyongyang in June 1999. Dr. Perry finally issued a public version of his report (and this policy review) in October 1999, the essence of which was a policy of engagement predicated on dealing with the North "as it is, not as we would like it to be," on the coexistence of two Koreas for another considerable period of time, a progressive lifting of the fifty-year-old American embargos against the North, a deepening of diplomatic relations between the two sides, and a substantial aid package for the North. The North, for its part, agreed to continue to observe the 1994 agreement freezing its plutonium facility, to suspend missile testing, and to continue talks with the United States about ending its missile program, including the sale of missiles to the Middle East.

Kim Dae Jung also believed that North Korea did *not* oppose a continuing U.S. troop presence in Korea if Washington were to pursue engagement with Pyongyang rather than confrontation (U.S. troops would continue to be useful in policing the border, that is, the demilitarized zone (DMZ), in assuring that the South's superior armed forces don't swallow the North, and in keeping Japan and China at bay). Secretary of Defense William Cohen seemed to echo such views in July 1998, when he declared that American troops would stay in Korea even after it was unified. Then at the June 2000 summit, Kim Jong Il confirmed this view, telling Kim Dae Jung directly that he did not necessarily oppose the continued stationing of U.S. troops in Korea. In this sense, President Kim's proposals constituted the first serious attempt in fifty years to achieve North-South reconciliation *within* the existing Northeast Asian security structure, largely built by the United States after 1945. (This remains today the best win-win alternative for U.S. policy toward the North.)

This summit, and the State Department's major review of policy, prepared the ground for a deal on North Korea's missiles that was deeply in the Korean, American, and world interest. North Korea was willing to forgo construction, deployment, and international sales of all missiles with a range of more than three hundred miles. If President Clinton had been willing to do Kim Jong Il the favor of a visit to Pyongyang, American negotiators were convinced that Kim would also have agreed to enter the Missile Technology Control Regime (MTCR), which would limit all North Korean missiles to an upper range of 180 miles (and thus remove a threat felt deeply in nearby Japan). In return the United States would have provided $1 billion in food aid to the regime.[5]

President Clinton wanted to go to Pyongyang, and his negotiators on Korea had their bags packed for weeks in November and December 2000. Indeed, I remember visiting President Kim with some other scholars in December, just a few days before Christmas, and he told me he still hoped Clinton would go to Pyongyang. But as Clinton's National Security advisor Sandy Berger later put it, it wasn't a good idea for the president to leave the country when they didn't know "whether there could be a major constitutional crisis."[6] After the Supreme Court stepped in to give the 2000 presidential election to George W. Bush, Bush's advisors made clear that they would not honor the missile agreement, whether or not Clinton journeyed to North Korea.

What is the lesson of Seoul's decadelong policy of reconciliation, and Washington's (more temporary and temorizing) strategy of engaging the North? First, the North froze its reactor and some eight thousand fuel rods, and thus had no access to plutonium for eight years (1994–2002). Second, top officials believed them to be also ready in 2000 to give up their delivery capability (assuming they had capability to make a nuclear warhead), in return for various inducements. Third, major progress on other fronts happened after Kim Dae Jung came to power, including the big export zone at Kaesong (where 40,000 North Korean workers are employed), and this "opening" was greatly furthered by the second North-South summit in October 2007, which put in place agreements to open up more ports and indeed the wealthiest part of the Democratic People's Republic of Korea (the southwest) to trade and manufacture. In short, the two biggest problems with the North—the military threat posed by its weapons and missiles, and its isolation from the world—could be eroded slowly in the context of engagement and reconciliation.

The United States and North Korea

The contrast between Seoul's policies since 1998 and the American stance *vis-à-vis* North Korea could hardly be greater. Soon it will be twenty years since a bipartisan consensus emerged inside the Beltway that the Democratic Republic of Korea (DPRK) would soon "implode or explode," a mantra that began with Bush I and lasted through Clinton and Bush II, right down to the present times. This was the hidden premise of the American pledge to build two light-water reactors to replace the Yongbyon plutonium complex in the 1994 Framework Agreement: since they wouldn't come onstream for eight or ten years, by then they would belong to the Republic of Korea (ROK).

Iraq War architect Paul Wolfowitz journeyed to Seoul in the aftermath of the apparent American victory over Saddam to opine (in June 2003) that "North Korea is teetering on the brink of collapse." In the intervening years we heard General Gary Luck, commander of U.S. forces in Korea, say (in 1997) that "North Korea will disintegrate, possibly in very short order;" the only question was whether it would implode or explode.[7] In this he was reiterating the slogan of another of our commanders in Korea, General Robert Riscassi, who never tired of saying Pyongyang would soon "implode or explode" (Riscassi retired in 1992). When does the statute of limitations run out on being systematically wrong? If "know your enemy" is the *sine qua non* of effective warfare and diplomacy, I think that the United States has been badly served by those who claim expertise on North Korea in Washington. But I know from experience that any attempt by outsiders to break through this Beltway groupthink merely results in polite silence and discrete headshaking. North Korea's "coming collapse" is still the dominant opinion today, reinforced by a Beltway consensus that some sort of "succession struggle" has been unfolding since August 2008.

The leading Washington pundit on North Korea is Nicholas Eberstadt, who has been with the American Enterprise Institute for about twenty years, and initially distinguished himself by using demographic data to pinpoint the wretched health care system and dramatic declines in life expectancy of the Soviet Union, several years before it

fizzled. Since at least 1990, he has been predicting the impending collapse of North Korea,⁸ but his views are best sampled in his 1999 book,
The End of North Korea. (When a *New York Times* reporter asked John
Bolton what the Bush administration's policy was on the DPRK, he
strode to his bookshelf and handed him Eberstadt's book: "that's our
policy," he said.) Finally, Eberstadt got tired of predicting the DPRK's
collapse and decided to do something about it: he argued that America
and its allies should waltz in and "tear this regime down." At the time,
he had excellent backing in such views from within Vice President
Cheney's and Don Rumsfeld's entourage, and especially from Paul
Wolfowitz and John Bolton.

Shortly after the invasion of Iraq began, Defense Secretary Rumsfeld
demanded revisions in the basic war plan for Korea (called "Operations
Plan 5030"). The strategy, according to insiders who have read the
plan, was "to topple Kim's regime by destabilizing its military forces,"
so they would overthrow him and thus accomplish a "regime change."
The plan was pushed "by many of the same administration hard-liners
who advocated regime change in Iraq." Unnamed senior Bush administration officials considered elements of this new plan "so aggressive
that they could provoke a war." Short of attacking or trying to force
a military coup, Rumsfeld and company wanted the U.S. military to
"stage a weeks-long surprise military exercise, designed to force North
Koreans to head for bunkers and deplete valuable stores of food, water,
and other resources."⁹ This is how the 1950 invasion began: North
Korea announced a long summer military exercise along the 38th parallel, mobilizing some 40,000 troops. In the middle of these war games,
several divisions suddenly veered south and took Seoul in three days;
only a tiny handful of the highest officials knew that the summer exercises were a prelude to an invasion.

Larry Niksch, a longtime specialist on Asian Affairs at the Congressional
Research Service and a person never given to leaps toward unfounded
conclusions, cited Rumsfeld's war plans and wrote that "regime change
in North Korea is indeed the Bush administration's policy objective." If
recent, sporadically applied, sanctions against the DPRK and interdic-
tion of its shipping do not produce a regime change or "diplomatic capitulation," then Rumsfeld planned to escalate from a preemptive strike
against Yongbyon (which Clinton came close to mounting in 1994) to "a
broader plan of massive strikes against multiple targets." Rumsfeld's plans
were discussed more than once in our paper of record, but no one ever
pointed out that North Korea might have good reason to fear the United
States. The same is true of Iran.

Whether this experience holds lessons for rapprochement with Iran is beyond my expertise. I have thought for twenty years that North Korea genuinely wants to come in from the cold and have normal relations with the United States, however hard it has been for them to change enough to get that done. Their revolution burned itself out a long time ago, even if their deep desire for independence and their touchiness (bordering on paranoia) about their sovereignty continues apace. No Israel exists in their neighborhood, instead the DPRK is the last remaining obstacle to the dynamism of the East Asian economies, whether run by communists (as in Vietnam and China) or not. For Pyongyang it is a matter of catching up to trends in the regional political economy set in motion a long time ago. It is not clear to me that a nonnuclear Iran can live with a nuclear Israel, and the main regional trend that Iran has joined is in the direction of Islamic fundamentalism and terrorism (through its support of Hamas and Hezbollah), whereas the DPRK is well poised to develop a series of export-led industries, if it wanted to and was helped from outside. Iran does not seem interested in that path (after all, it was pioneered in East Asia). Iran also has long desired to be the regional powerhouse of the Middle East, whether under the Shah or the Ayatollahs, and North Korea has no pretensions along those lines in its region.

Instead, what Pyongyang and Tehran share is the kind of bloody-minded, rigid, and fundamental desire for independence and sovereignty that was so widespread in the postcolonial nations after 1945. Sometimes I laugh out loud at the degree to which Pyongyang has so totally embraced the Western concept of national sovereignty, especially since it was violated so readily by the imperial nations who brought the concept to East Asia. But there is no question that the DPRK and Iran share this same orientation, it is the cornerstone of their pride and dignity, and it is one reason why they became close friends after 1979 (oil and missiles are the other reasons). The missile and satellite launches of both regimes are to demonstrate military prowess, of course, but they are also linked fundamentally to their desires for self-reliance and recognition, and to demonstrate to their people and foreigners that they are, well, *modern*. Pyongyang's first satellite attempt was directly connected to the fiftieth anniversary of the regime in 1998, and its second one this year was intimately involved with the opening of the Supreme People's Assembly after a long hiatus, and the public appointment of Kim's third son and likely successor, Kim Jong Eun to his first formal office. Yet few, if any, analysts in Washington pointed to these linkages, at least for the press, such that the media and the pundits

interpreted both events purely in terms of an alleged threat to Alaska
or the west coast. Simply beginning to acknowledge the highly nationalistic nature of these two regimes, rather than harping on communism
and terrorism, and doing small things to indicate recognition of some
of the values that both governments hold dear, would go a long way.
Here is where new American strategies of rapprochement can clearly
gain traction, in my view.

Psychology 101

How do psychiatrists deal with an angry, violent, insulting, aggravating,
recalcitrant, prideful, self-defeating patient? With concern, empathy,
understanding, deflection, subtle advice (usually through suggesting
alternative behavior), the setting of limits, on the one hand, and the
opening of avenues toward change, on the other. Think of Tony Soprano
and Jennifer Melfy (of the popular HBO TV series, *The Sopranos*): did
she call him a fat, slovenly, self-indulgent, and self-regarding criminal
thug? No, she treated him like a human being in pain, who needed help.
One book or article after another screams out that Kim Jong Il is an
Oriental-criminal-communist-despot, or that Iran's leaders are nutcases
and fruitcakes engaged in "nuclear *jihad*." This is not limited to the tab-
loids. President Bush called both regimes "evil" and called Kim Jong Il
a "pygmy" whose regime he would like to "topple."

Meanwhile, I have read the *New York Times* daily for forty years, and
I have never seen a serious investigative article on the origin, background, and nature of the North Korean regime. In fact, there is very
little good investigative reporting on North Korea or Iran. Hardly ever
do readers learn about what *we* have done to them—just what *they*
intend to do to us. This is such a serious problem, given the polarization of our politics since 1992, that the government itself is limited
and constrained by extreme public attitudes. Negotiate with Kim Jong
Il? Why, that's appeasement (John McCain)! Engage Tehran? They're
holocaust deniers who want to erase Israel (the American Israel Public
Affairs Committee)! It should be the government's responsibility to
inform the public honestly and thoroughly about the actual dimensions
of our relations with these two countries, just as a psychiatrist must
know intimately the background and experience of a patient, if there is
any hope of healing his mind.

A little-noticed program of academic exchange in computer science
between Syracuse University and North Korea shows that Pyongyang

can conduct mutually beneficial exchanges free of political interference. The American director, who asked not to be named, told me that the North Korean students were much more skilled than he expected (but happy to work on better computers here), polite and well behaved in every respect, and said that in all his work with the North the relevant officials have complied with his requests, and done what they promised to do. Beyond this, of course, are literally hundreds of westerners and other foreigners who have been delivering goods and services through one nongovernmental organization (NGO) or another to the North since the famine of the late 1990s. They do not find this country so strange and impenetrable, perhaps because of their wide experience in even worse catastrophes around the globe. They have valuable experience that could be drawn upon as the United States engages the DPRK.

Juan Cole expresses similar ideas in his new book, *Engaging the Muslim World*. Engagement does not mean surrender, appeasement, or even accommodation. It means "critique as well as dialogue, pressure as well as basic human respect," and the use of military threats or force as the last resort ("all options are on the table," says the world's greatest power with thousands of nuclear warheads, the only power to have used them in anger—and yet there is no workable military solution for Iran or North Korea). Cole also notes that the theocratic restrictions on personal freedom since 1979, resented by large sectors of the Iranian population, give the United States a significant advantage and possible leverage—the desire for pragmatism, stability, and ordinary relations with other countries is strong in Iran, and many opinion polls still show much admiration for the United States.[10] Given the history of British and American interference in the internal affairs of Iran, and palpable threats by the Bush administration, Cole also makes a special plea relevant both to Iran and North Korea: assure Tehran that the United States will not try to overthrow its government.[11] Other experts have made the same point, and had emphasized this before the erstwhile elections. More important for our purposes, though, President Obama's special envoy to North Korea, Stephen Bosworth, stated in Congressional testimony on June 16, 2009 that the United States had no intention to attack or overthrow Kim Jong Il's regime, and returned to William Perry's mantra: we should deal with the North "as it is, not as we would like it to be." Maybe that is a hint of where Obama's North Korea policy is headed—I hope so.

The Bush administration's reckless threats regarding North Korea and Iran have vastly reinforced the most reactionary forces in both countries, so we are still digging out of a hole rather than laying to rest decades of enmity. Now is a good time finally to shed the anachronistic polarized positions and mind-set of the cold war and to move in the direction of a calm, steady, nuanced, and persistent process of rapprochement with North Korea and Iran. Think of Jennifer Melfy and Tony Soprano.

Notes

1. James Der Derian, *On Diplomacy: A Genealogy of Western Estrangement* (New York: Oxford University Press, 1994).
2. Nazila Fathi and Alan Cowell, "After Obama Overture, Iran's Leader Seeks U.S. Apology," *New York Times*, January 29, 2009.
3. Many would see Iran as an exception, but I agree with Max Rodenbeck that it is really "a strategic featherweight." In a conventional war, a rather long list of countries would be able to devastate it, beginning with Israel, India, and Pakistan. See Rodenbeck, "The Iran Mystery Case," *New York Review of Books*, January 15, 2009, 35–38. This article also lists a number of excellent new books on Iran.
4. Ibid., 38.
5. See Michael R. Gordon's investigative report, "How Politics Sank Accord on Missiles with North Korea," *New York Times*, March 6, 2001, A-1 and A-8.
6. Ibid., A-8.
7. Naewoe Press, *North Korea: Uneasy, Shaky Kim Jong-il Regime* (Seoul: ROK Government, 1997), 143.
8. See his "The Coming Collapse of North Korea," *The Wall Street Journal*, June 25, 1990.
9. Bruce B. Auster and Kevin Whitelaw, "Upping the Ante for Kim Jong Il: Pentagon Plan 5030, A New Blueprint for Facing Down North Korea," *U.S. News and World Report*, July 21, 2003. http://www.usnews.com/usnews/news/articles/030721/21korea.htm.
10. See a particularly good column on this by Roger Cohen, "The Other Tehran," *New York Times*, February 2, 2009.
11. Juan Cole, *Engaging the Muslim World* (New York: Palgrave Macmillan, 2009), 5, 231, 244.

CONTRIBUTORS

Victor D. Cha received his PhD from Columbia University, he is director of Asian Studies and holds the D. S. Song Chair at Georgetown University. From 2004 to 2007 he served as director for Asian affairs at the White House National Security Council. Dr. Cha was also the Deputy Head of Delegation for the United States at the Six-party Talks in Beijing, and received two Outstanding Service commendations during his tenure at the NSC. He is an award-winning author of three books, and has published widely on U.S. policy in Asia including in *Foreign Affairs*; *Foreign Policy*; *International Security*; *and Survival*. His latest book is *Beyond the Final Score: The Politics of Sport in Asia* (Columbia University Press, 2009).

Bruce Cumings teaches modern Korean history, international history, and East Asian political economy at the University of Chicago, where he has taught since 1987 and where he is the Gustavus F. and Ann M. Swift Distinguished Service Professor and the chairman of the History Department. He is the author of the two-volume study, *The Origins of the Korean War* (Princeton University Press, 1981, 1990); *War and Television* (Visal-Routledge, 1992); *Korea's Place in the Sun: A Modern History* (W. W. Norton, 1997; updated ed. 2005); *Parallax Visions: Making Sense of American–East Asian Relations* (Duke University Press, 1999; paperback 2002); *North Korea: Another Country* (New Press, 2003); and coauthor *of Inventing the Axis of Evil* (New Press, 2004). He is also the editor of the modern volume of the *Cambridge History of Korea* (forthcoming, Cambridge University Press). He is a frequent contributor to *The London Review of Books*; *The Nation*; *Current History*; the *Bulletin of the Atomic Scientists*; and *Le Monde Diplomatique*. He was also the principal historical consultant for the Thames Television/PBS six-hour documentary, "Korea: The Unknown War." His new book, *Dominion from Sea to Sea: Pacific Ascendancy and American Power*, was published by Yale University Press in November 2009. In December 2009 it was ranked seventh among the top twenty-five books of the year by the *Atlantic Monthly*. He is also contracted to publish a new, single-volume synoptic edition of The *Origins of the Korean War.*

L. Gordon Flake is Executive Director of the Maureen and Mike Mansfield Foundation, a position he has held since February 1999. He was previously a Senior Fellow and Associate Director of the Program on Conflict Resolution at The Atlantic Council of the United States and prior to that Director for Research and Academic Affairs at the Korea Economic Institute of America. Mr. Flake is coeditor with Park Roh-Byug for the book *New Political Realities in Seoul: Working toward a Common Approach to Strengthen U.S.-Korean Relations* (Mansfield Foundation, March 2008), and coeditor with Scott Snyder for the book *Paved with Good Intentions: The NGO Experience in North Korea* (Praeger, 2003). He has published extensively on policy issues in Asia.

Rüdiger Frank is Professor of East Asian Economy and Society at the University of Vienna and Deputy Head of the Department of East Asian Studies. He is also an Adjunct Professor at Korea University and the University of North Korean Studies. He holds an MA in Korean Studies, Economics and International Relations and a PhD in Economics. Visiting Professorships included Columbia University, New York and Korea University, Seoul. He is a Council member of the Association for Korean Studies in Europe, Vice Director of the Vienna School of Governance, and Deputy Editor of the European Journal of East Asian Studies. He is coeditor of the annual book *Korea: Politics, Economy and Society* (Brill). His major research fields are socialist transformation in East Asia and Europe (with a focus on North Korea), state-business relations in East Asia, and regional integration in East Asia. See http://wirtschaft.ostasien.univie.ac.at/ E-mail: ruediger.frank@univie.ac.at.

David C. Kang is Professor at the University of Southern California, with appointments in both the School of International Relations and the Marshall School of Business, and director of the Korean Studies Institute. His latest book, *International Relations of East Asia: Five Hundred Years of Peace*, will be published by Columbia University Press. Kang is also author of *China Rising: Peace, Power, and Order in East Asia* (Columbia University Press, 2007), *Crony Capitalism: Corruption and Development in South Korea and the Philippines* (Cambridge University Press, 2002), and *Nuclear North Korea: A Debate on Engagement Strategies* (coauthored with Victor Cha)

(Columbia University Press, 2003). Kang has published numerous scholarly articles in journals such as *International Organization and International Security*, and *International Studies Quarterly*. He received an AB with honors from Stanford University and his Ph.D. from Berkeley.

Mark Manyin is a Specialist in Asian Affairs at the Congressional Research Service (CRS), a nonpartisan agency that provides information and analysis to Members of the U.S. Congress and their staff. At CRS, Dr. Manyin's general area of expertise is U.S. foreign economic policy toward East Asia, particularly Japan, the Koreas, and Vietnam. He also has tracked the evolution of terrorism in Southeast Asia and the environmental causes of security tensions in Asia. From 2006 to 2008, Dr. Manyin served as the head of the CRS' eleven-person Asia Section overseeing the Service's research on East, Southeast, and South Asia as well as Australasia and the Pacific Islands. Prior to joining CRS in 1999, Dr. Manyin completed his PhD in Japanese trade policy and negotiating behavior at the Fletcher School of Law and Diplomacy. He has written academic articles on Vietnam and Korea, taught courses in East Asian international relations, worked as a business consultant, and lived in Japan for a total of three years.

Han S. Park is a university Professor of Public and International Affairs and the Director of the Center for the Study of Global Issues (Globis) at the University of Georgia. Among his many publications are *Human Needs and Political Development: A Dissent to Utopian Solutions* (Schenkman); *North Korea: Ideology, Politics, and Economy* (Prentice Hall); and *North Korea: The Politics of Unconventional Wisdom* (Lynne Rienner), as well as more than one hundred journal articles and book chapters. Dr. Park has earned prominence on the world stage as a peacemaker, especially regarding the North Korea nuclear conundrum. He has visited the world's most reclusive system nearly fifty times over the past twenty years on scholarly and peacemaking (mediation) purposes. The chapter on *Songun* Politics is largely based on his personal observation and firsthand information.

Kyung-Ae Park holds the Korea Foundation Chair at the Institute of Asian Research of the University of British Columbia. She is a former president of the Association of Korean Political Studies in North America. Professor Park's areas of specialty include comparative politics and international relations, with an emphasis on East Asia. She is the author, coauthor, and coeditor of many scholarly publications on issues ranging from North and South Korean politics and foreign relations to gender and development, such as *Korean Security Dynamics in Transition* (Palgrave) and *China and North Korea: Politics of Integration and Modernization* (Asian Research Service). She also authored articles in a number of journals, including *Comparative Politics, Journal of Asian Studies, Pacific Affairs, Asian Survey,* and *Pacific Review.* Since 1995, she has made several trips to Pyongyang and hosted North Korean delegation visits to Canada, playing a key role in promoting Track-II exchanges between Canada and North Korea.

Gilbert Rozman is the Musgrave Professor of Sociology at Princeton University. His most recent books are *Northeast Asia's Stunted Regionalism: Bilateral Distrust in the Shadow of Globalization* (Cambridge University Press, 2004); *Korea at the Center: Dynamics of Regionalism in Northeast Asia,* coeditor (M. E. Sharpe, 2006); *Russian Strategic Thought toward Asia,* coeditor (Palgrave, 2006); *Japanese Strategic Thought toward Asia,* coeditor (Palgrave, 2007); *Strategic Thinking about the Korean Nuclear Crisis: Four Parties Caught between North Korea and the United States* (Palgrave, 2007); *South Korean Strategic Thought toward Asia,* coeditor (Palgrave, 2008); *Chinese Strategic Thought toward Asia* (Palgrave, 2009); and *U.S. Leadership, History, and Bilateral Relations in Northeast Asia,* coeditor (Cambridge University Press, 2010).

Scott Snyder is Director of the Center for U.S.-Korea Policy at The Asia Foundation, a Senior Associate with Pacific Forum CSIS, and an Adjunct Senior Fellow for Korean Studies at the Council on Foreign Relations. He is based in Washington, DC. He lived in Seoul, South Korea as Korea Representative of The Asia Foundation during 2000–2004. Previously he served as a Program officer in the Research and Studies Program of the U.S. Institute of Peace, and as Acting Director of The Asia Society's Contemporary Affairs Program. His publications include *China's Rise and the Two Koreas: Politics, Economics, Security* (Lynne Rienner, 2008); *Paved With Good Intentions: The NGO Experience in North Korea* (Praeger, 2003), coedited with L. Gordon Flake; and *Negotiating on the Edge: North Korean Negotiating Behavior* (USIP, 1999). Snyder received his BA from Rice University and an MA from the Regional Studies East Asia Program at Harvard University. He was the recipient of a Pantech Visiting Fellowship at Stanford University's Shorenstein Asia-Pacific Research Center during 2005–2006; received an Abe Fellowship, administered by the Social Sciences Research Council, in 1998–1999; and was a Thomas G. Watson Fellow at Yonsei University in South Korea in 1987–1988.

INDEX